A man lay sprawled across the bed. His head and face had been struck and smashed repeatedly. He'd been hit hard enough to shatter his skull and his brain had swelled out. His throat had been cut. Dennis Freeman had been hit so hard that his blood had spattered across the ceiling.

Down the hall, the police officers entered the bedroom of his twelve-year-old son Erik. His small fragile body lay in a lifeless heap on his bed, his face beaten to a bloody pulp.

In the back hallway, they found Brenda Freeman. She was lying on her side, her nightgown pulled up. There was a bloody knife on the floor next to her. She'd been stabbed in the back and a pool of dark blood had coagulated underneath her body.

On the wall behind Brenda's body, someone had scrawled two swastikas.

One of the family cars was missing. So was a shotgun.

The skinhead brothers, Bryan, 17, and David, 15, were nowhere to be found.

ORDINARY LIVES DESTROYED BY EXTRAORDINARY HORROR.
FACTS MORE DANGEROUS THAN FICTION.
CAPTURE A PINNACLE TRUE CRIME . . . IF YOU DARE.

LITTLE GIRL LOST (593, $4.99)
By Joan Merriam

When Anna Brackett, an elderly woman living alone, allowed two teenage girls into her home, she never realized that a brutal death awaited her. Within an hour, Mrs. Brackett would be savagely stabbed twenty-eight times. Her executioners were Shirley Katherine Wolf, 14, and Cindy Lee Collier, 15. *Little Girl Lost* examines how two adolescents were driven through neglect and sexual abuse to commit the ultimate crime.

HUSH, LITTLE BABY (541, $4.99)
By Jim Carrier

Darci Kayleen Pierce seemed to be the kind of woman you stand next to in the grocery store. However, Darci was obsessed with the need to be a mother. She desperately wanted a baby—any baby. On a summer day, Darci kidnapped a nine-month pregnant woman, strangled her, and performed a makeshift Cesarean section with a car key. In this arresting account, readers will learn how Pierce's tortured fantasy of motherhood spiralled into a bloody reality.

IN A FATHER'S RAGE (547, $4.99)
By Raymond Van Over

Dr. Kanneth Z. Taylor promised his third wife Teresa that he would mend his drug-addictive, violent ways. His vow didn't last. He nearly beat his bride to death on their honeymoon. This nuptial nightmare worsened until Taylor killed Teresa after allegedly catching her sexually abusing their infant son. Claiming to have been driven beyond a father's rage, Taylor was still found guilty of first degree murder. This gripping page-turner reveals how a marriage made in heaven can become a living hell.

I KNOW MY FIRST NAME IS STEVEN (563, $4.99)
By Mike Echols

A TV movie was based on this terrifying tale of abduction, child molesting, and brainwashing. Yet, a ray of hope shines through this evil swamp for Steven Stayner escaped from his captor and testified against the socially disturbed Kenneth Eugene Parnell. For seven years, Steven was shuttled across California under the assumed name of "Dennis Parnell." Despite the humiliations and degradations, Steven never lost sight of his origins or his courage.

RITES OF BURIAL (611, $4.99)
By Tom Jackman and Troy Cole

Many pundits believe that the atrocious murders and dismemberments performed by Robert Berdella may have inspired Jeffrey Dahmer. Berdella stalked and savagely tortured young men; sadistically photographing their suffering and ritualistically preserving totems from their deaths. Upon his arrest, police uncovered human skulls, envelopes of teeth, and a partially decomposed human head. This shocking expose is written by two men who worked daily on this case.

Available wherever paperbacks are sold, or order direct from the Publisher. Send cover price plus 50¢ per copy for mailing and handling to Penguin USA, P.O. Box 999, c/o Dept. 17109, Bergenfield, NJ 07621. Residents of New York and Tennessee must include sales tax. DO NOT SEND CASH.

BLOOD CRIMES

Fred Rosen

Pinnacle Books
Kensington Publishing Corp.

Some names have been changed to protect the privacy of individuals connected to this story.

The letters written by Nelson B. Birdwell I are reprinted with his kind permission.

PINNACLE BOOKS are published by

Kensington Publishing Corp.
850 Third Avenue
New York, NY 10022

Pinnacle and the P logo Reg. U.S. Pat. & TM Off..

First Printing: October, 1996
10 9 8 7 6 5 4 3 2 1

Printed in the United States of America

*With the greatest affection, this book is dedicated to
my teacher, my friend,
Professor John DiGiovanni of Hunter College.*

Acknowledgments

Carol Annunziata and Joe Gioia offered invaluable support in the writing of this book.

Paul Blizard opened doors that had remained closed.

Brian Collins gave support and friendship.

Wally Worth set me straight.

Dick Makoul offered wise counsel, a wonderful meal, and fashion advice; he gets the award for Allentown's best-dressed attorney.

Bob Steinberg offered perspective.

Naomi Halperin of the *Morning Call* chipped in with photographic assistance.

Dan Kelly, of the *Reading Eagle,* was a welcome face throughout the grim proceedings.

The gang at Starbuck's provided much-needed conversation during my daily fill-ups.

Finally, and most of all, I thank you, dear reader, for putting your hard-earned bucks down and buying this book.

PART ONE

"And a man's foes shall be they of their own household."

Matthew 13:6
New World Translation,
(Jehovah's Witnesses Bible)

Prologue

Midnight, February 27, 1995

Benny's heart raced with the excitement of the kill.

Crunching snow under his Doc Martens, he strolled over to wait by the driveway. A minute later, the front door burst open and David ran from the house.

David looks really scared, Benny thought, like he's seen a ghost. And he's changed—there's no more blood on his clothes. Benny looked down at his own jeans for any blood.

When Benny looked up again, Bryan was in the doorway.

Confused, Bryan looked around, listening. Save for the distant sound of the whimpering dog inside the house, he heard nothing. Making sure all the lights were out, he pulled the front door shut. Then he closed the outside screen door gently, so it wouldn't bang.

"Benny, let's go by your house to pick up some tapes," Bryan said cheerfully.

Benny nodded. He got into his car, parked at the curb.

"We'll take ours," Bryan told David, his younger brother.

There were three vehicles in the driveway. Bryan and David's father's van blocked the first of the two cars. Bryan started up the van. After the engine caught, he turned on the rear windshield wiper to clear the rear window of snow so he could see to back out of the driveway. He double-parked, went back, and started up the first car.

After the car was out on the street, David got in on the passenger side. Bryan then drove the van back up onto the driveway, hopped out, and went back behind the wheel of the car.

Benny pulled out. Bryan followed him through the silent snow-covered streets of Allentown, Pennsylvania. When they got to his house, Benny parked and got in the back seat of the other car.

"You got the money?" David asked.

Bryan rattled his pockets. He patted them for a moment, feeling not only a lot of change but piles of crumpled bills that filled them to bursting.

They stopped for gas and cigarettes at a 7-Eleven, then sped out of Allentown.

"Where we gonna go?" David asked.

"I don't know," said Bryan. "We'll probably just go up to Michigan and meet those guys."

"Who—"

"Frank," Bryan answered. "We'll go see Frank." He headed north on the Pennsylvania Turnpike. Inside of ninety minutes, they had reached Interstate 80, heading west. Bryan drove carefully, obeying the speed limit.

They made a few pit stops, but by 8:30 A.M. the

next morning, they had traveled 388 miles and were across the state line, outside of Youngstown, Ohio. Fearful that the police might be after them, they decided it would be a good idea if they lay low during the day.

"How about that place?" David asked, pointing at a motel that was coming up on their right.

Jesse Capece was behind the desk of the Truck World Motor Inn in Hubbard, Ohio, when the three walked in. Each was over six feet tall and weighed well over 200 pounds. They weren't men, really, but teenagers in the body of men. They wore combat boots and jackets. And their heads were shaved clean.

When they came over to the counter to register, Jesse noticed the tattoos on their shaved heads. Two of the boys had the word "berserker" tattooed near their hairline. The third boy, who was younger but bigger, had his forehead tattooed with the Nazi slogan *"Sieg heil." Who were these weird guys?* Just looking at them gave Jesse the willies.

The boy who filled out the registration card signed in as "Benny Birdwell." He listed the license plate number as "JZK 2291, Pennsylvania." He left the box for the make of car blank.

"What kind of car you driving?" Jesse asked.

"An Olds," said Benny.

"No, it's a Buick," said Bryan.

"Uh-uh, it's a Pontiac," said David, who knew cars.

"Let me see your license," Jesse asked.

Benny took out his license and let Jesse examine it.

"Well, it looks okay," Jesse said uneasily. "Awright, that'll be sixty-five dollars for the room."

Bryan dug into the pocket of his jeans and pulled out a bunch of crushed fives. He counted out thirteen of the bills. Jesse gave them the key to the room.

After they were gone, Jesse went outside to check out their car. It was a Pontiac, all right, with a Pennsylvania tag. But the number on the plate said "JNK 088."

They'd lied.

When seventeen-year-old Samuel Ehrgott set out on his paper route at dawn, Salisbury Township looked like a Norman Rockwell painting.

In a place like Salisbury, an Allentown suburb, snow doesn't turn to slush quickly because there just isn't enough traffic. The streets stay quiet and soft and nice, the houses peaceful and warm under the snow white covering.

Sam rode his bike up and down the streets of his development. Methodically, he stopped to put a paper on the porch of each subscriber.

Though they lived next door to him, the Freemans were actually one of the last families on his route. As he did every morning, he got to their place at 5:45 A.M. Today, though, Sam knew something was different.

Where was Mr. Freeman?

Mr. Freeman would always be coming down the stairs at that hour, or already warming up his truck. Not today, though. His van was parked in the driveway. That was strange. The man was never late. And he never took a day off. Sam felt something was wrong.

At school a few hours later, when his homeroom teacher took attendance, Bryan Freeman was missing. Then Sam remembered what Bryan Freeman had said a few days ago.

Something was *very* wrong.

One

Since 1978, Valerie Freeman had lived with her brother and sister-in-law. There was a bottle of twelve-year-old Scotch that Dennis kept hidden, to be opened on the day she got married. It wasn't bound to be any time soon.

Fiftyish and mousy-looking, Valerie had no prospective suitors. Still, you never knew. Whatever Jehovah wanted for her would be his will. *Thy will be done.*

It had been Jehovah's will that David and Bryan would rebel against their parents and pick on Valerie Freeman by urinating in her shampoo and leaving chicken bones in her bed. Dennis had seen what was happening and knew that Jehovah had chosen him, yet he felt powerless to stop the cruel way his sons were treating his sister. That was the usual thing with Dennis these days. He just didn't know what to do.

"Maybe if you move out, things might be better," Dennis had suggested. Not wishing to overstay her welcome and seeing that things had gotten out of hand, Valerie left. Still, she saw the family a lot. Her favorite nephew, Erik, was suffering the most. His brothers didn't treat him well. They felt that the younger boy, always kissing up to his parents, was spoiled, while they were held in nothing but the utmost contempt. David and Bryan picked on Erik, teased him, and chastised him for his religious beliefs. Erik was a devout Jehovah's Witness, and in him rested the one great hope that the line of Jehovah's Witnesses in the Freeman family would be redeemed. But clearly, Valerie realized, Erik had felt himself in some sort of jeopardy, and though he didn't say from whom, it was clear that he feared his older, more powerful brothers. They could be brutes when angered, and with the cruel use of their strength and size, could inflict tremendous pain.

All this Valerie knew when, at 5 P.M., her hand reached out for the front doorknob. She tried it. It had no give to it. That was unusual. Her sister-in-law, Brenda, always left it unlocked when she was home, and she was home most of the time. Valerie had a key, but before she used it, she decided to step around to the side and try the garage door. It was also locked. She looked over at Dennis's truck. It looked like it hadn't been moved.

Unusual. Dennis, a school janitor, never missed a day of work.

Growing alarmed, Valerie went around the side of the house and tried the sliding glass door. Unlocked, it gave easily.

Inside, the house was dark, very dark. It was cold enough to see your breath.

With a growing sense of dread, she ran down the hallway to Erik's bedroom. She paused for a moment before the closed door and then pushed it open.

A few minutes later, there was a frantic knock at the Ehrgott home next door. Samuel Ehrgott answered it.

"May I use your phone?" Valerie asked.

"What's wrong, Valerie?"

"Erik is dead," she said, in a shaky voice.

Sam's mother came to the door.

"Ma, Valerie says Erik is dead." Sam told her what had happened. She immediately dialed 911 to report a homicide.

A few moments later, the radio crackled to life in the blue and white. "Thirty-five. Thirty-five."

Officer Michael Pochran picked up the mike and pressed the button. Thirty-five," he responded.

"Proceed to Ehrgott residence on Gale Avenue. See a woman there about a homicide. Body of a young boy has been found."

"Roger."

When he got to the residence, Pochran saw people gathered outside the Ehrgott home. They motioned him across the way. Pochran followed their directions and parked his cruiser.

"Who's the owner?" Pochran asked the crowd.

"It's Freeman," said a small, mousy woman who stepped forward. She wore tortoiseshell eyeglasses that distorted the shape of her eyes. "Brenda and Dennis Freeman. My brother and sister-in-law."

"And you're—?"

"Valerie Freeman. I found Erik." She started to cry.

"How'd you get in?"

"Through the back door," she answered between sobs. "It was open. But I have a key, too." She gave him the key to the front door.

Officer Pochran walked slowly up the snow-covered driveway. He noticed that today's paper was still on the porch. In the driveway were two vehicles—a car, and parked behind that, a van. The rear window of the van bore the tracks of a windshield wiper, though the van looked like it hadn't been moved.

As Valerie had said, the front door was locked. He went to the back, where he found the sliding glass doors open, exactly as Valerie had left them.

He returned back to the front and waited for backup. When Officer Michael Reddings arrived, they used Valerie's key to gain entrance.

Their flashlights cut through the interior darkness. Halfway up the stairs, the beams picked out blood on the stairway carpet. At the top of the landing, they looked down and flashed their torches.

Below them was the living room, and beyond that the kitchen, where a silver aluminum baseball bat lay against a blue cabinet. The blood covering the barrel of the bat contrasted starkly with the cabinet's blue.

Still on the landing, they heard a dog barking and followed the sound to a closed bedroom door. Behind it, the dog sensed their presence and continued barking violently. They didn't open it. Instead, they entered the master bedroom across the hall.

A man lay sprawled across his bed.

His head and face had been struck and smashed repeatedly. So hard had he been hit that his skull had been shattered and his brain had swelled out through the cranium. His throat had been cut.

"Must be Dennis Freeman," said Pochran.

"Look." Reddings pointed up.

Dennis Freeman's blood had spattered across the ceiling.

"Damn," said Pochran.

"Let's check for the kid."

Down the hall, they entered Erik Freeman's bedroom. His small, fragile body lay in a lifeless heap on his bed. His face had been beaten into such a bloody pulp, they had no way of knowing that Erik had been a handsome boy.

Their grim footsteps made hollow echoes. They headed down to the basement, searching for Brenda Freeman as they went. On the floor in a narrow hallway they found a metal pipe covered with blood.

In the back hallway they found Brenda. She was lying on her side, her nightgown pulled up, exposing a large, fleshy body. There was a bloody knife on the floor next to her.

Brenda Freeman had been stabbed in the back. A pool of dark blood had coagulated underneath her bloated body. Behind her, on the wall, someone had scrawled two swastikas. *Is this some kind of hate crime*, Pochran wondered. *Can the victims have been Jewish?*

By that time, the rescue squad of the Eastern Salisbury Township Fire Department had responded. Finding that the victims were dead and there was nothing they could do, they milled around the crime scene, careful not to touch anything, lest they contaminate evidence.

"Looks like Bryan Freeman killed his parents and little brother," said Frank Johnson, one member of the rescue squad, addressing another, Harry Liste.

At 10:30 P.M, Trooper Joseph Vazquez arrived at the Freeman home. With his baby face and dark complexion and hair, he looked more like the archetypal Latin lover than what he was—a seasoned homicide investigator with twelve years of experience.

Wearing surgical gloves to prevent contaminating the crime scene, Vazquez took a look around the house, noting the angles at which the victims were lying, the types of wounds, stabbing or slicing, and the blunt-force trauma to the heads of Erik and Dennis. Most of all he noted the ferocity of the assaults. It was overkill.

A small army of technicians that accompanies any violent death in a large American city worked silently through the house. They dusted for prints, examined and photographed the bodies and crime scene, and eventually, when the detectives gave the okay, removed the bodies to the morgue for autopsy.

Detectives fanned out across Lehigh County to question those who knew the family. They called in after interviews with Brenda's sisters, Sandy Lettich and Linda Solivan. Both women said that there was bad blood between David and Bryan Freeman and their parents and little brother. At the crime scene, Valerie Freeman confirmed this. "David and Bryan had become skinheads," she added.

The police also learned that the family had kept a shotgun in the house. It was missing. Since Bryan and David and one of the family cars were also missing, along with their cousin Benny, and with the antagonism the boys had openly displayed toward their parents, it was a logical leap to conclude that they had killed their parents and were on the lam.

"Let's get the warrants to arrest them," said Bob Steinberg.

Steinberg was the district attorney of Lehigh County. Tall, slim, and well dressed, he also happens to be honest, the direct antithesis of a stereotypical small-town politician. He is a hands-on DA who not only prosecutes many of the cases his office handles, he also participates in active investigations. In one case involving a rapist/serial killer, Steinberg had actually discovered the body of a young girl the man had killed. He was no stranger to helping track down suspected criminals.

By late that night, Steinberg had his warrants and directed the police to contact the National Crime Information Center (NCIC). Fugitives are listed with the NCIC, and local police departments are expected to tap into their files on a regular basis to see who is wanted.

Soon, the NCIC computers had a complete description of the Freeman brothers and Ben Birdwell, a description of the car they were driving, and the license plate number.

By that evening, the local media had found out

that the Freeman family had been murdered and
that the suspects were their sons and their cousin.
The case was splashed across the front pages of
the *Allentown Morning Call* and the *Reading Eagle.*
"Skinheads Kill Parents," the headlines read. The
airwaves ran it, too. Besides the local stations, ABC,
NBC, CBS, CNN, and Fox all bannered the story
of the murders and the boys' escape.

Kate Blacke, a fifteen-year-old student at Salisbury High School, was in her home watching TV,
when the report of the Freeman murders came on.

"David and Brenda Freeman and their son Erik
have been found brutally murdered in their Allentown, Pennsylvania, home. Missing are their other
two sons, David and Bryan, and the family car. Police suspect that the missing boys, who are skinheads, are responsible for the crime. An all-points
bulletin has been issued for their arrest."

"Oh, my God, they did it!" Kate said aloud.

She couldn't believe it: they'd actually gone
through with it. And now they were on the run,
probably heading for Florida. At least, that's where
they'd said they wanted to go.

Florida.

In searching through Bryan's room, police came
upon a picture of a teenage boy. On the back,
someone had drawn a swastika. The picture of the
boy was immediately identified by rescue squad
members as Harry Liste. Liste was a squad member
and was one of those who had responded to the

emergency at the Freeman home. He was still on the scene.

Vazquez immediately had Officer Pochran and Trooper David Seip drive the teenager down to the Eastern Salisbury Firehouse for an interview. The time was 10:45 P.M. While Liste was being whisked in for questioning, across town in two homes, the grieving was beginning.

Linda Solivan and Sandy Lettich had just finished talking to the detectives. They had loved their sister Brenda dearly and were shattered by the news of her violent death. The deaths of Dennis and their nephew Erik made it all that much more difficult to bear. Yet they were devout Jehovah's Witnesses.

This was an attack directly from Satan. Only Satan could wreak such havoc on the Freeman household; only Satan could kill them so violently. But Satan could not, would not, win, because they were killed as Jesus was. To die for being a Witness is the ultimate joy. As such, their death was not so much a tragedy as an honor. Brenda and David and Erik were martyred Jehovah's Witnesses in the same way that the Christians were martyred in the Coliseum and the Jews at Masada.

Trooper Seip, though, was not concerned with affairs on the spiritual plane. His job was to get to the bottom of a triple homicide and get the perpetrators arrested. He began questioning Harry Liste.

"Where do you go to school?" Seip began.

"At Salisbury High School with Bryan. And David."

"How'd your picture wind up in their house?"

"Well, I'm a friend of Bryan's. We're regular friends, me and Bryan," he added.

"How long have you known Bryan?" Seip asked.

"About two years, though we hardly ever do anything outside of school. We pal around at school."

"Sort of like school friends," said Seip.

"Yeah. We have some of the same classes and we both go to Vo-Tech in the afternoon. Bryan's taking automotive classes."

"How well do you know his brother David?"

"Not well at all. I met David through Bryan."

"Did you ever hear either make any threats toward their parents?"

Liste nodded. "Bryan said a couple of times that he wanted to kill his parents."

"When did he make these threats?"

"Bryan's been saying that he wanted to kill his parents for the past two years. Bryan said that he had beat up his father in the past."

"Did he ever indicate why he hated his parents?"

"No, he never said," Liste replied. "He also said he hated his little brother and he would beat him up as well."

"How long were they skinheads?"

"About three years."

Seip realized if Liste was right, it meant that Bryan had been a skinhead since he was fourteen and his brother since he was twelve.

"Did Bryan have any of those tattoos the skinheads usually have?"

"He had several."

"Describe them."

"Well, he had the word 'berserker' tattooed across his forehead. Then there was a swastika made of bones on his neck, and a man half black and half white on his right arm. That means something in skinhead lore, but I don't know what."

"When was the last time you talked to Bryan?"

"On Friday. At school. It was in the morning sometime. I said I'd see him between classes and at lunch."

"Do you know how Bryan was doing in school?"

"He was in trouble, at least on Friday, because he wrote some obscene stuff on a state test he'd been taking. That had gotten him suspended for five days. Bryan told me that he didn't care if he got into trouble."

"Had he said anything to you about his plans for the weekend?"

Liste shook his head.

"What kind of mood was Bryan in on Friday?"

"Bryan seemed pissed off. I saw him trying to scrounge lunch money off somebody. The principal saw him and grabbed Bryan. Bryan pushed him away. That was the last time I saw him."

"Do you have any idea where Bryan might have gone to?"

"Well, about two weeks ago, Bryan said he was trying to get some money to go to Florida. He wanted to go there because of the mostly white population."

Seip didn't tell Liste that Bryan had been misinformed. Florida has a significant African American and Hispanic population.

"Bryan always talked about an uncle he liked a

lot." The uncle lived in Florida, but Liste didn't know his name.

"Did you see David on Friday?"

"Yeah. In the hall. He seemed okay."

"Now Mr. Liste, about that picture we found in the house—it was of you, and on the back there was a swastika."

Liste explained that he had drawn the swastika on the back.

"Are you a skinhead?"

"No way," said Liste. "I just wrote that stuff to be Bryan's friend."

"So what did you guys do when you palled around? Out of school, that is."

"It was about two months ago at the Whitehall Mall. It was me, Bryan, David, Beth—that's another friend of Bryan's—and Ben, his cousin. There were about twenty skinheads altogether. Dave and Bryan tried to pick a fight with some kid and they got bounced out of the mall."

"So where do you think they've gone to?"

"Like I said, they had this uncle they liked and they also said they liked their grandfather. Me, I think they took off and they'll keep going."

"Do you know if they have any weapons?"

"Bryan has a pocketknife with a blade. David might have a shotgun. Bryan said they'd been shooting the shotgun recently and that they got their shells at Tru-Value Hardware last week, maybe Thursday or Friday. A kid named Allan Hayward works there and might have sold them the ammo."

"Any idea what kind of car they're driving?"

"Bryan used to drive a gray Camaro, but his parents sold it about two weeks ago. He's been taking the bus since then. I think Bryan's driving a big blue Cadillac now."

"How'd he get it?"

"I think David bought it and Bryan was driving it until David got his license."

"Did you ever see either brother driving a black Sunbird?"

"No." On thinking further, Liste recalled, "Oh, yeah. It was a convertible. I only saw Bryan's mother driving it. I did see Bryan in the car, but only with his mom."

"You think Bryan killed his parents?"

"He hated them with a passion. Yeah, I think he killed them."

"What about David and Ben?"

"Maybe David did, too, but I don't know about Benny."

"When was the last time you saw Benny?"

"About two to three months ago at the Whitehall Mall. I didn't know him that well. I do know that Bryan and Benny got a job at a Wendy's on Tilghman Street. They started there last weekend and Bryan had to shave if he wanted to work there."

"You ever call Bryan?"

"Never. But he does have a pager and I might have the number. I'll try and find it and give it to you. Don't know if it'll do any good, though. I don't think Bryan will come back or answer a page from anyone except maybe Benny."

"Do you know where Benny is?"

"No. And I don't know how to find him, and even if I did, I don't think Benny'd talk to you."

"How about friends—girlfriends who might know where they are?"

"There were two girls, Maryann Galton and Jennifer Greener. They were skinhead girls who went to school with Bryan. Galton had a shaved head."

"Tell me something, David—did you ever hear of Bryan and David, as skinheads, doing any harm to people?"

"Two or three months ago, Bryan told me that he, David, and maybe Benny were driving in Allentown. They hit a black kid walking down the street with an eight-ball in a sock."

"You know anything else about that incident?"

"No."

"You said earlier that the last time Bryan said he wanted to kill his parents was Friday?"

"Yeah."

"About what time? Can you narrow it down?"

Liste thought for a moment. "Sometime like between 10:30 and 11:00. At lunch."

"Why did Bryan hate his little brother?"

"Because he was a Jehovah's Witness, like his parents."

The interview was over. The next morning, newspapers across the country, from the *New York Times* to the *Oregonian,* had the story on their front pages. Still, no one knew where the boys were; no one knew where they were headed.

* * *

At the crime scene, Trooper Vazquez had discovered that the Freeman brothers knew a boy named Marshall Fallon. Thinking that Fallon, like Liste, might have information on their whereabouts, Trooper Seip was dispatched to bring him in.

Fallon lived at a hotel on Hamilton Street. Seip brought the seventeen-year-old to the Salisbury Township police department for questioning.

"Yeah, I've known David and Bryan since May of 1994. I'm one of their closest friends," Fallon bragged.

"Where was the last time you saw them?" Seip wondered.

"Haven't seen either in the last week or two. I'd tried to get together with them, but ever since their parents sold their cars, we got no way to get together. They used to give me a ride to work."

"Where do you work, Marshall?"

"Alpo. I was just laid off."

"Don't you have a license?"

Although the legal driving age in Pennsylvania is sixteen, Fallon had neither a valid driver's license nor a car of his own.

"The brothers, they'd drive me and sometimes pick me up at work."

Fallon went on to relate that within the last month the Freemans had changed. "They've been talking about bizarre things lately. Like two weeks ago, the Freemans were talking to me about robbing a gun store, killing a cop, and splitting down South. That's what they said, 'splitting.' They also talked all the time about how much they hate their parents, the principal at their high school, and other skins. They talked about destroying these people and about getting 'berserker' tattooed on their forehead."

"What about those tattoos? What else did they say about them?"

"They said that when they had 'berserker' tattooed on their forehead, it would be the final straw. That tattoo would mean that they no longer cared about anything, that they would go on a 'path of destruction.' "

"What do you think about the Freemans now?"

"They're out of control! They'll hurt anybody who gets in their way."

"Including—"

"Police, yeah, including police. See, in the Skinhead Nazi organization there's a point system for certain crimes. You receive one point for killing a parent or a family member, killing a cop, and raping and killing a woman." Fallon added it up. "So the Freemans, they got three points each." One for Dennis, one for Brenda, and one for Erik, even though he was underage.

"Do you know Benny Birdwell?"

"Yeah, but I don't like him. I really don't know him much at all."

"Have either of the brothers called you since the murders?"

"No, but I'm staying at a hotel and last night into this morning, the pay phone in the hall rang all night. I didn't answer it, but I feel it was probably the Freemans calling me."

"Where do you think they're going?"

"Either down to North or South Carolina, or Florida."

The boys had chosen to stay in their room at the Truck World Motor Inn in Ohio, but by 10 A.M. they had gotten bored.

"Let's go next door to the mall and look around," said Ben.

On their way to the mall, they passed Sonny Converse, a trucker on his way to Pennsylvania. Gazing down from his eighteen-wheel rig, he noticed the three skinheads. They were hard to miss.

After the mall, the boys came back. Jesse Capece kept a sharp eye on them. They hung out in the lobby for a while, then went back to their room. Since they were paying in cash, a record was kept of their phone calls.

One, Jesse noticed, was to a local Domino's Pizza. The other was to Michigan.

"This is Bryan from Pennsylvania," Bryan said into the phone.

"Bryan *who* from Pennsylvania?"

"Remember in Detroit? You got my number."

On the other end of the line, Frank Hesse thought back to the last time he'd been in Detroit. It was only a few months before, at a New Year's Eve concert. Frank had gone to Detroit to hear a few white supremacist rock bands. That's where he had met Bryan, he remembered.

"I'm in Ohio," Bryan continued. "I got a couple of days off from work," he lied, "and I'm going up to Detroit and thought I'd stop up."

"Well, stop over," said Frank, "and we'll have a beer together."

As Frank gave the directions to his house, Bryan repeated them and David wrote them down on the receipt for the hotel room.

It was 7:58 P.M. when they checked out. Jesse Capece watched carefully as they pulled their Sunbird out onto the road.

Back in Allentown, the interviews by the police with friends of the Freeman brothers and Benny Birdwell were still going on.

"I've known Bryan and David Freeman for about three years," fifteen-year-old Deborah Miles told Trooper Eugene Derenick. "Bryan was an 'A' student until about six months ago when he began drinking alcohol constantly."

"Why?" Derenick wondered.

"He seemed to start drinking constantly when his cousin Benny dropped out of school."

Miles said she had been Bryan's girlfriend until about two months ago.

"Why'd you break up with him?"

"He got these tattoos—that, and the excessive drinking," Deborah answered. "It had gotten to the point where Bryan was drinking beer before he went to school."

She added that Bryan had spoken of killing his parents around Christmas. He was upset that his parents didn't believe in giving Christmas presents. She also remembered that Bryan and David didn't like their aunt Valerie. They tormented her by "pissing in her shampoo bottle" and wanted her to leave their home.

As for their skinhead beliefs, Deborah thought that Bryan Freeman was the leader and David and Benny Birdwell were followers. She said they also had a friend named Clark Hessler who was a skinhead living in Allentown who drove a red Honda XL.

Next up for an interview by Derenick was Bob Zelinski, another fifteen-year-old. He immediately informed Derenick that he was a skinhead and he had known the Freemans for about three years. "I got David to become a skinhead two years ago," he told Derenick proudly.

"And that's how the others became skins?" Derenick asked.

"David got Bryan and Benny Birdwell to be skinheads afterward," Zelinski explained. "David and Bryan hated their parents because they were Jehovah's Witnesses. Their mother had rules of no smoking or drinking alcohol in her house. Their parents had just sold Bryan's car recently. David said a couple of times recently, 'I would like to kill that fat bitch.' He was talking about his mother."

"Did Bryan say anything?"

"He said, 'We'll be out of here soon,' " Zelinski answered.

"How about his younger brother? Did either of them say anything about him?"

"David called his brother 'a piece of shit.' Oh, they also had beer in the fridge in their home and their mother would throw it away."

Zelinski related that he had heard a student

named Fred Simon received a call from someone who said "Fred" and hung up. He said that Simon believed it could have been the Freemans. He said that the last time he'd spoken to the Freemans had been yesterday. David had called and said he might stop by the bowling alley where he was going to be, but David never had.

Zelinski also related that recently he had been at a party at the Acorn Hotel and the Freemans had jumped him, saying he was Polish and not pure white. He said that the Freemans and another skinhead named Clark Hessler were now enemies.

By midnight, Sonny Converse had reached Murray, Pennsylvania. He took a coffee break at a truck stop and bought a newspaper. On the front page he saw the pictures of the three young men wanted for the murders of Brenda, Dennis, and Erik Freeman.

Sonny immediately dialed 911.

"Hey, I just saw those guys!" Sonny said excitedly.

"What guys?" asked the 911 operator.

"Those three guys you're looking for."

"Which three guys?" the dispatcher said with exasperation.

"The skinheads."

The dispatcher's voice suddenly took on a new edge. "Where?"

The police in Murray, Pennsylvania, immediately called the Salisbury Township police and told them that a trucker had spotted their suspects at the

Truck World Motor Inn in Hubbard, Ohio. When Vazquez called Truck World, he spoke to Jesse Capece.

"Yes, they were here," Jesse Capece acknowledged over the phone. "I knew there was something wrong with them."

She was asked where they had gone to.

"I don't know. They just pulled out of here a couple of hours ago. But they did make a phone call, to someplace in Michigan."

Vazquez alerted the Michigan state police that the Freeman brothers and Ben Birdwell, suspects in a multiple homicide case, were coming their way. He gave them their Pontiac Sunbird's tag number. They were to be considered armed and extremely dangerous.

Along with his partner, Salisbury Township detective Richard Metzler, Vazquez headed out to Allentown Airport and the first flight to Michigan. If the cops in the north country caught his suspects alive, he wanted to be there when they were questioned.

Two

Detroit is thought of the world over as "Motor City." It is here that many of America's automobile manufacturers are based and produce many of the thousands of automobiles that find their way onto the world market every year.

But to others, Detroit is known in another way, as the beachhead of the white supremacist movement in the United States. While places like Idaho and Montana garner greater headlines because of their much-publicized though isolated conflicts with white supremacists, it is in Detroit where Adolf Hitler's racist dogma is being disseminated to the white supremacists' main target: America's youth. Detroit is the battleground in what white supremacists describe as "rahowa," or racial holy war.

Detroit is a city polarized by racial tensions. The inner city's infrastructure has crumbled, leaving blacks and other disenfranchised minorities to live in crime-ridden neighborhoods.

In the bedrooms of some of the homes in the white suburbs are teenagers who see and feel their parents' hypocrisy and, like their parents before them, rebel against their elders' beliefs, looking, too, for a place to belong. And like their parents before them, they turn to music to express their rebellion. Once it was the Beatles and the Stones; today it is Nordic Thunder and White Terror, hate rock bands.

Hate rock began in England. Ian Stuart was a musician in British punk rock in the seventies who'd put together a band called Skrewdriver. They signed on with a small label in Britain and opened for a lot of acts, including the Police and Siouxsie and the Banshees. Eventually, the neo-Nazi National Front, a white supremacist group, pushed Stuart to publicize his political thoughts to attract sympathetic fans. Stuart agreed.

In that agreement, the symbiotic relationship between neo-Nazi groups, and what would later become known as "skinhead rock" was formed. While organizations that condemned Stuart set up a moratorium on his work, the National Front set up a record label called White Noise.

White Noise's first CD was also Stuart's first openly racist record. Called "White Power," it became the prototype for similar hate records to come. But distributing this type of music to a large audience in America proved daunting until Resistance Records came along.

Resistance Records is based in Detroit. The company records white power bands, and distributes their CDs. Unlike other companies that have tried to do the same thing, Resistance is not a bunch of fringe-group amateurs. Its owners and founders, George Burdi and Mark Wilson, have come up with a way of marketing these CDs with topnotch promotion and packaging.

George Burdi's own band, Rahowa, has an album out called *Declaration of War.* On the box is a picture of a Nordic warrior beefed up on steroids towering over the corpse of a black man. The lyrics are equally clear.

Resistance Records sponsored a skinhead concert that took place in Racine, Wisconsin, on September 30, 1994. Three hundred hate rock fans met in Memorial Hall, a huge, cavernous space wired for sound.

On the bill were White Thunder, Rahowa, White Terror, and No Remorse.

The band members shrieked racial epithets from the stage, and the crowd shouted back in chorus.

The concert closed with a selection from "No Remorse" entitled "Farewell, Ian Stuart." A few of the other acts joined them onstage. Some of the crowd cried in mourning, because Stuart had recently died.

After the concert, while most drifted back to their cars, Joe Rowan, leader of the band Nordic Thunder and a group of twenty to thirty skinheads, decided to go out partying.

Racine is probably best known as the home of the Racine Belles, the first team to win the Women's Professional Baseball League World Series in 1944, a feat immortalized in Penny Marshall's film *A League of Their Own.* Its most recent notoriety came from what happened next.

Rowan and the skinheads went into a local convenience store called Starvin' Marvin's to buy beer and pretzels. They were on their way to a party in Hartford, about an hour northwest of Racine.

Their adrenaline still pumping from the concert, Rowan and the jackbooted skinheads began to trash the place. The clerk tripped a silent alarm and then went to the back room to wait for the cops to arrive.

When police arrived, they found Rowan in the back of a pickup truck. Blood was leaking out of a bullet wound. The coroner later said it was a bullet through his back that had killed him.

The concertgoers were still milling about, shouting that a black man, Gene Flood, who was walking away from the store, had killed Rowan. The cops arrested Flood. He was later charged with first degree homicide.

After a brief investigation, police discovered that Rowan and his buddies had traded insults and racial slurs with a few of the store's black customers. One of those customers was Gene Flood, who, fearing for his life, took out a gun and fired wildly, hitting Rowan, who was taken outside and laid in the pickup truck to die.

Flood was later freed when the police ruled it had been a self-defense shooting. But to the skinhead movement, regardless of the ignominious way Rowan had died, he was a martyr to the cause, a victim of the race war in America and the ascendancy of the mud people, those who were not "pure" white.

Death is a solemn right in the skinhead movement, and Rowan was immortalized. He had died for the rights of free white men everywhere to protect their white homeland against the niggers and kikes.

David, Bryan, and Benny looked at Detroit as it passed from view.

"Cool place, Detroit," said Bryan.

"Yeah, our kind of people there," David added.

Despite the dragnet that had been set out for them, they slipped through it easily. Despite the many police cruisers who passed on their way north, not one stopped them.

The Sunbird hurtled through the night with the three teenagers wondering what was ahead of them. The idea began to drift into their consciousness that there was the possibility of being captured, but like all teenagers, they thought of themselves as immortal. If anything did happen, they'd survive. Still, it would be smart to have a story ready for the cops, just in case. Since Ben was eighteen and could be tried as an adult, Bryan and David would take all the responsibility for the killings. As juveniles (Bryan was seventeen and David fifteen) they'd be tried as such. Ben knew from his own legal problems that the penalties for a juvenile committing a crime were considerably lower.

"Not much jail time," they reassured each other.

Another important point. While Pennsylvania had the death penalty, it had not been invoked for thirty years. There was no reason to believe it would now. Besides, who ever heard of frying a kid, even for murder? It just didn't happen.

So they'd worked things out, the two brothers and their cousin. They got their story straight.

Traveling north into Michigan on the interstate, they stopped only for gas and cigarettes a few times. In the homes they passed, night owls stayed up, channel-surfing with their remote controls. Someplace in the middle of all that channel surfing and all those thousands of people watching TV in the early-morning hours, there were some who saw CNN's reports of the flight of the brothers Freeman and cousin Birdwell, the pursuit by Pennsylvania authorities, and the tension produced by the uncertainty of their capture.

In the reports, the three were described as armed and dangerous skinheads with an obvious propensity toward violence.

By the time Benny and the Freemans entered the town of Midland, Michigan, at 6:50 on the morning of February 28, they were the most wanted fugitives in America.

"You know, it's sort of early to call on Frank," David said.

"Yeah, I guess you're right," Brian answered.

"So let's check into a hotel in the meanwhile," said Ben.

Greg Pavledes was working the eleven-to-seven graveyard shift at the Holiday Inn in Midland, Michigan, when the skinheads walked in.

"We want a room for three," said Benny Birdwell. On the registration card, Benny wrote his name as "Mike Burr," with an address on Susquehanna Street in Allentown, PA.

The price of the room was $76.68, including tax. The boys reached into the pockets of their jeans and pulled out a big wad of five-dollar bills. After they'd paid, they went back to their car and proceeded to drive around to their room.

A short while later, the one with the *"Sieg heil"* tattoo on his forehead (David) reappeared.

"How do we get a key to the minibar in the room?" he asked.

Since they didn't have a credit card, Greg asked him for a $150 cash deposit. David reached into his jeans and came out with a whole bunch of ones, fives, and quarters and proceeded to count out the deposit. Greg gave him the key.

Their size and their tattoos had given Greg the willies before, but it was the method of payment that made him really suspicious. It was highly unusual for someone to pay for the room and minibar all in cash, and with low-denomination bills and change, at that.

After talking to the motel security guard, Greg called the Midland police department to report his suspicions. Officers Sam Delamater, a stockily-built cop in his early thirties and his partner, Officer Peter Delgaudio, were dispatched to the motel.

They met with the security guard at the front desk. The guard was concerned because three strange-looking young men with short hair and tattoos had checked into the hotel. They'd paid for their room in coins and small bills. The cops agreed to check it out.

Inside room 222, the three heard a sharp knock. They looked at each other. Who the hell did they know in this town?

"Who's there?" one of them shouted back.

"Police!" Delamater shouted back.

Cool as the proverbial cucumber, Ben answered the door.

"What are you fellas doing here?" asked Officer Delamater.

"Just visiting," said Bryan.

"And where'd you get those small bills you paid for the room with?" Officer Delgaudio asked.

"We're waiters," Benny answered smoothly. "We get a lot of small bills in tips."

Delgaudio stepped into the room while Delamater remained at the door. The cops' suspicious gaze roamed the room.

Bryan was in bed, the covers pulled all the way up to his chin. Within a minute, the toilet flushed and David came out of the bathroom. The cops could plainly see the words *"Sieg heil"* tattooed on his forehead.

All of the boys appeared sober. There was no alcohol evident, no drugs. The only palpable odor in the room came from half-smoked cigarettes that smoldered in ashtrays. The cops continued to ask them questions. Benny did most of the talking. When David and Bryan were addressed, they responded vaguely but politely.

"Why don't you pull those covers down?" Delamater asked, looking over at Bryan. He wanted to be sure the kid wasn't concealing a weapon.

"Sure," said Bryan.

As the covers came down, exposing his body, naked save for his briefs, the cops could see that he was concealing something, but it wasn't weapons.

Bryan's body had been tattooed extensively with Nazi symbols. Across his chest were two blue and red chevrons. Inside the one on the left side of his chest was the SS, symbol of Hitler's Storm

Troopers. Inside the chevron on the right was a swastika. Separating the two were the German words *"Weiss macht."*

Below the nipple on the right side was another swastika and a tattoo of what looked like a skull or a spider. It was impossible to tell without getting closer.

On Bryan's right arm was a cartoonish figure that was half white and half dark. On his neck was a swastika made of bones. There was a "berserker" tattoo on his forehead.

"Those are pretty interesting tattoos," said Delgaudio.

"Oh, you think so?" said Benny, brightening up. "One of them cost him a thousand dollars."

Benny showed the cops his tattoos. He had a swastika on his left arm, an iron cross on his right, a Viking holding an ax on his forearm, the word "anarchy" tattooed on his right leg, and the word "berserker" across his low forehead. In the process of his exhibiting himself, the cops noticed a cut in the webbing between his index finger and thumb.

"How'd you get that cut?" Delamater asked.

"Oh, I fell and cut it," Benny answered nonchalantly.

"How old are you?" Delamater asked David.

"I'm eighteen," David answered defensively.

"Well, you don't look that old."

"Well, I am," David answered quietly.

To the officers' credit, they were suspicious enough of the boy's story to search the room and the car for contraband, any sort of illegal substances. Finding none, they ran the kids' names through the police computer to see if there were any outstanding warrants.

The Midland County prosecutors' office would later claim that this check came up negative, that the bulletin on the search for the boys had not yet gone out over the wires.

"Have a good evening, boys," said Delamater.

"Oh, we will, Officer, we will," said Benny.

They watched them get into their squad car and leave.

"Boy, those cops are dumb," said Bryan.

"And how," Benny chimed in.

"Let's go see Frank," Bryan said.

"And party," David added.

Though he spelled it differently, August Hesse had a special place in the white supremacy movement. His surname was similar to that of Hitler's chief of staff and confidant Rudolf Hess. But unlike Hess, who parachuted into Britain during the early days of World War II in a misguided attempt to make peace, peace was the last thing on August Hesse's mind in December 1994.

Hesse had been shopping in a store in Midland, Michigan, when a black man had walked in. After shouting racial epithets at the man, Hesse threatened to kill him. Police were called, and Hesse proceeded to fight with them until he was taken into custody.

Down at the stationhouse, Hesse was charged with ethnic intimidation and resisting and obstructing a police officer. When the Freemans and Birdwell rolled into Midland, August Hesse was still awaiting trial. He would later plead guilty to the charges against him and be sentenced to a year in jail.

The countryside around Midland, Michigan, is verdant, but not in winter. Then it is a bleak place, the land lying wan, sometimes covered by snow, as it was on February 28, 1995. The Hesse property was in a rural area of Midland County, composed mostly of farms, where decent middle-class people tried to make a living off the land.

On the property was the main house, where Frank Hesse lived with his brother, August, and his father, Ronald. In the house were mailings from some of the country's neo-Nazi groups. The Hesse brothers appeared to be avid subscribers. While the Hesses had no direct links to neo-Nazi groups, or the Michigan Militia that is allegedly tied into the Oklahoma City bombing, prosecutors would later claim that in their basement were the makings for incendiary pipe bombs. As a kind of signature, someone had scrawled racial epithets on the pipes.

Down the road was the framework of a house that Frank had been painstakingly constructing for months. Frank Hesse, tall, handsome, with close-cropped hair and big hands, had gone down the road to work on his house. He was there, busily hammering nails into wood, when his father called down from the main house.

"Hey Frank, Frank."

His father's voice carried on the wind a full quarter-mile down to where Frank was. He looked up.

"You got visitors," his father continued.

Frank put down his tools, wiped his hands on his jeans, and strolled out to the road. As he walked up the hill to the house, he saw three guys standing outside a Pontiac. One of them he recognized.

"Hey, Bryan, you made it," he said with a ready smile, extending his hand in greeting to Bryan Freeman.

They shook hands and Bryan quickly introduced David and Ben. Frank had never met either before and while David seemed an easy, laid-back sort of fellow, Ben Birdwell immediately gave Frank the creeps.

"Well, like I said," Bryan related, "we took off from work and came up to, you know, hang out."

"That's great," said Frank. He always had a welcoming hand out to a fellow skin. He could not deny them the hospitality of his home.

"Come on inside," he told them brightly.

They went inside, had a few beers, and Frank showed them where to stow their gear. They appeared to be traveling light.

A little later in the day, he took them down the road to show them the house he was building. They helped in putting up some beams, but they didn't seem to be much good with their hands, especially Ben.

Back at the house that evening, Frank showed the boys his gun collection. He hunted game with rifles. Ben seemed particularly interested in his assault rifle.

Ben went on about how good a hunter he was,

what a dead shot he was, digressing to other areas where he was superior. *What a braggart this guy is,* Frank thought.

At no time during their stay with Frank did either Freeman brother or their cousin give any indication of what had happened back home. All three stuck to their story that they had gotten off "work" and just felt like taking a little road trip.

That night, Frank took them "malling"—the all-American pastime of going to the local mall, eyeing the girls, window shopping, and repetitive walking up and down the corridors of commercialism. When they returned back to the Hesse house, it was about 9 P.M.

Frank broke out six packs of beer. The boys proceeded to polish off the cans one by one. Frank let them listen to some of his music. Ordinarily, Frank liked to listen to country more than skinhead music, but his guests were into skinhead rock and Frank was nothing if not a polite host.

He played various cuts by two skinhead bands he favored, Bound for Glory and Aggravated Assault.

By 1 A.M. the boys were pooped and started to turn in. David was the last. He was stone cold drunk, so drunk that he had to step outside for a wintry blast of frigid Michigan air. That and vomiting in the field outside seemed to clear his head, and he went back inside. He smoked some dope and went to sleep.

The boys awoke to a sunny day. They breakfasted on coffee, cereal, and milk. David, in particular, needed the coffee because he was nursing a hangover. By 11 A.M., they were finished and went down to the river to go ice fishing.

Ice fishing is a peculiar custom in the north country. Unlike most easterners, who try to stay in out of the cold weather, and southerners, who can't tolerate it, denizens of Michigan's north country find something in every season to make sport of. Arctic weather is no exception. Using a special tool that cuts a hole in the thick ice of a river, the fisherman sinks a line in and waits patiently in the frigid cold for some fish to snap at the bait and be reeled in for dinner.

And that's what the four boys did that day, with Frank taking the lead in showing the other three what to do, for while David, Bryan, and Ben lived in a semi-rural area, they were essentially city boys.

So the boys fished. For the remainder of the afternoon, until about 3:30 P.M., they waited patiently for a bite.

By 4 P.M. they were back at the Hesse homestead, sans fish. It just wasn't their lucky day. The fish had refused to bite. The boys began to have a late afternoon repast when suddenly they heard a disembodied voice from outside, coming in loud and clear on a bullhorn.

"Frank Hesse. Frank Hesse."

"What the heck did you do now?" Frank's father Ronald asked.

"Nothing, Dad, I swear."

"Frank Hesse, we want you and David, Bryan Freeman, and Nelson Birdwell—"

"Nelson?" Frank asked.

". . . to come out with your hands up."

"What the hell did you guys *do?*" Frank asked. Bryan smiled.

Outside, the place was surrounded by cops, members of the Michigan state police, supplemented by officers of the Midland County police department. Sergeants Tom Mynsberge and Dick Harms of the Michigan state police watched as the door to the Hesse house opened slowly and the four boys slowly made their way outside. As soon as they had cleared the farmhouse, a cop barked an order for them to keep their hands overhead and hit the ground. They readily complied and uniformed officers moved in to quickly cuff their hands behind their backs.

In order to prevent them from concocting a story, all four boys were placed in separate cars.

"You have the right to remain silent. Anything you say can be used against you in a court of law. You have the right to the presence of an attorney . . ."

As the boys were read their rights, Ronald Hesse watched the squad cars pull out. Damn! He already had enough trouble with his son Auggie, over the charge that he had beaten a black guy at a local supermarket.

As his squad car pulled out into the road, Frank Hesse flicked his long hair back over his shoulder and looked back at his father until he was a lonely speck on the horizon.

Three

Midland has 43,000 people who live within its environs. In Midland County there are 88,000 residents. In the whole county, there are maybe two to three homicides a year.

The state of Michigan does not have the death penalty and has not had it for over a hundred years. But there are *federal* crimes that warrant the death penalty. The last man executed in Michigan was a federal criminal who was hanged sometime during the 1930s. The man who pulled the gallows lever was the sheriff of Midland County.

Norman Donker is the prosecuting attorney for Midland County, Michigan. A tall, serious-looking man with a dour demeanor, he had gone grocery shopping and had returned home to find four messages on his answering machine. One of them was from a Philadelphia TV station. They had heard that the Freeman brothers and Nelson Birdwell had been captured, and were looking for a comment.

Not knowing anything about this, Donker contacted the state police. They had been just about to call the prosecutor to let him know that the fugitives had been captured.

Frank would be questioned and released soon after his arrival at the Midland County Jail, an old building in the heart of the Midland metropolis. David was booked at 7 P.M., Bryan at 7:38 P.M., Ben at 8:06.

In Michigan, seventeen is the age of consent. If you're seventeen, you're an adult and can be charged as one—and questioned as one. Bryan and Ben were placed in separate interrogation rooms.

David Freeman, fifteen at the time, was still considered a minor. Police weren't sure, considering his age and the severity of his crime, what to do with him. Should he be held with his brother and cousin, or sent to the juvenile division? It was an unusual situation for the Midland police.

Out in the police garage, David cooled his heels in the back of a cruiser until the venue was sorted out. Finally, after consultation with Donker, it was decided to take David to a temporary holding cell, and he was transported to the Midland County Law Enforcement Center. Sitting alone, without his brother or his cousin, David felt desperate, hopeless, and most of all, alone.

They got me, they got me, I'm going down. That's it. What do I do? What do I do?

They had him and there was nothing he could do about it. Maybe, just maybe, now was the time to try to save Benny, as they'd planned, in case they were captured. Well, they had been captured, *dammit*, and inside, he felt like shit.

David waived his right to counsel and decided to give a statement. Detective sergeants Tom Mynsberge and Dick Harms took him into an interrogation room, once again advised him of his Miranda rights, and made certain that he was making the statement of his own volition. With the legal niceties done, it was down to business.

"Well, basically, what we'd like you to do is on Sunday, which would be the twenty-sixth of this month, can you tell us what transpired at your residence, and like we said, we want to make sure that you put the reasons and events leading up to what actually happened, if you would. Please."

Harms and Mynsberge were sitting in a plain seven-by-twelve-foot cinderblock room. It was a room used for questioning suspects, the kind of antiseptic, windowless interrogation room that differed little from state to state, where cops sat patiently waiting for suspects to spill their guts.

David sat in front of a scarred wooden table. A tape recorder had been placed in front of him and one of the cops had turned it on so its microphone would catch everything he said.

"Well," David began, "we were home that day. And we, we came home later. Our parents were asleep. They started saying, 'Oh, if you go outside, you're gonna be locked sleeping outside. You know you can't leave the house for anything after eleven o'clock.' They, they were just saying you're not allowed to be doing any of that stuff. 'Gotta follow our rules or you'll be out of here.' They kept making up all these new rules, like saying that if they don't like somebody, we're not allowed to be with them."

"This is your mom and dad saying this, Dave?" asked Harms.

"Yeah, that's right."

"Okay, go ahead."

"This, I don't know. It's like, if we couldn't follow the rules, we'd be kicked out of the house, and just, like, a lot of real strict rules, and we couldn't take it any more."

"So then there came a point in time when they had you leave the house?" Harms surmised.

"Yeah, we've left the house before."

"I mean this particular night."

"No, it was, was not that particular night."

"Okay," Harms said patiently, "then what happened?"

"Well, we was, a little bit later, my mom came downstairs. My brother took a knife and started stabbing her. I went upstairs and I was beating my dad in the face with a baseball bat and cut his throat. I went to my little brother and smashed his face in."

David Freeman's voice was curiously flat and unemotional as he described the human devastation.

"With?" Harms asked.

"A bat."

"So you were downstairs when this happened to your mother?"

"Yeah. For like, a couple of seconds."

"And what did you see your brother do? What did you see Bryan do?"

"Put his hand over her mouth and stab her."

"Whereabouts did he stab her?"

"In the back. Everywhere."

"How many times?"

"I, I was only down there for a couple of seconds."

"What kind of a knife did he have?"

"It was a steak knife or something. It was pretty big. After that, I couldn't come back downstairs or anything."

"So then you went upstairs while this was going on?"

David nodded.

"Did you see your mother fall to the ground?" Harms wondered.

"No, I went back downstairs once after that, but I didn't look at her," David replied, his head sinking down, his voice a monotone.

"And then you went upstairs, and that's when you had contact with your dad and brother?"

"Yeah, they were sleeping in their rooms."

"They were in separate rooms?"

"Yeah."

"And they were in their own beds?"

"Yeah."

"And then what happened?"

"After everything was done, we grabbed the car and left."

"No, I mean, you went into your dad's bedroom . . . ?"

"Yeah."

"First?"

"Yeah, I went into his bedroom first."

"And then what happened in there?"

"First I hit him in the face with the bat and cracked his skull. I hit him, like, two or three more times and I cut his throat."

The words cut like a knife, slicing through the air and chilling it until the only thing that wasn't frozen were the words themselves.

"And what did you cut his throat with?"

"A steak knife."

"And you got it from?"

"The kitchen."

"Did your dad do anything when you cut him?"

"No, he never woke up."

"You're pretty sure he was dead?"

"Yeah. He was dead."

"What happened then?"

"I went into my little brother's room and I—"

"What is his name?" Harms interrupted. It really wasn't very important now, since he was dead, but he liked to personalize the victims.

"Erik," said David.

"And what happened then?"

"I hit him in the face with a bat and he just died like that. He never woke up, either."

"There was somebody else with you in the house at the time?"

"Yeah. That was Ben."

"And where was he when Bryan went down to the basement with your mom?"

"He was down there, but I don't know for how long."

"Did he see what happened to your mom?"

"I'm pretty sure," David answered hesitantly.

"And then did he see what happened to your dad and brother?"

"Yeah, he's the only one that had to go back in their rooms for some stuff. He's the only one that would, that could do it."

But Harms was more interested if Ben had participated in the homicides.

"Where was Ben when you were doing your brother and your dad?"

"I seen him walk by once and look in, but—"

"Did he say anything?"

"No."

"Where was he when Bryan was doing your mom?"

"He was downstairs for a little bit and then I guess he came up."

"So then he eventually found out that there was something wrong with all three of them, your mom and dad . . ."

"Yeah, that's right."

"How did you learn that? What did Ben say?"

"Oh, after that, Bryan came upstairs and he said, 'Well, she's dead,' and you know, 'I got Dad and Erik.' "

"Who said that she's dead? Ben?"

"Bryan did."

"But what did Ben say?"

"He didn't say, he really didn't say anything at all. After we left, we didn't really say anything for a while," David continued.

"Did Ben know that they were dead then?"

"Yeah."

"How did he know that?"

"Oh, he went back in the room."

"You saw him go back in the room?"

"Yeah."

"In whose room now?"

"In my dad's, after he was dead."

"Did he go into your brother's room after he was dead?"

"No, but the door was open."

Harms had no way of knowing that when Valerie Freeman discovered Erik's body, the door to his bedroom was closed. David was lying to protect his cousin.

"You don't know for sure if he saw your brother or not?"

"Yeah."

"Yeah what? How did he know he was dead then?"

" 'Cause we told him."

"While you were still at the house?"

David nodded.

"And what did you tell him?"

"I told him everybody else was dead."

"And what did he say?"

"Nothing. He didn't say nothing."

"What did you do with all the clothes you guys were wearing and everything?" Mynsberge asked.

"They're still at the house."

"You left everything at the house? So, the clothes you have here you changed into, right?"

"That's right."

"How did Bryan cut his hand? Was that when he was killing your mother?" Harms continued.

"Not that I know of," David answered evasively.

"Did he actually fall?"

"He said he fell."

"Okay, what happened to the knives that were used to kill your family?" Harms said impatiently.

"We put them back in the sink, both of them."

"You clean up or anything?"

"I didn't," said David, almost defensively.

"How about the baseball bat? Where's that?"

"It's sitting in the dining room, I think."

"You guys ever use an ax handle?" Harms wondered.

"Yeah, that was used, too. It was a pick handle."

"Who used that?" Mynsberge asked.

"Me. I used that and there was, like, a real big gold baseball bat."

"Who did you hit with the ax handle?" Harms asked.

"Oh, that would have been my brother," David answered, totally nonplussed by the question.

"And did you hit him with the baseball bat, too?" Harms asked.

"I only hit him once."

"Pardon?"

"I only hit him once."

"With?"

"The handle."

"Okay, and you say that did something to his face or skull?"

"Yes."

"Have you told anyone else about this?"

David looked down and mumbled "No."

"Nobody?" Mynsberge pressed.

"No."

"You guys were just pretty quiet about the whole thing?" Mynsberge asked dubiously.

"Yeah."

"There was no talk going on, just wondering what happened?"

"No. We just kept asking, 'What the hell did we do it for?' "

"You wished it would all go away, huh?"

"Yeah." He was looking down.

"Hard to take it back once it's done."

"Yeah."

"And you came up here to Michigan, these guys Frank and August, they don't know you're on the run?"

"No, they didn't know anything about what had happened."

"Do you drink at all, Dave? When's the last time you had anything to drink?" Harms asked.

A confession by a suspect under the influence is inadmissible. The detectives had to make sure David was sober.

"A couple of nights ago," he lied.

"You're not on any medication, are you?"

"No."

"Okay. We appreciate you having told us what's happening. Is there anything else that you have to say?"

"That's it. That's everything."

"You're pretty much sure that they were, all three of them were dead when you left there?"

"Not really."

Once again, the two cops ignored the inconsistency of the answer.

"Did the money from your trip, is that what you went back in the bedroom for?"

"That's right. That's why I went back into the bedroom."

"Is there anything left in the car? Any money?"

"I have no idea."

"What do you think should happen now?" Mynsberge wondered.

"I don't know," David replied thoughtfully.

"Gonna wait and see?"

"Whatever happens happens. There ain't much I can do about that now."

"Could you use some help?"

"I just don't want to spend the rest of my life in jail."

"When Bryan did that to your mother, did something, like, kind of spur you to go up and do that to your dad?"

"Oh yeah," said David, suddenly remembering. "Bryan said, when she was coming down, 'Whoever pussys out, they're getting stabbed.' "

"Pardon me, I didn't hear that."

"My brother, he said when my mom was coming down, 'Whoever pussys out, they're gonna get stabbed, too.' "

"Who did Bryan say that to?"

"Me and Ben."

"So I guess you guys were just to the point after they kicked you out, basically it's pretty much in Bryan's mind that things had to be taken care of right then."

"Yes."

"Did he try and get you guys fired up a little bit?"

"I wasn't really fired, you know, I was just—"

"How about when it happened?"

"I still wasn't."

"Did you do that to your brother and dad because you were scared of Bryan?"

"Nah, I just—"

"Just like lost it for a while yourself?" Mynsberge finished.

"Yeah. Lost it," David agreed.

"So did you know before your mom came down that Bryan was going to do that, or did he just talk about it and you weren't sure he was going to?"

"Not really."

"Then you weren't really sure until that evening?"

"Nah. I didn't think he'd do it. I was hoping he wouldn't."

Mynsberge was trying to establish intent in David's mind. If he could do that, David could be charged with first-degree murder.

"Was Ben aware of what was going on before?"

"Sure."

"Was Ben afraid of Bryan?"

"I guess he was the same as me. He didn't think he'd do it."

"And then it just happened."

"And after he stabbed my mom, we'd be there anyway, we'd be the accessories anyway."

"So before she came down the stairs, he said he was gonna do this?" Harms asked.

"Yes. He said, 'When she gets down, I'm gonna kill her, and you guys go upstairs and get Dad and Erik.' "

"Where was the other brother at this time?" Harms asked.

"He was in his room upstairs, sleeping," David answered with puzzlement. He'd already answered this question.

"How come nothing happened to him?" Harms asked.

David looked at him like he was crazy. What the hell had he been talking about?

"Something did happen to him," David answered sarcastically. "I only have two brothers."

"Okay, that's the two, then," Harms replied.

"Yeah."

"Oh, I thought there was—"

"No, it's Bryan," said David.

"Bryan is his other brother, and then Erik," Mynsberge explained patiently.

"I thought there was two younger guys there," Harms answered, still not getting it.

"What time was it?" Mynsberge went on.

"I don't know what time it was," said David.

"Was it dark? Afternoon?"

"No. It was dark out."

"You told us before we went on tape that you'd gone to Wendy's earlier in the day and then a movie."

"That's right."

"Okay, when you came home from the movie, that's when all the shit hit the fan?"

"Yes."

"Okay. Is that when they were upset with you because you came in late?"

"We weren't late," he answered defensively. "It was just, we stopped outside to smoke. We went outside for five minutes and they tried to lock us out."

"After the killings, what time did you leave? 'Bout midnight?"

"It must have been around midnight," David confirmed.

"You guys got cleaned up, got the money together, grabbed what you needed, and left?"

"Right."

"Did you shower and everything?"

"We did at the motels."

"Did you stay at more than one motel in Ohio?"

"We stayed at the one in Ohio and the one Holiday Inn here. That's it."

"Anything else you'd like to add to this statement, Dave?" Harms asked.

"No. That's everything."

"Probably feel a little bit of remorse, now that you've done that and you can't take it back, right?" asked Harms.

"Yeah," David answered.

"Well, we appreciate your talking to us, and did you have something else to say? You acted like you were going to say something."

Mynsberge leaned forward. Maybe . . .

"No," David answered.

"What time we got, Tom?"

"Twelve fifty-five," Mynsberge answered, pulling back from the table and getting up.

"Okay, we're gonna end this tape at twelve fifty-five on March the . . ."

"Second, of 'ninety-five," Mynsberge concluded.

It was not a good interrogation. David had said exactly what the two Michigan cops had wanted. In fact, at times, they had actually put words into his mouth.

A cop is supposed to go over the suspect's story a number of times. The idea is for the suspect to keep filling in the blanks so when the time comes for trial, the confession is airtight.

The confession David gave was full of holes. For instance, there was no indication David had killed his brother, yet he was taking responsibility.

Mynsberge and Harms had no idea that David and Bryan had agreed beforehand to say they had whacked Dennis, Brenda, and Erik, in order to help Benny. However, at no time did the boys, in agreeing to what their story would be, actually talk about who did what. David might have been telling the truth.

Mynsberge and Harms felt that David had been completely honest and sincere. He seemed like a boy with a great deal of guilt who wanted it expunged so he could move on with his life, such as it was. He couldn't bring his family back, but at least the confession gave him relief. That's what they thought.

But cops are not family therapists. Their job is not to elicit a confession so the suspect gets relief. The idea is to *get him*, as surely as the suspect has killed.

By speaking readily, David might have helped Benny, but he was tightening the noose around his own neck. He had no idea as he was led back to his cell that he now stood a good chance of dying in Pennsylvania's death chamber.

Four

In Allentown, Donna and Nelson Birdwell II were shocked at their son's involvement in the Freeman murders. Donna just couldn't believe it.

Despite Benny's past troubles with the law, despite her husband's arrest record, she just did not believe that her son could be a murderer. Whatever he was, whatever he'd done in the past, he was still a good boy who would never, ever commit murder.

It was a particularly shattering crime for Donna, who had been very close to Brenda. At times, Brenda had assumed the roles of sister, best friend, and even mother. To think that her nephews Bryan and David had killed her, and Dennis and Erik as well—it was just too awful to fathom. Over time, though, she knew she would have to accept the reality. As for Benny, she would not even entertain the thought that he was in any way culpable.

"We need to support our son," she told her husband. "We need to be with him."

And so two more members of the Freeman/Birdwell family got into their car and in the dead of night, headed north to Michigan.

* * *

Being in a cell was nothing new; Benny Birdwell had been in and out of trouble with the cops for years.

Benny calmly smoked his cigarettes and thought about the time he and his mother and his father had traveled from their Allentown home to Hackensack, New Jersey, in 1988, when he was eleven year old. His father had taken them there for some reason, and then he had left them in this fleabag motel. It was just such a shiteating place, "deplorable conditions" were the words the cops used to describe it.

He recalled those cops at the door, telling him and his mother that his father was under arrest. His old man had been stopped for some traffic violations. The cops found drug paraphernalia in the car and charged him with illegally possessing the stuff. They threw him in jail and put his name into the computer, which showed his father had violated parole when he'd left Allentown. And was also wanted on a charge of retail theft, felony grade. After he was sentenced to a $1,000 fine and community service on the New Jersey charges, he was extradited back to Pennsylvania.

Benny had a juvenile record but at least that wasn't public information. Nothing major. It was sealed because he'd been a juvenile. But he was eighteen now and if he was tried, it would be as an adult. Pennsylvania had the death penalty for a murder one conviction.

Now, Benny Birdwell, a.k.a. Nelson Birdwell III, sat in a dank cell in the middle of God-knew-where in some Michigan hick town waiting for the local cops to take him in for interrogation. He calmly smoked cigarettes until finally, at a little after 2:30 A.M., they came to get him.

Benny was led down a corridor and into another interrogation room. It was a carbon copy of the one recently vacated by David. The tape recorder was set up, and once again, Mynsberge and Harms took their positions for the interrogation, across from Benny.

"This is a taped statement between Nelson . . ."

"Benjamin," Harms added.

"Benjamin Bernell, better known as Ben, at the Midland County Jail."

"What's your last name?" Harms asked.

"Birdwell," Ben answered.

"Birdwell, occurring on . . ."

"How do you spell your last name?" Harms questioned.

Ben spelled it out.

"And this interview," Mynsberge continued, "is taking place on March 2, 1995, at approximately two forty-five A.M."

Mynsberge droned on with the preliminaries until finally he got to the point. "Okay, just talk right into the mike," Mynsberge pointed.

"Oh, all right," Ben said testily.

"As a matter of fact, you can just sit down if you want to."

"All right."

"Give your name and—"

"My name is Nelson Birdwell, and what shall I say, how did it happen?"

"We want you to just tell us about what happened, it was on Sunday evening, after you returned from the movies with Bryan and David."

"All right, were, they said that they had to go back to the house, so we went back and—"

Harms interrupted. "You went to Bryan and David's house after the movie?"

"Yes, we went back to their house."

"Go on."

"And we all went downstairs and Dave got something to eat and he came back downstairs with a plate of cookies, and his mom came down and like started bitching and shit like that, getting on our case, and he just stabbed her."

"Where did he stab her?" Mynsberge asked. He did not get Ben to qualify who did the stabbing.

"I didn't see."

"Okay."

"And he screams, 'You guys puss out, I'll kill you both.' "

"Who screams that?" Harms asked.

"Bryan, Bryan," Ben said loudly.

"Bryan screams that at you, and—"

"Snuff."

"Snuff?" Harms said, looking at his partner in bewilderment.

"Snuff," Ben repeated. "It's Dave's nickname."

"Okay."

"And Dave ran upstairs," Ben continued in a rush of words, "and I went in the other room and Bryan ran up behind them. All I heard was noise upstairs. Bryan said something and I ran upstairs, and Bryan came out. He was like covered with blood, and Snuff barely had any blood on him. We just looked at that. Dave puked up their stairs and I don't know what happened with the weapons or anything. I didn't hit no one or stab no one. Nothing like that. And after that, we just left."

"Who changed clothes before you left?" Mynsberge questioned.

"Bryan did. Dave kept his clothes on."

"Where did Dave throw up at?" Harms asked.

"In the dining room area. And then you go out to the deck. He puked on the deck, and in the dining room area. Right by the sliding glass doors."

"Backing up just a little bit now, when David and Bryan's mother came downstairs, do you remember what it was she was saying?" asked Harms.

"No, not really. She was like bitching about me being there, and like, she thought they were drinking again. She said they come home drunk, and I guess they just like lost it that night."

"Where was Bryan when she came downstairs?"

"Bryan was in his room downstairs."

"So you and David were in David's bedroom?"

"Yeah."

"And Bryan was in his own bedroom?"

"Yeah."

"Can you see in one bedroom from the other?"

"They're right across the hall, but if you stand by the door you can see."

"So Bryan's mother came down and approached Bryan's room?" Harms asked.

"Snuff's room," Ben corrected.

"And was yelling at Dave and Bryan at the same time?"

"I guess she was yelling at both the same time, but she was looking in Dave's room."

"And you were in Dave's room at the time?"

"Yeah. And Dave, he was yelling back at her."

"What was he yelling?"

"I have no clue."

That was strange. If Benny was there, why didn't he hear what was said? Harms pushed on.

"Okay," Harms continued, "and he comes out of the bedroom—"

"After Bryan stabbed her."

"So did you actually see the mother when Dave's stabbing her?"

"Bryan stabbed her," Benny corrected.

"Oh, I'm sorry," said Harms, apologetic, "when Bryan's stabbing her?"

"Bryan grabbed her from behind."

"Like putting his hand over her mouth."

"Yeah, he put her hand over her mouth and Bryan was behind her . . ."

"Bryan's got his hand over her mouth," Harms repeated.

"Over her mouth, and . . ."

"Bryan's behind her?" Harms asked, still not getting it.

"Behind her. She like dropped down to the ground and—"

"The mother dropped down to the ground," Harms repeated.

"Yeah. I didn't see where he stabbed her or anything like that."

"But you did see a knife or something?"

"Bryan had a knife in his hand when he came to her."

"Which hand did he have the knife in?"

"That would he his right hand, because he's right-handed."

"So he had his left hand over her mouth?"

"Something like that, yeah, because he's right-handed," Ben repeated.

"Did you see him make a motion with the knife?"

"I seen him come out of the room with the knife, but after that—"

"Out of his bedroom?" Harms repeated.

"Yeah, after that I didn't see none of it."

"At the time he grabbed her, did you see the knife?"

"No," Benny said firmly.

"But there wasn't anybody else around, there was just Bryan and his mother?"

"Yeah, and me and Dave in the room."

"And then you see the mother kind of fall you say?"

"She like dropped to the ground and started screaming."

"What did she scream?"

"Huh?"

"Did you hear what she screamed?" Harms clarified.

"No, she just screamed, 'cause he had his hand over her mouth."

"Did you see any blood at any time? On her?"

"I seen it on the ground after I came out of the room, and Bryan was upstairs screaming."

"She was—"

"Laying."

"What position was she in when you came out of Dave's room?"

"Her head was in towards Bryan's room. The room towards us going upstairs, like, right by the radiator, in that hallway."

"Was she on her back, or . . ."

"On her side. She was on her side."

"Where did you see the blood?"

"Well, it came out. I seen some on her night-gown."

"Was there any blood on the floor?"

"Not that I could see. I didn't really go over and check."

"Did you actually see Bryan leave her to go up-stairs?"

"Well, after Bryan grabbed her, I guess he must have stabbed her, 'cause she dropped to the ground."

"But you didn't see the knife move?"

"I didn't see the knife move or nothing. I went in the other room. They went upstairs."

"When Dave left his mother, how did he walk?"

"Fast."

"Did he say anything?"

"No. He had a really scared look on his face."

"And he was yelling something as he went up-stairs?"

"No. Bryan was yelling," Benny corrected.

"Okay, Bryan was yelling. Oh, Dave's the one that looked scared," Harms continued, finally getting it.

"Yeah, Dave looked scared."

"And Dave walks toward where you are?"

"Yeah."

"And he looks scared?"

"Yeah. And Bryan, Bryan says, like, 'If you guys puss out, I'll kill both of youse.' "

"And then what does Bryan do after that?"

"He goes up after her, after Snuff. Follows Snuff upstairs."

"What's the next thing you see or hear?"

"All I hear is footsteps, and talking upstairs, and then I heard this banging."

"Could you hear what they were saying upstairs?"

"No."

"What kind of banging?"

"Like a knocking sound."

"How many knocks did you hear?"

"Like, three or four."

"How far apart were they? Seconds or minutes?"

"Seconds."

"Did you hear any screams?"

"No screams at all."

"No screams," Harms repeated. "And then what's the next thing you see or hear?"

"I hear Bryan upstairs screaming."

"And?"

"And I go upstairs and see what it is. Bryan's, like, his hands were covered in blood."

"What's he screaming about?"

"I didn't really understand what. When I got upstairs, he stopped screaming."

"Did it sound like he was screaming at somebody?"

"Yeah. It was like that."

"Okay. You got upstairs and Bryan stopped screaming."

"Yeah."

"You get to the top of the stairs. Can you see David and Bryan at the same time?"

"Yeah."

"Are they standing?"

"Dave was right, Dave was puking at that time."

"He's over on the deck area, throwing up?"

"Actually, he threw up inside first. Right by the sliding glass doors."

"Where's Bryan?"

"Bryan was standing in the kitchen."

"What's he doing?"

"Nothing, really, just covered in blood."

"Where's the blood on him?"

"On his pants. The front. There was a lot on both legs."

"So he's standing there covered with blood. Is he holding anything in his hands?"

"No. He's not holding nothing in his hands."

"And what's Bryan doing?"

"Just standing there."

"Did he say anything?"

"No, he was just smoking cigarettes."

"Which way is he facing?"

"Toward the sliding glass doors, towards Snuffy and me."

"Does Dave have any blood on him?"

"No. Not that I seen."

"Do you see any ball bats around?"

"No."

"Do you see any ax handles around?"

"No."

"Any knives around?"

"No."

"See any kind of weapons around?"

"Just what's in the drawers."

"Okay, now we're to the point where David is vomiting, and you're standing there by David, and Bryan's looking at both of you, then what's the next thing that happens in sequence?"

"I just wanted to get out of the house. I'm like,'I'll be outside.' "

"So you said, 'I'll be outside,' and how do you exit the house?"

"Right out the front door."

"Where are they when you leave?"

"They were still upstairs in the house."

"When did you next see them?"

"Like, a minute later."

"Who came out first?"

"Dave."

"What's he doing? Carrying anything?"

"No. He's just really scared, like he's seen a ghost."

"Okay."

"Whole facial expression changed there on him."

"And then you see Bryan come out?"

"Bryan comes out right after he does."

"Did they say anything as you left?"

"Nothing. They couldn't. No one talked till that afternoon."

"Had Bryan changed clothes?"

"Yeah. He'd changed his jeans."

"So when you left the house, where did you go?"

"We drove by my house to pick some tapes up. Bryan wanted to."

"To get some tapes?"

"I told them if we go by there, I'm just gonna stay home, I'm not gonna come with you guys, so we didn't stop by my house then."

"And then where did you go from there?"

"Right on the highway up to here."

"Did they plan this trip ahead of time or did the trip just happen?" said Harms. A "yes" answer would establish premeditation and all but ensure the death penalty.

"It just happened," Benny answered smoothly. "I don't think they planned it ahead of time because I would have known about it before that."

"So what kind of conversation is going on in the car that makes you think they didn't plan it out ahead of time?"

"Well, Dave goes to Bryan, 'Where we gonna go?' and Bryan's like, 'I don't know. We'll probably just go up to Ohio and meet those guys.'"

"Did he mention which guys?"

"Just Frank."

Harms and Mynsberge knew he meant their buddy Frank Hesse.

"What did they say about what happened during the trip?"

"They didn't say nothing."

"Did they ever threaten you again?"

"No."

"Did they ever say, 'Don't say anything, don't talk to anybody'?"

"No."

"Who did they tell at Frank's house when they got there? What happened?"

"They didn't tell no one."

"You sure?"

"Yeah. I don't think they told anybody."

"Did you tell anybody?"

"No," Benny hastily replied.

"Did they have a lot of money with them?"

"Pretty much."

"Where did they get that?"

"I have no clue."

"How much money did they have?"

"About two hundred dollars."

"And who had that?"

"Both of them did."

"Split up between them?"

"Yeah."

"Did you have money with you when you left?" Mynsberge asked.

"I had about twenty."

"I can tell by talking to you that you feel a lot of remorse, at least more so then when you first started telling us about this, and we appreciate your telling us," said Harms. He was sincere. He really felt that Benny was feeling remorse for whatever his participation in the murders had been.

"This is your statement. If there's anything you want to add to that that we might not have asked . . ." Harms continued.

"Okay, we appreciate you telling us the truth, Ben. We're gonna stop the tape. What time is it?"

"It's three-oh-five," said Mynsberge, "this tape

concludes at three-oh-five," and he clicked the tape recorder off.

Mynsberge and Harms felt that Benny, just like David, was telling the truth. Mynsberge, who is a gentle man, felt that the boys were being sincere and cooperative, humble and remorseful. Nothing in their manner made Mynsberge believe either boy was trying to mislead them, despite the fact that there were contradictions in the two statements.

After a long, exhausting twelve-hour drive, Donna and Nelson Birdwell arrived in Midland, Michigan, on March 4. Donna immediately sought out the Midland County Jail, where she spoke with her son.

"Ma, I didn't do anything," Benny declared.

"Was it—"

"It was Bryan," he interrupted. "Bryan and Dave. They did it. They killed them. They forced me to come along, Ma. Ma, I was so scared!"

Donna believed her son. Benny continued to talk, telling her details about what had happened in the Freeman house.

Donna left his cell. *How could she help him get out from under a potential murder charge?* Realizing that the only way was to campaign in the media for his release, she granted an interview to a reporter from the local paper, the *Midland Daily News*. She revealed what her son had told her about his involvement—or really, lack of involvement—in the murders.

Donna told the reporter that Benny had told her that he'd hidden in a bedroom while his aunt, uncle, and cousin were slaughtered, and that he was not involved in any way in the murders. "My son is willing to cooperate with authorities," she continued.

Benny's account of the crimes, as related by his mother, went something like this.

"They were downstairs making noise when Brenda went down to ask them to be quiet. When it all happened, Ben hid in the bedroom. He (Ben) was in shock. He only left with them because he was scared. He thought they (Bryan and David) would kill him, too.

"None of them knew it was going to happen. Sunday afternoon, Ben was home washing his Wendy's uniform for work the next day."

Donna did not condone what had happened. She said, "We are a very close family, and we support our son. He's a wonderful, loving boy."

She neglected to mention that her "wonderful, loving boy" was a white supremacist with a juvenile record, the word "berserker" tattooed on his forehead, and Nazi symbols festooned over his body.

That night, the *Midland Daily News* scooped every paper in the country. They had the first purported eyewitness account by one of the three boys involved in what was now being called "the skinhead murder case."

Deep in the bowels of the Midland County Jail, the Freeman brothers huddled over a copy of the March 5 edition of the *Midland Daily News*. They read the interview Donna Birdwell had given to the paper, and her son's account of what had really happened. As they read, the anger began. It was never too far below the surface for either brother, and it took little to set it off. But if Benny had been in the cell with them—he had his own separate cell in another part of the building—they'd have wrung his neck and saved the state the cost of extradition and trial.

They had taken the rap because it had been agreed beforehand; Benny had convinced them that if they were captured, the authorities would only try the brothers as juveniles. If he (Benny) was blamed for what happened, they would try him—at eighteen, the oldest—as an adult. He could get death.

"You guys take the blame, okay? They'll let you off. Besides, with Bryan's history of emotional problems, nothing'll happen to you anyway. After all, a guy can't be held responsible for something he does if he has a history of mental stuff, right?"

That's what Benny had told them. And they'd bought it, because they had loved their cousin and they wanted to protect him. But now, now! That son-of-a . . .

They needed to tell the authorities that David's confession was concocted, that the statement was mostly a lie. And Bryan, who hadn't said anything yet, wanted to put his two cents in.

Their fucking aunt Donna. She'd opened her big

fat trap and out had come Benny's lies. She'd do anything to protect Benny. Now that she had said all that bullshit, they had to cover their own asses.

"Hey guard, guard!" they shouted.

Guard "Bull" Brand lumbered down the dank, narrow hallway and stopped before their cell.

"Tell the district attorney we got something to tell him," David shouted.

"Don't scream. You already made your statement," Bull yawned.

"Well, wake him up! And get our lawyer down here," Bryan yelled.

"You don't have a lawyer," said Bull.

"Then get us one," David shouted. "Tell 'em all we got a lot more to say, and this time it's the truth!"

Bull looked at his watch. It was late, but this seemed important. He didn't want to get in trouble if he didn't report what was happening immediately.

"I'll go call Donker," Bull said, shuffling back down the corridor.

"Yeah," Bryan shouted after him. "Yeah! Yeah! Tell him we got lots to tell him."

"Lots," David chimed in.

PART TWO

"He that troubleth his own house shall inherit the wind."

Isaiah 1:5

Five

Brooklyn Heights,
Fall 1966

It is 8:55 in the morning.

Walking down the hill to the edge of Henry Street are scores of young men and women, mostly blond and blue-eyed, but with an occasional brunette in the bunch. They are well dressed in shirts and ties, and in dresses that deliberately do not accentuate the human body. They talk little among themselves and pay little attention to their surroundings. They have a purpose, a specific destination, and a glazed look in their eyes.

Within the crowd on this day in 1966 is Dennis Freeman, a handsome resident of Allentown, Pennsylvania. Dennis is a tall, strapping young man of twenty-five.

Unlike most people his age, Dennis does not care about protesting against the Vietnam War. He has no interest in protesting for civil rights for blacks. He has no interest in voting for Robert Kennedy for president, or Richard Nixon, for that matter. He knows nothing about "free love." He has never smoked marijuana; he's never even inhaled a cigarette. Dennis's only concern is serving God as a Jehovah's Witness, just like his father, Clarence and his mother, Ruth.

Since 1900, the Heights, as it's known to Brooklyn residents, has served as the international headquarters for the Watchtower Bible Society, the parent organization of Jehovah's Witnesses. The Watchtower administers many different programs, including the door-to-door proselytizing that Jehovah's Witnesses are best known for. Dennis has done his full share of such proselytizing and continues to do so. In his free time, Dennis works the Clark Street IRT subway station in the Heights, greeting travelers with a message of salvation, should they choose to worship God the Witnesses' way, the only way, to seek salvation on judgment day. But unlike other religions, which view Armageddon as an abstract concept, the Witnesses have set a date for the conflagration.

Armageddon has been prophesied by the Witnesses Governing Body, a group of a dozen wise men who speak for God. The Governing Body says that Armageddon will occur seven years hence, in 1975. When it occurs, only the faithful, Jehovah's Witnesses, will survive to inhabit the "cleansed earth." All non-JWs will be destroyed by God.

Dennis knows and accepts that the Watchtower's way of salvation is based upon good works, and not on the saving grace of Jesus Christ's blood. This system, selling Watchtower books and magazines in public places and door to door, puts Dennis and other Jehovah's Witnesses in a position to be saved if they are faithful to the organization and do as they are told. Faithfulness to the organization involves adhering to the rules and regulations, that Watchtower elders enforce.

As for nonbelievers, those who believe in other religions—they will all be condemned and annihilated.

It makes no difference to Dennis that Watchtower materials said that Armageddon was supposed to happen in 1914 and in 1925. There were logical reasons those prophecies did not come to pass. Whatever the Governing Body says is now the truth. If they say Armageddon will occur in 1975, that is what will happen because God has decreed it.

It would never occur to Dennis to question the prophecy, for if he did, he would be disfellowshiped, banished from the Jehovah's Witnesses forever. His mother, father, sister, cousins, aunts and uncles, all of whom are Witnesses, would not be allowed to speak with him, to see him, even to go to his funeral, should he die. As far as the Witnesses were concerned, if he was disfellowshiped, he would cease to exist.

But that is not a problem for Dennis, who obeys his elders and does not question church doctrine.

While Armageddon will be a worldwide event, the Heights is the bastion against the evil that roams the world in the form of other religions. The best way to get the message out of God's kingdom on earth is through the printed word. The *Watchtower* printing plant is at the bottom of Henry Street, on the edge of the Heights, where it produces *The Watchtower* and *Awake!,* the two banner publications the Witnesses use to espouse their cause on street corners in cities all over the world.

Strolling down the street, Dennis was on his way to the *Watchtower* printing plant next to the Brooklyn Navy Yard. He would put in an eight-hour shift, with an hour off for lunch, and then, at precisely 5 P.M., he would trudge back up the hill to his quarters in one of the former hotels that dot the area.

Dennis was housed at the Margaret Hotel on Clark Street, one of the many Belle Époque hotels that catered at the turn-of-the-century to travelers who stayed in the Heights prior to trans-Atlantic trips on one of the great Cunard or White Star ocean liners that docked in New York Harbor. But over the years, as planes took the place of steamships, the hotels became a place for transients and fell into disrepair. The Watchtower had bought them for a song, restored them to their Victorian glory, and used them to house their workers. Though gilded from the outside, bespeaking the Witnesses' wealth, the rooms where the workers stayed could best be described as spartan, furnished in simplicity, with a bed to sleep in, a desk at which to study Watchtower theology as interpreted by their founder, Charles Taze Russell, and a bathroom.

Night after night, Dennis sat quietly at his desk, studying his New World Translation, memorizing its passages, thanking God for the revelations He brought forth through "God's organization."

Russell, Dennis, and all Jehovah's Witnesses deny that the body of Jesus Christ came to life after it had been entombed for three days. They claim that Jesus was resurrected as an "Invisible Spirit Creature" and that no one knows what actually happened to his body. Rather, they think, Jesus returned to earth invisibly in 1914.

The Witnesses deny that the return of the Jews to Israel is a fulfillment of biblical prophecy. Ezekiel's prophecy regarding the return of the Jews to their land is said by the Watchtower to be fulfilled in *their* organization.

The Jehovah's Witnesses began as a religious sect in 1879 when a Pittsburgh haberdasher named Charles Taze Russell used Hebrew and Greek translations of the Bible to interpret God's plan for salvation. A charismatic man, Russell shared his interpretation with other members of his community during Bible study classes.

Members of the sect were originally known as Russellites, but with the ascendance of Joseph Franklin Rutherford as Russell's successor in 1916, the Russellites became known as Jehovah's Witnesses. Rutherford built a large house in San Diego and had deeds drawn up holding the property in trust to Abraham, Isaac, and Jacob, who would return to earth in 1925 after Armageddon and would, presumably, live on Rutherford's property.

Jehovah's Witnesses spread out across the states and then the world, delivering "God's message," according to Russell's interpretation. Those early Witnesses were such effective proselytizers that before long, there were Jehovah's Witnesses on all seven continents. Russell went corporate, forming the Watchtower Corporation in 1889. Russell moved his sect to Brooklyn Heights at the turn of the century and a printing plant was set up that today publishes millions of handouts and Bibles that have been used to educate members and to convert. The Watchtower officially claims there are more than 3.5 million Jehovah's Witnesses worldwide, but that figure is popularly considered to be conservative, with total worldwide membership probably closer to 4.5 million.

The Watchtower's accumulated wealth makes it the single largest landowner in terms of property value in Brooklyn Heights, one of New York City's most exclusive residential areas. The Watchtower buys up property for future use, and if residents refuse to leave, Watchtower will try to buy them out.

Dennis was not interested in how the Watchtower conducted its business. He knew that the church did whatever it did in the service of Jehovah, and the people who lived in the buildings the Watchtower bought up were heathen. They would perish on judgment day.

It did not bother Dennis that the Watchtower had an autocratic hierarchy that exercised dictatorial control over its flock. Nor did it bother him that the Watchtower said one must come to Jesus through the Watchtower organization, thus inserting itself between an individual and Jesus. And he did not find it difficult to harmonize the organizational self-approval, self-praise, and self-identification as God's channel, with its simultaneous calls for humility and meekness on the part of everyone else. Dennis just did not question. He was obedient.

* * *

Dennis worked at the Watchtower printing plant from August 1966 to November 1970. While the death of his mother in 1969 had made him sad, he had found the woman to spend the rest of his life with. Her name was Brenda Birdwell.

Brenda was a tall, strapping girl of twenty-two. She had come to the Heights from her Allentown home to serve the Lord. Her parents, Nelson and Peggy Birdwell, originally hailed from Kentucky, but they had moved to Allentown, where economic opportunities were greater.

Brenda was very close to her sisters, Sandy and Linda, and her brother, Nelson, II. They were a close and loving family, and they faithfully executed the duties of Jehovah's Witnesses, proselytizing, going to Kingdom Hall on a regular basis, and reading and accepting church doctrine as the truth.

Five times a week—twice on Sunday, once on Tuesday, and twice on Thursday—the Birdwells and all their JW brethren in Allentown and all over the world trooped to their local Kingdom Hall. It was here at Kingdom Hall, the Jehovah's Witnesses' church, a plainly furnished auditorium, that the Witnesses gathered for Bible and literature discussion.

The Birdwells, the Freemans, and all JWs are required to purchase the literature produced by the printing plant in Brooklyn Heights. They discuss specific pieces of literature, articles, etc., during their literature discussion sessions.

The Watchtower articles Witnesses discussed in-

cluded "Young People Ask: Is Star Trek Harmless
Fun?" in which the author offers the thesis that
the *Star Trek* TV series and films only serve to pro-
mote ". . . a worldly attitude of Satan." Other
Watchtower articles discussed included those that
rationalize why Witnesses do not believe in blood
transfusions even when a life is in jeopardy.

Dennis and Brenda believed what the Watchtower literature told them. They returned to Allentown together to get the blessing of the Elders, the
JW equivalent of pastors or ministers, but with in-
finitely more influence over congregates' daily lives.
Elders have the power to take away salvation, re-
strict prayer life, and interrupt family communication or anything else they believe will bring a
wayward Witness to repentance. In the worst-case
scenario, when a Witness has betrayed the Watchtower in action or belief, the Elders recommend
one be disfellowshiped.

Like all the other Witnesses in their Kingdom
Hall, Dennis and Brenda reported the time they
spent doing society work, that is, door-to-door
proselytizing, to the Elders, who put that information into a file. There is a file on each member of
the congregation. This file also contains information on major sins a congregate has committed. All
information related to a Witness's private life is
kept in master files in Brooklyn Heights. They are
never destroyed.

Dennis and Brenda told the Allentown Elders of
their love for each other and asked for their blessing to be married. Looking at this couple who had
been put on earth to perform God's good works,

who'd come from families of Jehovah's Witnesses, the Elders knew immediately that these two would only extend the bloodline of Witnesses who create God's kingdom on earth. Without reservation, they gave them their blessing, and Dennis and Brenda married.

Jehovah's Witnesses are strongly discouraged from attending college. Serving God's will, especially at headquarters in Brooklyn, is more important. Dennis and Brenda, praying for the knowledge of God's will every day and every night, understood that the best way to please God was to go back to the Heights and work hard to spread the Jehovah's Witnesses gospel to nonbelievers. They returned to Brooklyn Heights in 1973 and took up residence in one of the converted hotels.

As the Armageddon year of 1975 approached, their work in the printing plants, in proselytizing in the subways, and of going door-to-door in Brooklyn's neighborhoods became more important toward making certain that on judgment day, Dennis and Brenda would be among the chosen few spared from Armageddon's destruction, to live on the "new earth." For their labors, they were each paid $14 a month.

By late 1974, thousands of Witnesses worldwide had cashed in their insurance policies, abandoned careers, and sold their possessions to spend the short time remaining in the ministry work before the end of the world. Dennis and Brenda stepped up their door-to-door works, trying to convince people that they must become Jehovah's Witnesses to please God and perhaps receive salvation.

On New Year's Eve 1974, the dark clouds gathered for the Armageddon that was imminent—1975 was here; the world was coming to an end. Dennis and Brenda held tight, waiting for the die to be cast, for Gabriel's trumpet to sound, for Jehovah to destroy all those but the true Christians, the Witnesses of himself.

Nothing happened.

The world kept on. Realizing that Armageddon was not happening, the Governing Body came out with a complicated pronouncement for their error while not admitting it had been a mistake. This was an opportunity, a *further* opportunity, to do good works, to serve the Watchtower and Jehovah before Armageddon. This time no date was set.

Dennis and Brenda felt profound relief. They had a new opportunity, a new light, a new day to serve. Dennis, who had developed into a wonderful public speaker, was dispatched to Allentown, where he appeared as a keynote speaker during a summer assembly of Witnesses at the Allentown fairgrounds. Dennis addressed a crowd of 12,000 and those who were there, said he touched the hearts of the people in his invocation of biblical prophecy.

Dennis enjoyed being home again; he had to admit he had gotten homesick and so the following year, in 1976, he and Brenda left the Heights for good and went back to Allentown to raise a family. This was the way to best serve Jehovah. To raise children to adhere to his precepts, Witnesses who would do good works, and worship at Kingdom Hall with their brothers and sisters in the organization.

For years Allentown had been one of the most

blessed of Jehovah's Witnesses congregations in the world, for it was from this small city in the heart of Pennsylvania's Lehigh Valley that Nathan Knorr hailed. Knorr would take over for Rutherford as president of the Watchtower in 1992. He would head the Governing Body and as such become the most powerful Jehovah's Witness in the world.

Dennis idolized Knorr. When he had decided ten years earlier to go to the Heights, Knorr had sent him a personal letter in which he'd told the young man ". . . you are going to get a wonderful four-year advanced theocratic training which is far better than any secular education you can get."

The fact that he had worked for years in the holy land of the Heights only served to embellish his reputation. When they returned to the provinces, those who'd served at headquarters were looked on as the most holy of the holy, venerated because they had been to the Promised Land, had served Jehovah at his core, and had been close to the Ruling Council.

In 1976, Dennis, all of twenty-eight, was nevertheless venerated and given the rank of Elder. He was looked on as a pious man with a deep understanding of the Bible and its meaning, with a quiet ability as a teacher to communicate that knowledge to even the most recalcitrant of pupils.

As he gained status in the congregation, Dennis as an Elder must have been exposed to and trained in some of the undercover work of the Elders. This would include following members of the congregation who were suspected of wrongdoing; and accessing congregation files, which revealed inside information on all the congregates, including his wife, parents, in-laws, and siblings, and eventually, his own children.

Two years later, in 1978, Brenda gave birth to their first child, whom they named Bryan. After his father died that same year, his sister Valerie came to live with him, Brenda, and the new baby she helped to care for.

Two years later, Brenda gave birth to their second child, David. She would give birth once more, in 1984 to Erik.

The family settled in a house on Ehrets Lane, a quiet street in Salisbury Township only a few miles from downtown Allentown. It was a two-story ranch house that some developers like to call a "splanch." There were two bedrooms, a living room, a kitchen, and a bathroom when you entered. Walking downstairs, you came to a narrow corridor into which two more bedrooms and another bathroom opened.

Ehrets Lane was a peaceful place. On any given day it was quiet enough to hear the wind chimes from a house nearby. To add to the rural feeling, in the corner window of her bedroom, Brenda put a picture of a rooster that could be seen from the street. The location, though, had been picked for more than its serenity or property value.

Down the block and across the street was the local Kingdom Hall, the locus of their family life, the source of their sustenance, the wellspring from which the bounties of Jehovah flowed.

Dennis and Brenda were doing good works. They had formed a loving family. Now, all they had to do was live happily ever after.

Six

It was not an uncommon sight in the 1980s for an Allentown resident to open his door and see Dennis Freeman on the porch steps, accompanied by his redheaded children Bryan, David, and Erik. They were there to proselytize by selling copies of *Awake!* and *The Watchtower.*

Always, the Freemans would appear fresh scrubbed and clean cut, with sunny smiles and even sunnier dispositions. They were only too ready to answer questions about Jehovah's Witnesses and to enlighten the uninitiated. Sometimes, Dennis would convince the Allentown neighbors he met through the door-to-door ministry to attend Kingdom Hall study sessions.

Dennis was nothing if not obedient, and he wanted his children to be that way, too. And for a while, they were. They attended all the study sessions with their parents and when their parents wanted them to, did their door-to-door ministry.

From the outside, things looked normal in the Freeman family. The Freemans had a basketball hoop out in the driveway and neighbors used to see father and sons playing ball. They seemed to have a good relationship. But appearances can be deceiving.

The Jehovah's Witnesses are not supposed to drink alcohol. Yet according to court records, alcohol was brought into the house in the form of beer. Starting at six, David began drinking beer.

Despite the prohibition against alcohol, there is a big problem with alcohol abuse among Jehovah's Witnesses. The contradiction between JW policy and the consumption of liquor David and Bryan could see in the community must have been terribly confusing to them.

The boys' outside lives were made difficult by their parents' religious beliefs. Children who grow up as Jehovah's Witnesses grow up in an atmosphere of isolation. They are not allowed to participate in afterschool group activities. Friendships with schoolchildren who are not Witnesses are prohibited. On the rare occasion when David and Bryan questioned their parents' beliefs, which had been imposed on them, they were answered with biblical quotes from the Witnesses' version of the Bible that supported their beliefs. Obedience was the watchword.

Because Witnesses do not believe in government, the Freeman brothers were the only ones in their classes who did not salute the flag and say the Pledge of Allegiance every morning. While it was their constitutional right to do so, it nevertheless alienated them further from the other children. Jehovah's Witnesses are also prohibited from engaging in sports and other forms of competition.

On Christmas morning, there were no presents

under the Christmas tree for David and Bryan because there was no Christmas tree. Jehovah's Witnesses do not believe in established holidays. December 25 was like any other day. The Freeman boys never had the joy on that day that their friends at school had told them about. Neither did they celebrate Easter or that most pagan of American holidays, Halloween.

The Freeman brothers never got birthday presents either, because celebrating birthdays is prohibited under Watchtower doctrine. They had to listen to their friends' stories about how wonderful their parents treated them on their birthdays. The brothers were told that their present was being "in the truth," as Witnesses refer among themselves to their beliefs.

"Why can't we have birthdays?" David asked.

"Why can't we have Christmas?" Bryan asked.

"Why can't we trick or treat on Halloween?" Erik asked.

It was the rest of the world that was wrong, Brenda would tell them; the only correct religion, the only religion acceptable to God, is Jehovah's Witnesses, Dennis would say stoically.

But all this paled before the deadly decision that would await their parents should they ever be hurt and require a blood transfusion, for Jehovah's Witnesses do not believe in blood transfusions. Should a transfusion be the difference between life and death, their religious beliefs would have obligated Dennis and Brenda to watch their children suffer and die rather than transfuse blood into their veins. No matter how much they suffered as parents over such a decision, being Witnesses would come first. Only state intervention could allow such a transfusion to take place.

David and Bryan, and later Erik, were left on their own. Scripture became their one true salvation.

By the time David and Bryan were eight, they knew the scripture verses cold. Bryan took after his father: he was so smart that even at eight, he could give a Bible talk for six minutes and have the Elders spellbound.

Dennis and Brenda loved their children. They were raising them as they had been raised, under the organization's wing. They would grow up to do good works, to minister as adults from door to door. Their further schooling after high school would be discouraged, as it had been discouraged for Witnesses for generations.

The idea that education leads to a more substantive place in the economic hierarchy of society, or simply that with education you can make a better living, is anathema to the Witnesses. Only nonbelievers believe that, and besides, they're going to be destroyed by Jehovah at Armageddon regardless of their education, so further schooling is unnecessary.

As to their more formal religious education, when Witnesses attend Kingdom Hall, it is for the purpose of discussing Watchtower-produced publications, be it passages from the Watchtower version of the Bible or sections of the Watchtower annual yearbooks.

The 1974 Jehovah's Witnesses yearbook must

have been especially interesting to Bryan and David, because it put a revisionist spin on the Watchtower's anti-Semitic record under the Hitler regime.

The yearbook recalls that on or around September 1936, prior to an international convention of the Witnesses held in Lucerne, Switzerland, Joseph Rutherford and his eventual successor, Nathan Knorr, ". . . had come to Germany . . . in order to see what could be done to ensure the safety of the Society's property, had prepared a declaration."

Rutherford, who had made anti-Semitic rants in the past, wrote a document known as the "Declaration of Fact." "It was a protest against the meddling of the Hitler government into the preaching work we were doing," the '74 yearbook states.

But the "Declaration of Fact" did not read like an anti-Nazi document. "It was the commercial Jews" who had "built up and carried on Big Business as a means of exploiting and oppressing the peoples of many nations," the declaration read in part.

At the convention itself, a large number of Witnesses refused to adopt it, perhaps because of the brown-nosing to the brownshirts and revulsion at the document's anti-Semitism. But adopt it they did. "The conventioneers . . . took 2,100,000 copies of the declaration home with them, however, and distributed them to numerous persons in positions of responsibility. The copy sent to Hitler was accompanied by a letter that, read, in part:

"The Brooklyn presidency of the Watchtower Society is

and always has been exceedingly friendly to Germany. In 1918, the president of the Society and seven members of the Board of Directors in America were sentenced to 80 years' imprisonment for the reason that the president refused to let two magazines in America, which he edited, be used in war propaganda against Germany."

Because at the time the Witnesses officially refused to renounce religious meetings, Bible evenings, and the recruitment of new members, they would later claim, as the Freemans were taught, an honorable record in opposing the Nazis. Yet there is no evidence of concrete action on their part against the Nazi regime in those early days of Hitler's power, when he was the most vulnerable.

The Freeman brothers must have listened fascinated as the Elders told them how it was only when the Witnesses refused to make the "Heil Hitler" salute in 1935, or refused to serve in the Army, that the sect's officials and a large part of its membership adopted a clear posture of opposition to the regime. That led to the first wave of Witnesses arrests in 1936 and 1937, and their imprisonment in concentration camps.

After the outbreak of the war, more large-scale arrests occurred, and again in 1944. However, the number of Witnesses in the concentration camps were relatively small, staying to themselves in close, compact groups. They were conspicuous for the order, cleanliness, and discipline that they maintained in their barracks. Since they refused, because of their religious beliefs, to cooperate with "illegal" political groups and to escape from the camps or offer

active resistance to the SS, the SS came to exploit
them for its own purposes.

On the orders of SS head Heinrich Himmler, the
Witnesses were used to gather mushrooms and fruit
outside the camps because there was no danger of
their trying to escape or attacking the SS. As a result
of that change in SS policy, the situation for most
of the Witnesses in the concentration camps im-
proved, and most survived until liberation.

At best, it was a checkered record, but the Witnesses in their prayer meetings extolled the virtues
of nonintervention with the Germans. If someone
of another religion died, it was not their place to
intervene.

Bryan and David may have wondered about this
dichotomy: how can you sanctify one life but not
another because of religious belief? Maybe the Jews
deserved to die because they had not embraced
God in the right way. It was perplexing. But questions were not encouraged; obedience was.

While Jehovah's Witnesses do not believe in formal government, they try to be model citizens who
are encouraged to obey the laws of the land in
which they live. Regardless of any judgment one
may make about the Freemans as parents, one
thing can be said of them in absolute truth, and
that is that they never broke the laws of the land.
The same, however, could not be said about
Brenda's brother.

Nelson Birdwell II has been in and out of
trouble with the law for years. His crimes ranged

from burglary to receiving stolen property. In this respect, he was not a good role model for his son, elson Birdwell III, whom everyone called "Ben."

Once, in 1987, Nelson was wanted by the Whitehall Township Police (Whitehall is adjacent to Allentown) on a felony theft charge. Birdwell fled the state with his wife Donna and their ten-year-old son, Ben. Living in a van, they wound up in New York, a faceless family moving through the masses, just three of the thousands of homeless that call the Big Apple home. After a few months of this rootless existence, they traveled across the Hudson River and took up residence in a fleabag motel in Teaneck, New Jersey. Leaving Donna and Ben behind, Birdwell hit the streets. He was arrested for possession of drug paraphernalia and motor vehicle violations and held on $10,000 bail. When his name was put through the computer, it spit out his record and the outstanding charge in Whitehall, Pennsylvania.

Seeing that her husband was going to be detained for a while, Nelson's wife, Donna, was forced to call Birdwell's father, Nelson Birdwell Sr., also a Jehovah's Witness, who drove up from Allentown to bring his daughter-in-law and grandson home. The elder Birdwell was so concerned about them that he asked that a representative of Lehigh County check on the family's living conditions to make sure they were okay. Birdwell II, meanwhile, was taken back to Whitehall to face justice.

Nelson Birdwell II has been arrested fourteen times and convicted thirteen times. His son, Ben, watched his father closely and began emulating him. As Ben grew up, he began getting into trouble. Eventually, he had a juvenile record.

Bryan and David Freeman watched not from afar but close up as their uncle, and then their cousin, with whom they were close, went through their criminal troubles. They saw the way both father and son flouted authority, the way they broke the law, and the way the law continually reprieved them. Once again, it was terribly confusing: all the Birdwells were raised as Jehovah's Witnesses.

And then there was their grandfather. Bryan and David were extremely fond of their grandfather. Nelson, in turn, loved his grandkids. However, the elder Nelson Birdwell stopped being a Jehovah's Witness around 1986. After some sort of unspecified dispute he refuses to talk about, he stopped being a Witness.

Did he leave because he was disfellowshipped? Or did he leave by his own volition? Regardless, how Brenda explained to her children her father's departure from the fold remains undisclosed.

Despite all the problems that shook the Freeman family, Bryan and David kept to the straight and narrow. Not once were they arrested. Not once were they charged with a crime. They never had a criminal record of any sort.

Even as police in three states hunted them, the Freeman brothers' criminal record remained pristine.

Robin Manners was a member of the Salisbury Township Kingdom Hall. A Jehovah's Witness for eighteen years, she remembers Dennis Freeman as a mild, quiet, respectful man.

"My husband, who was not a Witness, used to go over to the Kingdom Hall and plow out the snow for Dennis. And Dennis, he always sent us a lovely thank you card. That's something you remember, when a man has manners like that."

As an Elder, Dennis sometimes led the discussion at the Salisbury Township Kingdom Hall, where there were five meetings a week. "Dennis was so nice and down-to-earth; he would always come over and shake our hand."

Dennis, meanwhile, began turning his back on family problems. In 1986 he took a job in the Southern Lehigh School District as the bus terminal manager. When a position opened up as school custodian, Dennis was asked to serve in that capacity. Always obedient, always ready to help out, Dennis agreed.

Dennis quickly became known among his coworkers as a gentle man with a quiet sense of humor. He had a nickname for everyone, whether it was Sally Kneller, middle school head custodian, who he called "Sweet Sal," or Ray Seifert, district heating, ventilation, air conditioning, and plumbing supervisor, who Dennis nicknamed "Macho."

Dennis became known around the school as a confidence builder. He'd always tell Macho, "You can do it. You don't belong here. You should be going on to bigger and better things." It would never occur to Dennis to do the same himself.

Ray and Dennis developed a strong friendship and mutual respect. During lunch, they played basketball or stickball and sometimes lifted weights together. Once they went out to shoot bow and arrow.

Ray later recalled that Dennis set him up. "He never told me he was on his high school archery team."

Being involved with school sports is a practice that is frowned upon by Jehovah's Witnesses, so Dennis was taking a chance that he would be remonstrated by the elders if they found out he was an archer.

Around the school where he worked, Dennis quickly developed a reputation as an erudite man. He always seemed to be reading something. Away from Kingdom Hall, he indulged a passion for the classics, reading Plato and discussing the philosopher with his co-workers.

In Plato's *The Republic,* the philosopher examines the nature of justice within the state. Considering that Jehovah's Witnesses disavow the state, and justice would play a major role in the future life of the Freeman family, it is ironic that of all the philosophers, the one whose work Dennis chose to pursue was Plato.

Seven

January 1995

When Floyd Cochran answered his phone, the woman on the other end of the line announced excitedly, "I've lost control of my boys."

"They're out of control, and so is my household," Brenda Freeman continued, barely controlling the hysteria in her voice.

Aryan Nations is one of the more prominent neo-Nazi groups in the United States, and Cochran had been an Aryan Nations spokesman and organizer in Idaho. Brenda was calling because she just didn't know what to do and Cochran, who now counsels parents whose children are caught in the neo-Nazi web, had no easy answers to her predicament.

Brenda needed easy answers. Maybe she'd go closer to home. She dialed again.

"Can I help you? This is Barry Morrison. I'm the head of the Anti-Defamation League here in Philadelphia."

"Yes, I hope so. I'm at my wits' end. I need help with my boys."

"But Mrs. Freeman, we're the ADL, we—"

"I know, you monitor and track hate groups.

Well, my sons, Bryan and David, they're skinheads."

Morrison was interested. The ADL in Philadelphia kept close track of skinheads across the state.

"What seems to be the problem, Mrs.—"

"Freeman. Brenda Freeman. I'm calling from Allentown. I was referred to you by one of our local agencies. I just don't know where to turn. You see, my sons—I can't control them any more."

"Are your sons violent, Mrs. Freeman?"

"Well, one time they assaulted my husband during a counseling session."

"Counseling for what?"

"Substance abuse and psychological problems. Both of my boys have . . . problems, but I love them. I can't control them and I just don't know what to do."

Brenda went on to describe other violent incidents: when the brothers took her hostage and police had to talk them into releasing her; when Bryan pinned her to the floor and threatened to kill her with a hatchet.

"Did you press charges?" Morrison wondered.

"No," Brenda answered. "I'm just trying very, very hard to get them counseling and help them."

Morrison didn't know what he could do. It sounded like whatever social welfare agencies Brenda Freeman had been dealing with, they just didn't understand the immediate threat the Freeman brothers posed to their mother and probably their father as well. The real question was how strong their skinhead beliefs were. The more strongly they believed in white supremacy and fascism, the more violent they would be.

"Do your boys ascribe to Mark Thomas's doctrine?" Morrison asked.

Thomas was the local hatemonger, a Hitler wannabe, probably the most powerful neo-Nazi in the state.

"They been there, to his farm, I mean. They wear the swastika on their clothes, and they have the Nazi medals and such. They are also tattooed."

"With Nazi symbols?"

"Yes. On their foreheads."

The whole situation was too typical. While some skinheads come from lower-class backgrounds, by and large, they are teenagers from middle-class homes who have grown disillusioned with their families and are seeking out some sort of substitute. The camaraderie of the skinhead cause serves as a replacement family, despite its roots being twisted and evil.

"Are they involved with any other skinheads?"

"Someone told me about skinheads in the York area. David was seen there after hours in possession of beer. He was spotted with this other boy who was under the care of the state. He was an emancipated minor."

She was afraid her son was thinking about doing the same thing.

"Then there's Ben."

"Ben?"

"Their cousin. Older cousin, he's eighteen. He's a skinhead, too."

"Well, what is it you're seeking?"

"Just some suggestions about how to handle them. Mr. Morrison, they have, uh, threatened me, too."

She needed to do more then "handle them." Her boys were racists. One had already gotten violent, the other was getting ready to act out. But Brenda Freeman was ignoring all that. Mrs. Freeman felt she had an obligation for her sons' well-being, despite the fact that violence was already present in the family dynamic. Morrison recognized a pattern of avoidance.

"What about your husband. His name is—"

"Dennis."

"Dennis. Has he been able to help through all this?"

"Dennis, he's had his problems. He was severely depressed after his father died recently."

That struck a chord. Many times depression was an inherited disease.

"Do either one of your boys have problems with depression?"

"Yes, Bryan does. He has . . . violent tendencies. He had been on medication to control it, but then he stopped taking it."

"Mr. Morrison," Brenda added, "I also feel that my boys have engaged in behavior I just can't condone, like harassing and beating up minorities."

"Well, let me give some thought to it. Maybe I can make some suggestions down the road."

"Thank you. I'd appreciate that."

Morrison took her number, and a few weeks later, he called to say that while he had no suggestions yet for how to cope with the situation her sons had put her in, he was not neglecting her.

The fact was, he just didn't know what to tell her.

For her part, Brenda was in constant anguish. She didn't know what to do. She couldn't control Bryan and David anymore. She had tried everything. Even going to the Anti-Defamation League, which was a violation of Watchtower doctrine. Everything was supposed to be kept within the church. If anyone found out what she'd done, she would certainly be remonstrated by one of the Elders.

Brenda went into her bedroom and took the *Death Book* out of the top drawer of her dresser. It was a scrapbook that she had found in Bryan's dresser. As she had many times, she opened its pages and began to look through it. And as she looked, her face grew grimmer and grimmer, her heart grew heavier and heavier, and even though it was midday, it seemed like God had taken all the light out of her life:

KEVIN IZBICKI CONVICTED OF MURDER

MAN JAILED IN MACHETE ATTACKS ON 3

SKINHEADS RAMPAGE, ATTACK FOREIGNERS

SENTENCE IS LIFE IN RACIAL KILLING

WHITE SUPREMACIST GETS LIFE FOR
KILLING PERSIAN GULF VET

12 HOURS NEEDED TO DIG UP BODY

PROPOSAL MAY END ANIMAL SACRIFICES

SUPREMACIST'S SLAYING ROCKS SMALL WISCONSIN CITY

The headlines of the *Death Book* read like a who's who of murder and racism, tied to the skinhead movement internationally, with a little Satanism thrown in for good measure.

Also in the book were mailing labels with the name "Eastern Hammerskins" on each one. Eastern Hammerskins is a skinhead group with an active gang in nearby Stewartstown.

After she had put the book aside, Brenda realized that she and Dennis were in real danger. There was the possibility, however remote, however unexplainable, that her children, David and Bryan, might—

No, she just couldn't give voice to her fears. But in case she wasn't around, she was going to explain the *Death Book*. Brenda found a sheet of paper and began to write.

"Found on December 3, 1993 book in middle drawer of Bryan's desk—called *Death Book*.

"Inside cover article about girl who started fires and other destructive things through demon possession—on blue construction paper in block letters the words, 'Help me! Please!'

"Inside sheet pasted with articles like trial for Izbicki, who killed his mother. Also an ad for cremation service, also obituary listing, also articles about a teen who kept a diary in which she plotted her father's death because he resented his 'meddling' in her love life. Also about 2 girls who showed no remorse about killing their mother because she punished them for sneaking out at night—occult literature was found in the house. Also article about Exxon exec who was abducted and killed. Article about man who eluded police but was finally captured in Arizona. Various little articles about young people who killed or raped without remorse.

"Some articles about deaths in Serbia, an article about a priest who was expelled from his order for his beliefs that involved mysticism.

"An article about the deaths involving heavy metal music and Satanism in Arizona. Various other articles, some yet unpasted.

"Most disturbing to see and read."

That last line was probably the most understated thing Brenda had ever written in her life.

Rules, rules, rules. Nothing but stupid rules. That's how David and Bryan felt about their home, and they hated rules.

There were rules on who they could socialize with, when to go out, when to come back. Rules not to smoke, not to drink, not to talk. Erik went along with the rules. Ass kisser.

If the Freeman brothers were asked at exactly what moment they began rebelling against their parents, their family, and their religion, they would not be able to answer. The truth was that their thoughts had begun to rebel many years before they physically grew strong enough to defy their parents.

The seeds for the rebellion had been laid in their formative years and it was upon hitting their early teens that they began to act out, that is, to begin to blatantly defy their parents' edicts and to take their growing anger out on the society that they found themselves in.

Their active rebellion began in 1991, when Bryan was thirteen and David eleven. The boys decided that they would no longer attend Watchtower meetings. Some of the Witnesses in the Salisbury congregation believed that the boys' listening to heavy metal music—heavily laced with violence—accounted for their intransigence. Dennis and Brenda didn't know why, just that the rebellion had started.

Jehovah's Witnesses know that their salvation depends on what they do on earth during their corporeal lives. Even if they have served Jehovah with all the power of their heart, only the chosen few will be spared on Armageddon Day, which they believe is imminent.

If Dennis could not get his boys to conform, if they continued to act in such heinous ways, he, Dennis, would not be allowed the privilege of being saved from destruction and live on the paradise earth.

Dennis knew what was at stake: his very life. If he could get his boys to conform, he at least had a chance. *They* had a chance. He needed to preach to them more, to get them to accept the teachings

of the Elders like he had as a child. That was the
only thing to do, and that would take time.

Dennis preached and two "brothers," (the term
Witnesses use to address each other) would come
to the Freemans' house on Ehrets Lane and reason
with the boys, using scriptural passages to have
Bryan and David accept Jehovah and come back
into the fold. To come back into the fold meant
life; to resist meant death.

Such efforts were to no avail. The Freeman
brothers continued their rebellious ways. At that
point, the boys were "marked" as a bad association. The rest of the congregation in Allentown
could not associate with them. They were effec-
tively isolated from the community they had grown
up in.

To David and Bryan, being marked meant nothing. They had been marked since they'd started
school and associated with kids who were not Witnesses. At this point, it was probably a pleasure to
have once and for all pissed everyone off enough
that they didn't have to deal with their parents'
beliefs and their asshole friends anymore.

Whether Dennis Freeman was forcibly removed
as an Elder or resigned of his own accord is unclear. Why is also unclear. Dennis's father-in-law,
Nelson Birdwell, says that Dennis stopped being an
Elder because "it was something of a personal nature between Dennis and his peers. The boys became aware of this and lost respect for their father.
The boys respect strength."

Whatever the reasons, one thing is clear: once
Dennis stepped down from the Witnesses' ruling

echelon, getting his sons to conform became his top priority. It was either that or face destruction.

Dennis was a big man, six feet and over two hundred pounds, but he was weak emotionally. He set boundaries that his sons trampled. He could never tell them, "Do not come home late" and *mean* it. No matter what he said, they did the exact opposite. Controlling them was something he just could not do. So Dennis abdicated that responsibility, withdrew into himself, and let Brenda become the disciplinarian. It was a task she threw herself into with great zeal.

Brenda established a series of rules David and Bryan had to live by. If they didn't, they were punished.

It didn't work.

One night in 1992, Valerie Freeman came into her room, put on the lights, and found someone had put animal parts in her bed. It seemed to be some sort of Satanic ritual.

Brenda and Dennis could not believe it, but there was the evidence, right in front of them. When twelve-year-old David was confronted by his mother and father, he confessed to having done the act.

"Satan!" Dennis shouted. "You are doing Satan's work!"

"Yeah, right," said David, unimpressed by the religious rhetoric. He picked up a beer and took a long, slow slug of it.

Upset, Dennis and Brenda sought counseling from the Elders, who visited the Freeman home and tried once again, to show David the error of his ways. David did not take too kindly to that.

During one incident, David was sitting on the couch in the family room when Valerie came in to confront him about his behavior toward her. David stood up, his bulk towering over the small woman. Dennis and Brenda came in and watched the two standing toe to toe, arguing vociferously. The argument lasted the better part of two minutes.

"Do you want a shootout?" David finally screamed.

Bryan was standing by the doorway, quietly observing, a bemused smile on his face. In subsequent confrontations with Valerie, David would not threaten her, but he did punch holes in the wall and throw furniture around. To his parents he snarled on at least one occasion, "I'm going to kill you both."

David had already begun rebelling at school. Against the express doctrine of the Witnesses, he had reached out into the sinful world and joined his school's football team. But in November 1992, he had a violent disagreement with his coach and threatened to kill him. He was suspended from school for ten days.

What to do! Brenda fretted about her child. Dennis had grown more and more withdrawn as the troubles got worse and worse. She had been left to shoulder the responsibility of seeing that her child did no harm to family and others.

The Elders were summoned again to put the fear of God into David, again to no avail. That left Brenda no other choice.

On November 13, 1992, David was committed as an inpatient by his parents to a renewal center at nearby Quakertown, where he was to receive rehabilitation counseling for his alcohol problem. It was during this rehabilitation that David claimed to have been abusing not only alcohol, but other drugs as well. He was discharged a month later on December 14, 1992, and came back into the welcoming bosom of his family.

David was furious! Who the hell was his mother to get rid of him so easily because she didn't like what he was doing?

David got into a pushing match with his mother. He knocked her to the floor and jumped on her.

"I'm gonna kill you, I'm gonna kill you, I'm gonna kill you!"

Who broke up the fight is unclear. Maybe it was Dennis, coming out of his shell long enough to protect his wife. He was bigger than his two sons, and he could take care of himself, and if need be, physically stop them from acting out.

Regardless of who stopped the conflict, it was clear to Brenda that David needed to be institutionalized again. On December 23, 1992, David was voluntarily committed to First Hospital at Wyoming Valley. To David it was an incarceration, but it lasted only a month. He was released on January 26, 1993, with a recommendation that he be put in a residential placement. That same day, he was sent to the Reed Shelter Care program in Womelsdorf, Pennsylvania, to await admission to a residential program.

In legal documents, Dennis and Brenda stated that the reason for this longer-term placement was that they felt "unable to control him at this time and fear(ed) for their safety as they cannot provide the structure and supervision he needs." The state proceeded to adjudicate him a dependent so he could be institutionalized for proper care. He was placed in the Paradise School for Boys.

The Paradise School for Boys is a Catholic institution in Abbottstown, Pennsylvania, that the state uses to place children who have become wards of the state. Their parents have temporarily given up their parental responsibilities because they can no longer control their children and are asking the state to straighten their kids out. In previous generations, the Paradise School would have been called a reform school.

Carol Lynn Crutchley is a psychiatrist at the Paradise School. In February 1993, she was in her office when David Freeman went to see her. The purpose of the interview was a psychiatric evaluation designed to determine the extent of his problems and what kind of treatment the young man needed.

David proceeded to describe to Dr. Crutchley his family relationship. Afterward, Dr. Crutchley filed her report.

"David does not have some connectedness or relationship to his family. He did describe having wanted to kill his parents for several years extending back to either 1990 or 1991."

In 1990, David was ten years old and still attending prayer meetings.

"He related that he had an older brother who really had not related much with David except when they had on one occasion, of being in agreement about beating up their father. He also related that he had a younger brother he really did not care for. He described him as an 'asskiss.' "

Dr. Crutchley detailed what David told her about his rebellion.

"He would smoke outside of the home." Jehovah's Witnesses are prohibited from smoking. "He wanted to shave his head. This was not in accordance with the parents' wishes or the rules of the home. Most of the activity that he did outside the home that would be regarded as antisocial, of course, was not in keeping with his parents' values.

"Some amount of theft, drinking; he was using marijuana, getting stoned, he was engaged in vandalism, spray painting Nazi symbols." A loner, David "felt that it was unsafe to do any of these things with others involved because they might turn on him or tell on him. So he kept these activities to himself."

Dr. Crutchley went on to state, "There was an element of criminal sophistication in his activities. He knew things that would create a greater liability for apprehension and he could plan accordingly. He also had a good knowledge of how to carry out what he wanted to do without getting caught. That was one of the reasons he did not have an arrest record and history of offenses such that he would have been more likely to been adjudicated delinquent."

As to when his rebellion began, "David relates that there was a time where he decided to disobey parental rules, about one and one half to two and one half years ago. By the end of '90, the beginning of '91, David is aware of being in an ongoing adversarial relationship with his parents. His drug use increased then. He wouldn't obey parental rules about returning home."

The alcohol that had been in the house since he was a child had turned out to be a tremendous problem for him. The doctor's report continued:

"He had been drunk way back. He started quite young. He told me he had been abusing alcohol since he was six years old. So that was an ongoing defiance of parental rules and expectations, but that (alcohol abuse) increased because of parties (he attended) and additional drugs he'd use."

David not only had problems with alcohol, he had problems with hard drugs as well.

"He said he used every street drug he could obtain except heroin and inhalants during the two and one half years prior to the time when I saw him. He said he didn't form any particular affinity for drugs. (Instead, it was) poly-substance abuse."

In his own words, David Freeman described to Dr. Crutchley how, beginning between the time he was ten and eleven years old, he was making buys of all commonly available street drugs, including uppers, downers, angel dust, mescaline—the usual range of drugs available on street corners in America. Yet his parents remained either ignorant of his substance abuse, or turned a blind eye and a deaf ear to it, because they could not believe what was happening.

Dr. Crutchley continued:

"David said that he's always disliked his parents.

The discord with his parents extended back in relationship to their religion. The ongoing thing of setting limits and trying to tell him what to do and what not to do. A primary example of not following parental rules was (his) staying out at parties and doing whatever street drugs he could obtain and continuing his alcohol usage. He also began antisocial activities during that time period of stealing, vandalizing."

What was gradually emerging was a picture of a boy with a secret life. On the surface, through his adolescent years, he was charming and gracious; he went to church and obeyed his elders. But inside, he had developed a hate toward the authority figures in his life, specifically his mother, father, and the Watchtower. That hate imbued itself in every facet of his life. It had caused him to rebel not only in the home, but outside it as well, for example, when he threatened his football coach.

As for his relationship with his brother, that also began to take on another interesting dimension. Dr. Crutchley wrote:

"One unusual thing was the way he described his older brother, because he was a druggie and he tends to trust druggies." But if "any of these (other) druggies tried to turn him in for something, that he would be able to turn the tables on them and incriminate them more than they could incriminate him. That's why he was trusting the persons that I and others would think risky to trust, meaning the druggies, so it was more like he could gain (the) upper hand . . . the amount of evidence that he would have available at his disposal versus the amount they'd have at theirs, which impressed me as showing far more thought and planning and feelings of control than the average resident I see at Paradise School."

David had made certain to have the goods on his drug-dealing and using friends. If they were ever busted, they wouldn't even think of turning him in as part of a plea bargain because they knew he had additional stuff on them that he wouldn't hesitate to use.

"In my interview with him and in prior psychological testing, which was intelligence testing," the standard IQ tests administered to kids in school, "I found that he's above average in intelligence, or on the high side of the average range."

David had an estimated intelligence quotient of 110, which was in the high end of the average range. "I had no doubt that he was in the above average range, the higher range, a little brighter or more intelligent than most people."

She went on to describe a scenario they discussed, in which David passed a burning building. Would he go in and rescue anyone? David answered, "No."

He said that he liked to listen to heavy metal music and favored the music of a group called Storm Troopers of Death. He was particularly anxious to see them at a live concert.

Dr. Crutchley concluded her report in a most ominous manner. She said, "I put down that he had high risk for the future development of antisocial personality disorder. Prognosis was very guarded. David Freeman does not have empathy for others."

The last was a telling remark. A classic psychopath does not feel guilt, does not feel what it is like to be someone else which allows them to inflict pain and suffering without any feeling for the other person.

Dr. Crutchley had described the formation of a psychopathic personality. This in itself is not unusual, but in an individual who is already starting to act out, as David Freeman was, the chances of antisocial acts increasing to the point of violence increase in direct proportion to the degree of psychological problems.

David Freeman was an accident waiting to happen. But early intervention sometimes works, so there was some hope.

David would remain in the Paradise School for a full year. When he was released in the spring of 1994, he had received at least one good citizenship citation from the school. He had fit in well there, and away from his family environment, he had prospered. Maybe his antisocial tendencies had been derailed. Maybe he wouldn't act out anymore.

When David was discharged, he went home, back into his family. It never occurred to either Dennis or Brenda that they were laying the seeds for their own destruction. They did not realize that every part of a family system reacts to every other part, that David and Bryan were reacting to something present in the household, just as Dennis and

Brenda were reacting to what they had been taught.

Had they sought intervention as a family and stayed with a therapeutic program, things might have turned out differently. But to do so would have been to admit that the teachings of the Jehovah's Witnesses were not enough to get them through their family crisis. To do that would have been to repudiate the religion and risk disfellowship and damnation.

Dr. Crutchley's report contained references to David Freeman's white supremacist activities. It did not go into detail on how he formed this apparent affinity for neo-Nazis. Had she been searching for that answer, it might have led her back to Bryan.

Bryan Freeman would later be portrayed by the media as a hulking, incoherent brute, six feet tall and 215 pounds. They only got his physical description right.

If David was of above average intelligence, Bryan was even smarter. He had an IQ of 120 and did so well in school, he consistently made the honor roll. He was quiet, friendly, and respectful of his friends, but at home, he was totally different.

At least five times the Salisbury Township police were called to the Freeman home to break up interfamily fights. Bryan was in the middle of many of them, yet despite evidence of physical confrontations between parents and son, no charges were brought. Bryan's record stayed clean.

These two sides of his personality made him seem like a Jekyll-and-Hyde. Brenda felt that Bryan's abuse of alcohol, like his brother's, made matters worse. She sent him to alcohol treatment centers a few times, hoping Bryan would respond and their lives would be better.

Bryan spent long nights alone, staring up at the ceiling, feeling unloved and unwanted, wondering what he had done that was so wrong to end up confined against his will. Alienated from his parents and their beliefs, which had further served to alienate him from his peers, his future looked bleak. Nowhere did he belong. And then Seth Monroe came into his life.

Seth was a fellow inmate at one of the rehab centers Brenda and Dennis had banished him to. Seth had tattoos of skulls and crossbones on his arms and legs, and swastikas. When Bryan asked him what they were about, Seth told him, "I'm a skinhead, and if you know what's good for you and the white race, you'll become one, too."

In the remaining time they served together, Seth told Bryan what it meant to be a skinhead and all about the skinhead movement in America.

Eight

The skinhead phenomenon originated in England, where gangs of menacing-looking youths, with shaved heads and in combat boots, began to be seen in the streets in the early 1970s. Their style was meant to symbolize tough, patriotic, working-class attitudes in contrast to the sissyish, pacifistic, middle-class views of the hippies.

It was a time when England received a flood of immigrants from third world countries and "skins," prompted by a sagging economy, blamed these "nonwhites" for England's problems. It was classic hate rhetoric: when times are tough, blame anyone but yourself for getting you into the fix in the first place. Do not accept responsibility for your own lot in life; it's the other guy who's causing the problems. Solution: get rid of the other guy. His elimination will solve our problems. Then, and only then, will we be free to prosper.

The racist and chauvinistic attitudes that prevailed at the time among many skins later evolved into a crude form of Nazism. From the beginning, skins drew public notice for their bigotry and taste for violence, exemplified by their frequent assaults on Asian immigrants, attacks that came to be known as "Paki-bashing."

In the years that followed, as the Thatcher government of Britain took the country down a path of fiscal conservatism and trickle-down economics, the skinhead movement spread from England to the Continent and beyond. Racist skins are found today in almost every industrialized country whose majority population is of European extraction. Those attracted to the movement are primarily white youths between the ages of thirteen and twenty-five, with males outnumbering females. While skins attempt to maintain the mythology of the movement's working-class origins, in reality, skins come from a broad range of socioeconomic backgrounds, favoring the middle class.

Most skinhead gangs range in size from fewer than ten to several dozen members. To those devoted to the movement, being a skinhead is a full-time way of life and not simply adherence to current fashion.

Neo-Nazi ideology combined with the gang lifestyle provides skinheads with a seductive sense of strength disproportionate to their actual numbers, a sense of group belonging and superiority over others who are not fortunate enough to be white and embrace the skins' lifestyle. Skins also like to style themselves as modern-day Vikings. Invocation of Viking imagery offers the skinhead a perception of himself as a racial warrior.

Skinheads glorify Hitler and aspire to create his vision of a worldwide pan-Aryan reich. These strands, a sense of power, of belonging, and of destiny, combine to create the appeal the skinhead movement holds for disaffected and disenfranchised youngsters like Bryan and David Freeman and Ben Birdwell.

Neo-Nazi skinheads first appeared on the streets of America in the mid-1980s, about the time that the Freeman brothers' personalities were in their formative years. From a membership of a thousand in twelve states in early 1988, their ranks grew, approaching four thousand by 1993. These numbers have held steady.

While the numbers do not seem overwhelming, skins are violent disproportionate to their numbers. American skins began using boots, guns, and knives in their violent activities and they have since graduated to firearms. Despite the recent passage of the Brady bill, the ease of obtaining a firearm in the United States has made the American skins second only to their German counterparts in the ferocity of their attacks.

This propensity toward extreme acts of violence is reflected in the dramatic rise in the number of murders committed by skins in the United States. From December 1987 to June 1990, there were only six such killings; the overall total now stands at at least 37.

Most of the murder victims of the skinheads have been members of minority groups: Hispanics, blacks, Asians, homosexuals, and the homeless. Some deaths have resulted from in-group violence, with skinheads killing fellow gang members over petty disagreements. American skins also commit lesser crimes: beatings, stabbings, shootings, thefts, synagogue desecrations, and other forms of mayhem and intimidation.

There is no single national skinhead organization. Instead, loosely linked networks of skinhead gangs operate in scattered communities. In Pennsylvania, one skinhead gang more well known to law enforcement authorities is the Eastern Hammerhead Skins. It was their mailing labels Brenda discovered in Bryan's *Death Book*.

Gangs frequently change names and network affiliations. Individual members are often highly mobile, with little to tie them to a particular location. It is not uncommon for a group to leave a city and resume activity in another locale after feeling pressure from law enforcement and the community.

The most commonly perceived misconception about Skinheads is that they come from lower-class homes, from parents who are poorly educated, who have not been able to imbue in their children a strong sense of morality. While this can be used by sociologists and others to explain crime in general, in this country it does not apply to the skinhead phenomenon.

American skinheads, who claim to represent working class youth, frequently come from middle-class homes. Their roots lie not so much in economic decay as in domestic instability. This instability can take the form of broken homes or single-parent families, or as in the Freeman case, a home where religious intransigence and a failure to acknowledge that the family system has broken down, leads to the child seeking a surrogate family elsewhere.

Those skins who live with their families often do so under tense conditions. Parents like the Freemans rarely approve of their skinhead children's views or way of life. Those skins that live among their own do so in communal homes and apartments.

As Seth explained to Bryan what it meant to be a skinhead, Bryan became attracted to the skinhead Nazi ideology, which essentially offers alienated youth self-esteem through the degradation of others.

The more Dennis and Brenda tried to get Bryan to conform, giving the message that he was not good enough, the angrier Bryan got and the more he wanted to take out his anger on somebody. The skins' glorification of violence provides a sense of power; the pack mentality provides a sense of security lacking in the family.

Skinheads in America pattern their dress on the original British model: combat boots or Doc Martens, thin suspenders, and bomber jackets. They wear their hair close cropped. Some American skins are drug users, and most, like Bryan and David, are heavy beer drinkers. Drinking binges often precede hunts for purported "enemies."

The politics of hate do not provide for exclusivity. Skinheads march in Klan demonstrations. For instance, at a January 1993 march in Pulaski, Tennessee (the birthplace of the KKK), about a hundred skinheads marched with the KKK, shouting anti-Jewish and white supremacist slogans.

Skins tend to be young, but as they reach their mid-twenties, some outgrow their group and join the KKK. Skinheads have also linked up with such old-line hate groups as the Aryan Nations, the Church of the Creator, and White Aryan Resistance (WAR). These older groups refer to the skins as their "frontline warriors."

The Aryan Nations has for years hosted youth gatherings at its rural Idaho compound. These events, usually held in April to coincide with Hitler's birthday, have attracted numerous skinheads. They meet to drink beer, spout Nazi slogans, and hear white supremacist rock bands in concert, popular bands like Bound for Glory, Christian Identity Skins, and Odin's Law, a Canadian group.

As targets, skinheads usually seek out the "mud" people, those who are not "pure" white. Jews in particular are looked at as being "mud" people. This follows Hitler's ideology that made Jews the scapegoats for every calamity that ever fell upon mankind's collective head. Today, skins take the same view.

The skins hatred also extends to blacks, Hispanics, Asians, and others of nonwhite blood. What all these groups have in common is that they are the enemy of the skins, who are united in their desire to wipe them off the face of the earth and finish the job Hitler started.

American skins have repeatedly acted out their racial warrior fantasies in acts of exceptional violence. In August 1990, about the same time the Freeman brothers' rebellion against their parents began, in Houston, Texas, two 18-year-old Skinheads stomped a 15-year-old Vietnamese boy to death. The last words of the victim, who had emigrated to the United States were: "God forgive me for coming to this country. I am so sorry."

In June 1991, as David Freeman got more and more into alcohol and drug use, three 16-year-old members of the Confederate Hammerskins killed a black man in a drive-by shotgun slaying as the man sat in the back of a truck with two white friends.

Skinheads belonging to the Aryan National Front (ANF) were responsible for two separate killings of homeless black men in Birmingham, Alabama, on December 24, 1991, a Christmas Eve when David and Bryan Freeman sat home, their anger burning inside them that the next day, their parents would not allow them to celebrate Christmas.

In July 1993, while David Freeman was in the Paradise School for Boys, eight people were arrested by federal authorities and charged with a variety of conspiracy offenses in connection with a plan to incite a race war by, among other things, bombing an African-American church, sending a letter bomb to a rabbi, and assassinating several well-known African-American figures.

Among those involved in the latter plan were members of the Fourth Reich Skinheads group.

American skinheads do not confine themselves to ethnic hatred. They have been held responsible for several murders and countless assaults based on their hatred of homosexuals. Fatal skinhead attacks on gays have occurred in New York City, in San Diego, St. Louis, Salem (Oregon), and Reno.

Skins have killed their nonracist counterparts in gang brawls as well as unprovoked attacks. In August 1990, a fight between racist and nonracists skinhead factions in the parking lot of a Sacramento club resulted in the stabbing death of a SHARP (Skinheads Against Racial Prejudice). Then, in August 1992, two neo-Nazi skinheads stabbed and bludgeoned to death a seventeen-year-old nonracist skinhead of mixed Asian and white background in Olympia, Washington. The boy's only crime was that he was not "pure" white.

When times are slow and there are no "mud" people around to assault, or any other skin gangs to rumble with, or when their courage has not peaked for physical conflict, skins turn their attention to the dead—they attack the graves of Jews.

A skin and two accomplices were charged with the April 23, 1993 desecration of a Jewish cemetery in Revere, Massachusetts. In addition to overturning a hundred tombstones and spray painting swastikas, the skins scrawled a birthday salute to Hitler on a nearby wall. The three were sentenced to two years in prison.

Other Jewish institutions have also been attacked by skinheads.

On March 20, 1994, two skins shot several rounds from a high-powered semi-automatic rifle into the stained glass windows of a Eugene, Oregon, synagogue. The shooters were eventually sentenced to terms of 54 and 57 months.

Seth Monroe answered Bryan's questions about the American skinhead movement. If skinheads are bound only by loose alliances in various parts of the country, how would skins in Pennsylvania, for example, keep contact and maintain ties with their brethren in Oregon?

Over the years that problem was initially solved by a number of publications that all skins had access to. They were crudely made magazines. Some only ran for a few issues.

Some of the more popular skinhead magazines in the 1990s include *Blood and Honor,* out of Long Beach, California; *National Socialist Skinhead,* published in Saint Paul, Minnesota; *Iron Will* and *Skinhead Power* from North Carolina; and *The Berserker* of Levittown, New York, though this is more a newsletter than a full-fledged magazine.

The " 'zines" focused on skinhead music that carries the message of hate to a larger audience, but racist commentary is included throughout each issue in editorials and interviews. Typical of the views espoused in these interviews are those of members of the band Das Reich:

"We must expose the Zionist-controlled media and institutions to the rest of the white 'sheep' in America . . . we would like to salute all the white stormtroopers that are fighting daily for our struggle."

In the nineties, the skins took to using a more immediate way of keeping contact: the Internet and the World Wide Web. There are numerous skinhead sites on the Web where skins can keep in touch with each other, whether they're in Maine or Mobile. These Internet hate groups are not composed of beer-guzzling, potbellied, illiterate morons. They are a highly motivated, intelligent group of people who make hate their life's preoccupation.

Stormfront is an example of a skins' home page.

"*Stormfront* is a resource for those courageous men and women fighting to preserve their white Western culture ideals and freedom of speech and association, a forum for planning strategies and forming political and social groups to ensure victory," claims the first paragraph of *Stormfront's* home page.

Articles featured in one edition of *Stormfront* included *OKC Bombing and America's Future,* by William Pierce; *What Is Racism?,* by Thomas Jackson; and *Racial Realities: My Indian Odyssey,* by David Duke.

David Duke is the former presidential candidate, former Klansman, and Louisiana state legislator known for his white supremacist views.

In *Stormfront's* online library annex are "archived articles of interest to white nationalists," and "a collection of (hate) graphics and symbols" that readers can easily access for their own use. These are well-thought-out racist messages designed to attract the disenfranchised like Bryan Freeman, in much the same way that Hitler's philosophy of national socialism did in 1930s Germany.

In addition to actual articles, there's a section called "Internet Mailing Lists." Included are the "*Stormfront* Mailing List," which is "a moderated discussion forum for white nationalists," and "Canadian Patriots Network," which includes "current events of interest to Patriots in the Great White North."

For those who are more aggressive and want to interact, there are "Newsgroups of Interest to White Nationalists," where Net browsers can talk online, live, to those of like-minded views. And, like any business that wants to leave its customers satisfied, *Stormfront* has a list of "Dial-In Bulletin Board Systems"—one can dial into specific bulletin boards broken down regionally, including Chicago's "Cyberspace Minutemen," Portland's "Banished BBS (Bulletin Board System)," which specializes in Holocaust revisionist material, and "Digital Freedom, Canada's Newest White Nationalist Board."

But actions speak louder than words, or E-mail, and skins look at members of their own who are charged with hate crimes as prisoners of war. Among these so-called prisoners of war are David Lane and Gary Yarbrough. Both are currently serving long sentences for their role in the neo-Nazi terrorist group The Order. Matthew Hayhow, a skinhead is serving twenty-five years for armed robbery.

Resistance Records, the major producer of skinhead or hate rock music in America with its home in Detroit, puts out a magazine that focuses on skin music in the United States and Canada. It claims circulation of "12,000 and growing." They have a site on the Internet through which skins may mail-order their favorite Resistance Records releases.

The Resistance Records site is a masterwork of marketing. You can listen to excerpts of songs from some of the top hate rock bands, order records, or just relax with a cup of coffee and get into the hate rock movement. White power music has become so popular that MTV has already done a special on hate rock. Even kids who are not skinheads or white supremacists listen to the music because it deals with the alienation many in their generation feel.

Bound for Glory is perhaps the most influential American skinhead band. Led by Ed Wolbank, director of the neo-Nazi Northern Hammer Skins in Saint Paul, Minnesota, the band has recorded for Resistance Records and the German Rock-O-Rama label and has toured in Europe with Skrewdriver. A member of the band summarized the underlying message behind their music: "All of our music has a racial theme and that is 100% White."

Detroit, that hotbed of skinhead activism, boasts an active music scene. Two local bands, Max Resist and the Hooligans and Rival, performed frequently at the Westside Clubhouse in Detroit, where Bryan met Frank at the New Year's Eve concert.

The Clubhouse also served as the hangout for the Detroit skinhead gang the West Side Boot Boys. Out-of-state bands also frequently played at the Clubhouse. Among those advertised to appear in a tribute concert to the slain Joe Rowan were Bound for Glory, Centurian, the Voice, Aggravated Assault, and Shamrock. A recent flier, however, announced the closing of the West Side Clubhouse, allegedly for reasons of "security"; it claimed that alternative venues would be found for future concerts.

But Bryan Freeman lived in Pennsylvania and as he slowly learned from Seth about the skinhead movement, he discovered that Pennsylvania is also a hotbed of skinhead activity.

* * *

Across the state in Pittsburgh, skinhead activity
is largely limited to the Oakland area of the city.
Two skinheads, Steven Stanley and Francis Mercuri,
were arrested in July 1991 at an apartment where
police found an assortment of loaded weapons,
bomb-making instructions, a Nazi flag, and photographs of Adolf Hitler.

Mercuri was placed under arrest as a fugitive and
extradited to Florida, where he was convicted in
connection with an attack on a Jewish teenager.
Stanley pleaded guilty to hindering apprehension
of Mercuri.

Pittsburgh's skins are linked to a Pennsylvania
hate group alliance called the Pennsylvania Aryan
Independence Network (PAIN). There is also
something of a skinhead club and record scene in
the city itself. But it was across the state in eastern
Pennsylvania, in Bryan Freeman's home country,
that considerable Skinhead activity occurred.

In Shamokin, Pennsylvania, just miles from Allentown, eleven skins were arrested in April 1993 and
charged with ethnic intimidation, riot, and disor-
derly conduct. Five of the eleven were juveniles. The
arrests came about as a result of a confrontation with
state troopers. The skins had for several weeks been
terrorizing the downtown area of Shamokin.

In East Stroudsberg, also just miles from Allentown, a homeless white man asked for a ride from
two neo-Nazi skins. They were charged in his stabbing death in July 1992. East Stroudsberg police classified the killing as a "hate crime." A twenty-year-old

male from Pocono Pines, adjacent to Allentown, was convicted of criminal homicide and aggravated assault. Edward Rice, twenty, of Mount Pocono, pleaded guilty to reckless endangerment and testified for the prosecution against him in the case. Rice has also been accused of attacking a black taxi driver in Allentown. He and Pete Dalton, twenty-one, of Allentown, allegedly attacked and stabbed the driver, according to Allentown police. Both were charged with attempted homicide and Rice was turned over to Allentown authorities.

Other violence in Eastern Pennsylvania by skins:

A twenty-eight-year-old Coatesville gutter installer, was murdered on October 12, 1990, by a skinhead angered because he had taunted him about his appearance. When the installer left the bar where the verbal confrontation occurred, he was beaten with a crowbar, kicked in the head and face, and stabbed to death by two skinheads (nineteen and twenty-two). They were both convicted of first-degree murder by a Chester County jury.

In January 1992, a group of fifteen to twenty skins appeared in front of Upper Darby High School shouting *"Sieg Heil! Sieg Heil! Sieg Heil!"* and thrusting their arms out in the Nazi salute.

Two adults, and twelve juveniles were arrested. One adult pleaded guilty to criminal conspiracy and assault and received a year's probation. A judge dismissed charges against the other because the prosecution failed to establish that he had participated in the attack. The twelve juveniles were convicted of assault in juvenile court. Because they are juveniles, their records were sealed.

A month later, a brawl erupted at a benefit concert in Pottstown, Pennsylvania. Skinheads shouting *"Sieg Heil! Sieg Heil! Sieg Heil!"* were set upon by the crowd.

In Bucks, Montgomery, and Chester Counties, forty to fifty active skinheads are known to law enforcement authorities. In addition, there are some fifteen to twenty skinheads active in York County, including an Eastern Hammer Skins gang in Stewartstown. Another active group is the United White Skinheads, located in Wayne.

A neo-Nazi skinhead rock band, the Voice, is based in Philadelphia, where it maintains a post office box. Members of the band are connected with the Eastern Hammer Skins and the Christian Posse Comitatus. The Christian Posse Comitatus is perhaps the largest and strongest neo-Nazi group in Pennsylvania.

Nine

In his rehab facility, Bryan Freeman listened intently as Seth Monroe inculcated him with skinhead rhetoric.

It was a revelation. Suddenly, Bryan's mind was alive with a philosophy of life that made his hate into a positive force, a hate that would free him from the bonds of his parents and religion, hate that he could channel into violence against minorities who he believed were really responsible for his problems and those of society.

A mother can expect her teenager to rebel and decorate his room with posters of rock stars, pictures of gorgeous models, and other accoutrements of adolescence. But in the Freeman house, the eldest boy took the interior decorating of his room to new levels.

Swastikas appeared on walls, pictures of Hitler, photos of white supremacist rock bands on the Resistance Records label. The sounds of Bound for Glory, Rahowa, Nordic Thunder, and other white power bands filled the house. One day Bryan was your average teenager, and the next he was the indoctrinated member of a Hitler youth group.

"We have to get rid of the 'mud' people," Bryan told his brother, David.

"Jews and the Zionist conspiracy and the niggers are responsible for all our problems," Bryan said to Benny.

Like the stormtroopers, there is a uniform for today's skinheads, and Bryan quickly adopted it after his release from rehab. Dennis and Brenda could only watch in disbelief as Bryan shaved his head, bought Doc Martens, wore a cool leather jacket, and began spouting racial invective.

His parents protested his newfound conversion. Elders from the Kingdom Hall showed up on more than one occasion to try to get Bryan back into the field. They preached the doctrine of Jehovah. Unless Bryan repented his sinful ways, he would be destroyed on Armageddon Day with all the disbelievers. He just laughed.

Dennis continued to withdraw from his parental responsibilities, leaving the discipline of his children to Brenda. To her credit, Brenda tried setting boundaries: there would be no smoking or drinking in the house. There'd be curfews, and keeping up with studies at school. In record time, Bryan broke as many of the rules as he could.

Bryan was determined to be a full-fledged skinhead, and that meant tattooing. He found Brandon Johnson, a tattoo artist who had a storefront in the central part of Allentown. Brandon created fine skin art. Over the next few years, Bryan became a regular customer of Brandon's, and the tattooist indelibly printed on Bryan's skin the images of Nazi Germany that had terrified a full generation of people in the heart of this century.

Bryan also began an extended weightlifting program. The boy who had once delivered God's words vanished forever, replaced by a menacing, hulking youth who deified Hitler, a teenager devoted to the survival of the white race and the destruction of the Jews, blacks, and "mud" people.

Bryan had finally found someone who accepted him. In Hitler he found his surrogate father, someone who had channeled hate into something constructive: no less than the destruction of anyone who was different. It was a philosophy with broad appeal, which is why it stood the test of time and now, fifty years later, after Hitler had died, his legacy was the hate in Bryan Freeman's heart, hate that was born from rigid, unloving parents, hate born from a religion that demanded he stay an outsider, hate born from kids looking at him funny because he didn't have a birthday or Christmas dinner, hate born from too many tears and too little love. But *now,* he was accepted in the white Aryan brotherhood of man.

Anyone who stood in his way—*anyone*—would be wiped out in the path of destruction he would cut.

It apparently did not take long for David to ally himself with his brother against his parents and younger brother Erik and accept the skinheads as his one true family. He came from the same home as his brother and he had the same background. He felt the same way toward his parents, and while there was a time when he was younger when he'd felt alienated from *everyone* including his brother, Bryan had now taken a leap of rebellion that David yearned to do also. He cut his hair, bought the boots and jacket, and tattooed his body, and soon, two of the three Freeman brothers were full-fledged skinheads.

Erik quaked in terror before his older brothers. They terrorized him on a regular basis and made him feel unsafe in his own house, in his own bed. He never knew when one or the other might reach out to hit or threaten him. While he was the apple of his parents' eye, they couldn't be around all the time to protect him. Life in the Freeman house for the youngest brother became a minefield. Erik fell victim to Bryan and David's sadistic impulses.

Benny, meanwhile, visited the Freemans regularly. He was not indoctrinated the way Bryan was. For him, becoming a skinhead was just something to do. His sense of what was right and wrong had already been affected by his father's past and his own juvenile troubles.

The local paper reported that Benny was convicted on juvenile charges of theft, burglary, receiving stolen property, and trespassing which stemmed from the thefts of a .357 Magnum revolver and a .22 caliber Ruger semi-automatic pistol. His first probation officer, Karen Hammer, was quoted as saying, "He (Ben) indicated that the guns were going to be sold for drugs."

As one part of Benny's probation, Judge Reibman made him watch the film, *Schindler's List*. When he finished seeing it, Benny claimed the Holocaust was made up.

After Hammer, Jason Weaver, a Lehigh County juvenile probation aide, took over Benny's case. "Ben seemed angry. I couldn't tell why. I fear his skinhead activities are going to catch up with him soon," he wrote in his notes.

Benny's troubles were not confined to the legal system. He was also having problems in school.

He attended Whitehall High School. He cut classes a lot, was suspended, and "particularly had a problem with minority students," according to Karen Hammer. He carried a copy of *Mein Kampf,* and turned in essays on the Ku Klux Klan and white supremacy. He carried a KKK key ring.

He was later transferred to the Parkland School District and attended Lehigh County Vocational-Technical (VoTech) School before finally dropping out in the fall of 1994.

He had no positive belief system, and his family had problems, ranging from his father's repeated arrests and convictions to his grandfather's falling out with the Jehovah's Witnesses. Benny was ripe for the skinhead message Bryan and David offered. He would join. If anything, it sounded like fun.

Benny shaved his head and bought the clothes. The tattoos would come later. Now, there were three members of the Freeman/Birdwell family who had embraced white supremacy and neo-Nazism.

They began hanging out with Allentown's skin-head gangs. The Freemans and Ben Birdwell were frequently seen with their skinhead brethren harassing blacks and other minorities at the Whitehall Mall in the Allentown area.

They were boys without a moral compass. Three

teenagers looking for action. Three young men with the strength to kill and the will to do it.

All it would take now was a channeler, someone who could translate those feelings into action. That someone was already in the neighborhood.

Twenty miles outside Allentown is a farm that looks like any other from the outside, but what grows there fouls the soil. The crop is hate.

Mark Thomas's farm is a gathering place for his Christian Identity Group, the Christian Posse Comitatus, a loose congregation of Klansmen, racist skins, neo-Nazis, and white supremacists of other persuasions who travel there each weekend from across the state to hear him preach his version of white supremacy. As many as fifty gather on any given weekend, with that number swelling to two hundred on summer weekends and even more for his Oktoberfest every fall.

Thomas is an extremely intelligent and lucid man with the craggy face of a frontier pioneer. He combs his hair across his forehead like his idol, Hitler. With the square-cut mustache adorning his upper lip and his dark eyes, he looks astonishingly like the former head of the Third Reich.

Thomas describes himself in an article as "a philosopher and to most conservatives, a renegade. The only thing I really hate is Judaeo-Christianity and any political system that puts the love of money before the love of people. I am a humanist, a liberal, and an old hippie, if you follow the original definition of those words, and I have become a stranger in a strange land," the last an apparent reference to Robert Heinlein's science fiction classic about an alien with a benign interest in cannibalism.

Christian Identity is a movement within the white supremacy movement that uses scripture, among other things, to prove white superiority. Thomas is a Christian Identity minister, ordained by Robert Butler, a founding father of Christian Identity, at the Aryan Nations compound in Hayden Lake, Idaho, in 1990. Civil rights watchdog groups like the Anti-Defamation League and the Alabama-based Klanwatch view Aryan Nations as one of the country's most violent white supremacist groups. Thomas, though, has publicly denounced violence to achieve his goals.

Thomas believes that blacks, Asians, Hispanics, and other nonwhites will be relocated to their places of origin. If they refuse to go peacefully, they will be made to go. As for Jews, they will be cast into the fires of hell. Thomas, though, does acknowledge that not all Jews are the devil. Just most.

Thomas believes that white supremacy is the will of God, that there will be an imminent race war that will cleanse the earth of racial corruption and restore God's white Christian kingdom to its rightful place as ruler of the universe.

Bryan, hearing this from Thomas himself and other skins, realized how Thomas's ideology compared astonishingly well to that of the Jehovah's Witnesses. Like the Witnesses, Thomas believed in an eventual Armageddon, but at the end of his, only whites would be left standing, regardless of whether they were of the 144,000 to go to heaven. In Thomas's world, even if you were not in that number, you would not be allowed paradise on earth if you were a nonwhite. And if you believed in Thomas's doctrine, all that was required was to channel the hate inside you, much easier than the discipline required to be a Jehovah's Witness.

Mark Thomas has a site on the Internet where he writes extensively about his beliefs. The Freeman brothers and their cousin Ben were attracted to Thomas because he is a very intelligent man who couches his anti-Semitic, racist beliefs behind logical arguments "derived" from the Bible. To children like the Freemans and Birdwell who grew up on the Bible and knew it forward and backward, and who had a perverted value system, Thomas's scriptural interpretation was the same as the Witnesses', only more palatable.

In an article on his Web site, Thomas deified the Unabomber, making the terrorist's manifesto analogous to the United States after the Civil War. Thomas writes, "It is a glorious fact that the Ku Klux Klan saved the White race from oblivion in the conquered South following the Civil War." He believes Germany built "the kingdom of God" in the 1930s. To some, Thomas's arguments for the supremacy of the White race seem plausible.

Thomas has managed to attract a loyal following. David, Bryan, and Ben were just following the crowd in embracing Thomas's rhetoric.

When David and Bryan began publicly extolling their neo-Nazi beliefs, Principal Michael Platt at Salisbury Township High School was quoted as saying, "The reaction around here varied. There were some faculty members who just said they were going through a phase and others who wondered how much we should tolerate. From a legal standpoint, I don't believe there is anything we could have done as long as they did not interfere with the educational process."

As far as the students were concerned, the Freeman brothers' conversion to white supremacism was looked on with something between curious interest and apathy. Still, regardless of what one thought, they made quite a sight, what with their shaved heads, combat boots, and camouflage jackets. One student in particular was intensely interested in their belief system.

Jack Kramer was a Salisbury student who saw in Bryan Freeman a particularly good story. Bryan was a good student, bright and articulate. Clearly, he and his brother were not ignorant idiots embracing a far right political belief because they could not distinguish between right and wrong, or because they did not understand the implications of the hate that spewed forth from their lips.

Jack wanted to get them on video tape. He set up an interview session at Bryan's house. David couldn't make it, but Benny, their initiated cousin, could.

The tape opens with Bryan sitting by a window. His huge form is silhouetted against bright sunshine. Bryan's fresh-scrubbed features and powerful body fitted into overalls, his immense tattooed arms and tattooed forehead dominate the frame. A swastika armband was prominently displayed on his left upper arm. Benny sat next to him with a cold, bemused smile on his face and an SS swastika armband covering his upper arm.

"When did you become involved in the white power skinhead movement?" Jack began.

"I've been hanging out with the skinheads for about a year," Bryan answered.

"What about you?" Jack turned to Benny.

"About six months."

"Why'd you become involved?"

"Well, after I got out of lock-up," Bryan answered patiently, "I had long hair, I was still pretty much white power, and I started hanging out with all the skinheads. It seemed pretty cool, so I shaved my head."

"Do you feel that all communication with other races is off?" Jack asked.

"Yes," Bryan answered firmly. "We should have no contact at all; they're the enemy."

There was no emotion in his voice, just calm, slowly delivered hate. For the rest of the interview, Benny remained silent, a smirk on his face, while his cousin took center stage. It looked like Bryan relished every moment.

"What bothers you or frustrates you about these other races?"

"Well, the biggest thing that I think is a problem is the fact that they can call racism on anything and we can't. They have Negro college funds, Chinese college funds, Indian college funds—you don't see a white man's college fund anywhere."

"Have you ever had any personal experiences with minorities that caused you to hate?"

"Well, I have a cousin who's a half breed."

"Do you know any of the history of the skin-heads?"

"I know some of it, yeah."

"Such as?"

"I know that pretty much George Lincoln Rockwell was the founder of the movement in the United States. Rockwell was the founder of the Nazi Party in America."

"How do you feel about whites who try to act black or dig minorities?"

"I think it's disgusting," Bryan said, with obvious loathing. "Especially the race mixers. They have the gift of being white, but they're willing to throw it all away to breed with animals."

Bryan's answers were beginning to sound rote, like he was spitting out propaganda that had been implanted in his head.

"How do you feel about those who associate with blacks?"

"A crime punishable by death. To all involved."

The interview was over.

Ten

Neither Brenda nor Dennis was eager to give their two problem children an allowance. All they'd do with the money was buy more drugs and beer, or some awful Nazi flags and armbands and iron crosses they kept in their messy rooms.

Along with Benny, Bryan took a job as a counterboy at a nearby Wendy's. There Bryan worked with his school friend, Kate Blacke, who also knew David. From her emerges a different picture of the skinhead all of Allentown would come to hate.

"Bryan was always nice to everybody. He never really had any problem with anybody," Kate recalls.

That was on the outside. Inside, Bryan was roiling. During one of his rehab stays, he had been diagnosed as suffering from depression. The drug lithium, frequently used to treat manic-depressive disorder, had been prescribed, but Bryan had refused to take it.

Kate and David were both high school sophomores—so she had ample opportunity to observe and interact with him. "David was always quiet. He kept to himself . . . (and) he actually got good grades. (In particular) David's social studies teacher, Mr. Hammer, liked him because he was quiet and got good grades. He used to sleep during class and wake up and pass the test. I think both brothers were on the school honor roll."

When they attended school, as opposed to the rehab facilities their parents sent them to, both Freemans excelled in their studies. Studies, though, were different from home life.

Kate remembers that "most of the time, they were kinda pissed-off at home, angry all the time, because they went through different phases . . . I know they did drugs, but they didn't do it while they were skinheads, because when you're a skinhead, you drink, but you don't do drugs. Skinheads are totally against drugs.

"They drank beer sometimes, and Jack Daniels. I remember when we were all high at someone's house one night and they had Jack Daniels and beer."

Boilermakers. The eighty-proof bourbon, or its hundred-proof version, also available, plus a chaser of Rolling Rock, make for a powerful combination. Since both boys looked older than they were, it was easy for them to go into any liquor store and purchase the beverages that should not have been available to them until they were twenty-one.

When the boys were in middle school, Kate recalls, they experimented with various drugs. "I think when they came to the high school they got into a different scene." As for their conversion to white supremacy, "They became skinheads because, I think, they felt left out because their family didn't care about them." The boys made it clear to Kate and probably their other friends that this was in truth how they really felt about their parents and younger brother.

Brenda and Dennis were intelligent people. They could not have been unaware of how their sons felt, yet they apparently did nothing to show them love. Quite the opposite, as Kate vividly recalls.

"One night, I went over there (to the Freemans' house). Their mom was making spaghetti. When it came time to have dinner, they asked me, 'Have you had dinner?' I said, 'No.' They said, 'You're welcome to eat here.'"

The invitation was polite but cold.

"They invited everyone to eat at the table, me and my friend that was with me, everyone except Bryan and David. And we were like, 'Don't they get dinner, too?' And I guess they just weren't good enough or something. It was an eerie feeling. They were not welcome because they were too bad; they were being punished."

This incident took place during the summer of 1994, around the time Brenda took up the "tough love" mentality of being strict with your kids and setting limits to get them to understand that you as the parent will not tolerate aberrant behavior. The denial of the privilege of eating dinner with family and guests may have been one part of Brenda's tough love platform.

"Erik sat at the table without his brothers," Kate continues. "The brothers noticed the preferential treatment he was getting." Kate believes that "the parents loved Erik because he was young and following along with their religion. And since Bryan and David were skinheads, they didn't believe in that."

While Brenda, David, Erik, Kate, and her friend ate, David and Bryan stood outside, smoking cigarettes. After dinner, the girls joined them and they went over to a friend's house to hang out. Benny soon joined them.

Cruising along in Bryan's car, he'd snap a cassette in, and out would come skinhead rock. White Power and Aryan Nation were just some of the bands Kate recalls they listened to. Skinhead rock is not popular just with died-in-the-wool skinheads. It is popular with disaffected teenagers all over the world. "I would hang out with them because I am proud of my heritage and I am white," says Kate. When she listened to the music, "I'd understand what they (the bands) were saying. There's good and bad in both races."

Kate had no way of knowing, because Bryan never told her, that until he was about ten he had been a devout Jehovah's Witness, with an intimate knowledge of the Bible, which he could still quote if he wanted to. "They didn't usually sit and talk about their parents, and Bryan said nothing about his split from the religion."

The religion, though, really wasn't the problem. It was the rules that their parents set up for them, rules the teenagers thought were unrealistic. "The only thing they ever got pissed-off about (on a regular basis) was like, if we went out after work, they had to be home at eight P.M., or earlier. They were not allowed to stay out. They'd come home and probably sneak back out again because they weren't allowed to do much."

After a while, their frustration turned to threats toward their parents. "Everyone heard them (make threats)," Kate observes.

They didn't make threats that often, but when they did, they were specific. They'd say something like, "I'm just gonna get so sick of it, I'm just gonna have to kill 'em or something."

The threats didn't sound truly serious to Kate. "You're not gonna do that, you're just angry," she would tell Bryan after one of his threats. And then Bryan would drop it, like he hadn't said anything.

"They were just mad and had these rules to follow," Kate states for emphasis.

They were close to losing control, but on the outside, anyway, David was his usual laconic self and Bryan exuded warmth.

Both before and after his institutionalizations, and after he became a skinhead, "Bryan was so nice to everybody."

Underneath, they were spoiling for action. Still, Kate recalls, they kept their racist beliefs to themselves. "The only time anything ever started is, say, if a black person started something with them. Then they would get angry." Racial invective would follow, and in the worse-case scenario, a fight between the racist brothers and their victims of color. "Otherwise, they wouldn't say anything to a black or Puerto Rican person unless something was said to them first."

The brothers Freeman got as good as they gave. "I've seen them in racial street fights. Either they got beat up," Kate says, "or they beat up black people because of what they were."

They might taunt their victim by calling him "nigger," and then the punches would fly. Sometimes it would just be a push and a shove and sometimes a full-fledged fight.

Kate also recalls her relationship with Ben Birdwell, who would sometimes fight with his cousins, and Ben's relationship with his cousins.

"I hung out with him a couple of times. When we worked at Wendy's, sometimes he'd drive up and pick them up if Bryan didn't have his car. He was around a little bit because he turned into a skinhead eventually himself.

"Ben was so sweet to everybody. I knew he got along with their parents because he is related in some sort of way. He never said anything about wanting to hurt them at all because it wasn't his place to because he didn't live there, know what I mean?

"Out of all of them, Ben was the nicest to me, and then Bryan. David was always really quiet and kept to himself. David just seemed like he was always angry inside. He wasn't mean," she hastens to add, "just angry. There was just a lot of hate building up (in both brothers) over the years from childhood because they missed out on a lot of things they should have had when they were little, like Christmas presents."

When their birthdays came around, they downplayed the occasion. " 'Well, I'm seven today, or eighteen, they'd say," like it meant nothing.

"They (Brenda and Dennis) cared a lot about

Erik. And the brothers, they got mad and were always picking on him. 'You think you're so special,' and stuff like that.''

Kate's friend Deborah Miles told her that Bryan and David had gotten so angry at Erik on one occasion that they had gone after him with a hatchet. Another time, Kate heard that David and Bryan . . . used to choke him, stuff like that.''

If it was true, the razzing of their little brother had gone into the realm of overt violence. Kate, though, had sympathy for David and Bryan.

"No one was there to love and care about them," Kate says.

Away from the job and school, the Freemans and Birdwell liked to party and drink. Fred Simon was a friend of theirs. They knew each other from school, talked frequently on the phone, and shared more than a few brews together.

"I want my mother dead," Bryan said on more than one occasion while they were drinking.

"I'd like to kick the fucking whore down the stairs," David chimed in.

They wanted to get away from "those assholes," but despite the threats toward Brenda, they never made any threats toward their father or brother, at least within earshot of Fred.

Fred, Bryan, David, and Ben used to get together and drink at a bar called the Wooden Keg off Tilghman Street in Allentown. It was a working class bar, and the boys and their cousin liked to have their beer there. From what Fred remembers, they drank heavily.

At about this time, Fred also recalls that both

Freeman brothers traveled to Detroit, to concerts at the Westside Clubhouse. Living up to their confrontational nature, the skins' clubhouse was situated on Joy Road, in a black neighborhood in northwest Detroit.

At the Clubhouse, the skins reveled in being the shock troops fighting for a new order based on the supremacy of whites. As the bands blared out their racist lyrics, the Freemans took it all in and slugged back their beers and smoked their cigarettes and looked through the smoky haze of the Clubhouse at each other and knew that finally, they were truly home.

When they returned from their trips to Detroit, trips Brenda felt powerless to stop, the boys were primed with hate. Their emotions had been aroused. They became more vocal with their friends about their antagonism toward their parents.

Bryan attended Lehigh County VoTech, where he took technical classes with other students, including Dan Hawthorne. Bryan, who could be personable and soft-spoken when he wanted to be, became friends with Dan. To Dan, Bryan seemed, despite the skinhead get-up, like a decent, intelligent guy, until Bryan let loose with his real feelings.

"I hate my parents," Bryan told Dan many times.

"I'm gonna kill them," Bryan said, as Dan listened, astounded. "One day, people'll see me on *America's Most Wanted,* after I kill 'em," Bryan bragged.

Another time, Bryan told Dan, "I beat up my

dad because he wouldn't let me smoke." There appears to have been some truth in that brag.

The Freeman family had gone to counseling sessions in an effort to try and resolve their problems. Far from doing that, one such session turned into a brawl when Bryan attacked Dennis. Dennis ended up with a dislocated shoulder. As for Benny and David, Dan knew of them, but he had seen them only a couple of times at the Whitehall Mall.

Hal Jordan also had classes with Bryan and had known him for two years. Bryan often talked to him about how he hated his parents and was going to kill them.

"My mom's a fat slob, and one day, I'm gonna kill her," Bryan said.

When Bryan wanted to make fun of other kids, he would do so by saying, "You slept with my mother, that big fat asshole, didn't you?"

To Barry Allen, Bryan said, "My mom and dad, they're both fat blobs. I hate them. I would like to kill them someday."

Barry was friends with Bryan for two years. Despite his threats, to the outside world he was always nice. To Barry's knowledge, he never hurt anyone.

Outside of school, Bryan and David began acting out. They told Fred Simon about an incident in which Bryan threw a molotov cocktail at a house across the street from St. Mark's Church on Susquehanna Street. The throw was bad and did not hit the house, but Bryan's hooded sweatshirt caught fire. They pointed out to Fred the house where this happened.

Another time, Fred, the Freemans, Benny, and some others were at Heath Barkley's apartment and the Freemans wanted to do some heavy drinking. Heath wouldn't allow it in his apartment. Fred said that he broke into a house under construction behind the apartments in the hills of the Devonshire development. Fred did not stay with them, Bryan, David, and Benny, but he was told that they trashed the place.

Back in the Freeman home, Brenda and Dennis were convinced that they were under attack from Satan himself. Satan, the angel thrown to the lower depths by Jehovah was attacking them through their sons Bryan and David.

Persecution by Satan. But it was not something to feel badly about. On the contrary, Jehovah would not let their children become skinheads unless the Freeman family was loved by Him. What better way for the devil to get them than through their sons?

Brenda accepted this rationale, because it was part of her religion to do so. But that didn't change the reality of what she felt. She was scared for her sons, scared for herself, scared for her family.

The boys had already had a strained relationship with their Aunt Valerie. Now, it just got worse with arguments and threats. There were violent arguments that Brenda had with the boys, where they threatened her physical being, while she set down rules they had to live by. The more she tried to discipline them, the more they rebelled.

They began spending more and more nights out with their skinhead friends, coming home from their debauchery in miserable shape. Brenda turned for help to Nick Palumbo, the student assistance program director for the Salisbury Township Schools. Brenda had her sons go see him.

During their sessions with Palumbo, the Freeman brothers expressed a "severe hatred of their parents." After consulting with Brenda, Palumbo assisted Brenda in placing the boys in various treatment facilities.

In addition to the Paradise School, over the next few years, Bryan and David Freeman found themselves interrupting their studies for stays at various Pennsylvania drug rehabilitation and behavior modification facilities, including Eastern States Hospital Renewal Center, the Richard J. Karon Foundation, and First Hospital in Wyoming. They were reevaluated every six months. "They knew how to play the game and did whatever was necessary to stay out of placement," Palumbo later recalled. Apparently, though, their playacting was not all that effective, as the record of their continued placement shows.

With all that traveling, the boys' social lives suffered. They had long ago left behind the Witnesses edict not to become friends with non-Witnesses. But they had not been social butterflies, either, and they always felt like outsiders. But their skins friends, contacts they maintained throughout their placements, *understood*. Their fellow skins could see the manipulation that was going on.

As the years passed, the brothers had trouble

even within the Allentown skinhead community. They wound up feeling alienated from it, to the point that they discussed with Benny forming their own skinhead crew.

Conformity was clearly something they did not like, yet something that everyone, family and school, required of them. Unlike other kids, though, the price of their nonconformity was their freedom.

When they did not conform to what their parents, in particular, their mother wanted, she sent them off. Placement was just another form of prison for them. There were no bars, but they didn't have a choice about being there. If they tried to run away, it got worse.

They had no place to go, no one to run to, but they were learning what to say to Palumbo so they'd stay out of placement. And if they could do that, then maybe, well, who knew?

Eleven

The cars began arriving after daylight, a few at first, but then, as morning wore on and the bright autumn sunshine cast down its golden rays on the farm, carload after carload of young men, with a few middle-agers along for the ride.

They had come from all over Pennsylvania, in cars loaded up with beer and guns. Some favored the smaller revolvers that could easily be concealed and pulled at a moment's notice to strike at a state trooper or other state representative impinging on their constitutional rights. Others sported rifles held in place in their pickups and vans by gun-racks, rifles that were primarily used to hunt game in the woods, but under the right circumstances, could be pressed into service to defend them against the encroaching "mud" people who surrounded them now wherever they went.

The farm they entered was ringed with barbed wire, which provided an unwelcome appearance at first. Those who knew what was beyond the wire, knew that they would be welcomed into the bosom of the Christian Posse Comitatus, to Mark

Thomas's Oktoberfest, an annual gathering that white supremacists from all over Pennsylvania put on their calendars as a date not to be missed.

Some of those who arrived had been there before, to spend weekends with Mark Thomas and hear him preach his gospel, while others had come for a bit more activity; Thomas reportedly gave classes on his property in survival training, which he termed "firearms safety training." During these sessions, his followers reportedly participated in target practice with automatic and semi-automatic weapons. State police at the nearby Reading barracks said that they had been called to Thomas's twelve-acre property numerous times over the past fifteen years to investigate neighbors' complaints of gunfire at the rear of the property. Despite this, no one had ever been charged with carrying illegal weapons or illegally discharging a weapon there, according to police.

Thomas has been concerned with police and other law enforcement officials getting the wrong impression of the activities on his farm, primarily the fear that they might force a confrontation like the firefight at the Branch Davidian compound in Waco, Texas, that ended with a blazing conflagration that burned the whole place down.

Thomas has maintained publicly that he does not have a heavily armed compound, that he stockpiles no illegal weapons, that he is not involved with a fortification of any kind. "The police have no reason to come in and shoot up the place," he told a local paper. But, he added, "It wouldn't be a real good idea to come in here and bother me.

I have children, and I'm not going to put up with any kind of nonsense."

The weapons he does have, primarily hunting rifles, he claims, are protected by the Constitution's Second Amendment and are necessary to protect against an encroaching federal government controlled by Zionists. Thomas has claimed that a federal agent of some kind exploded a pipe bomb on his property, blowing out the windows in his kitchen. Luckily, no one was harmed, but he did post armed guards on subsequent nights. No further incidents occurred.

When state police were told of Thomas's bombing claim, they responded that had a bomb of the magnitude Thomas described gone off, there would have been more extensive damage to his quarters. To Thomas, though, the bombing incident brought home his need for weapons.

"If the police aren't going to protect me, naturally I'm going to keep a gun around," he was quoted in print.

Food was stockpiled in the basement of Thomas's house in preparation for a racial holy war. The Christian Posse Comitatus minister had also built a bomb shelter out of a bus that he buried on his land.

For those familiar with Thomas's gospel, it was as inspired as it was complex. Thomas's religion is based on the first chapter of the Bible. Thomas claims that Jews are descended from the fratricidal Cain, who in turn was descended from the devil snake and Eve. White people, on the other hand, God's chosen people, are descended from Abel, the good brother, who was the progeny of Adam and Eve. That leaves the world with two main races: white people and Jews. Everyone else falls into the classification "beasts of the field."

Three of the visitors that October day had been there numerous times before and had heard the gospel according to Thomas: Bryan and David Freeman and their cousin, Benny Birdwell. Once again they saw Thomas's chapel, actually a trailer that had been turned into a chapel. A Nazi flag hung in the chapel, its stark brick red and black colors a vivid reminder that Hitler's genocidal dream was alive and well and being nourished in the state where Washington fortified his troops to fight the British.

For the event, Thomas had raised a tent to accommodate his guests because the chapel was too small. Scattered throughout the tent were Nazi flags. The crowd heard the racist speeches and the heavy metal music of skinhead hate-rock bands. But that was all a prelude, a warmup, to the charismatic speaker who now took center stage.

Mark Thomas stood in front of a giant cross, its surface covered in gasoline-soaked burlap. His craggy, weathered face looked more taut with emotion than usual. His hair parted to the side, his mustache clipped short, just like Hitler's, he stood up ready to address the crowd that had gathered at his Pennsylvania farm for Oktoberfest '94.

Thomas's intense eyes scanned the three hundred faithful before him. Scattered in the crowd were Nazis and Klansmen of all denominations— the Kew Castle Kounty Night Riders, the White Ar-

yan Revolution, the Bechtelsville White Knights—
and the young racist skinheads who belonged to
no group in particular. But regardless of age and
allegiance, their common bond was an intense hate
for those who were different than they were, and
a common solution—violent death for the "mud"
people, an Armageddon of free-flowing blood for
all those who are different than they are.

Reportedly, Thomas preached, "There is no possible hope for political reform or compromise. My
Bible says that the Jews are the people of Satan, and
our God has commanded us to exterminate them!"

A roar of approval swelled up from the crowd;
the most vocal were the skinheads. Their elders,
the aging homegrown Nazis and Klansmen whose
hearts and minds and bodies have corroded from
too much hate, looked on with pride and envy.
The young skinheads are the shock troops of the
New Order.

When the Apocalypse comes, which Thomas believes will happen in our lifetime, the Posse Comitatus warriors will be called to arms to actively
overcome evil and create a kingdom of Christ on
earth that will last a millennium. This kingdom will
be ruled by white Anglo-Saxons, the true people
of Israel and of God.

"I think the Jews and whites are going to strug-
gle until one has subjugated the other. Right now,
I think the Jews are head and shoulders ahead,"
Thomas preached.

The crowd roared. David and Bryan Freeman
and Ben Birdwell were among those faithful followers taking in everything Thomas preached. Over-

Three-year-old David (left)
and five-year-old Bryan
(right) Freeman in
December 1983.
(*Photo published with the kind
permission of Nelson Birdwell*)

Erik Freeman at seven
years old.
(*Photo published with the kind
permission of Nelson Birdwell*)

Two-year-old Bryan with his parents Brenda and Dennis in 1980.
(*Photo published with the kind permission of Nelson Birdwell*)

Dennis and Brenda
Freeman on their wedding
day. (*Photo published with
the kind permission
of Nelson Birdwell*)

Bryan Freeman at 17.
(*Photo courtesy* THE MORNING CALL)

The family home in which the Freeman brothers were raised.
(*Photo courtesy Fred Rosen*)

The building which once served as the Kingdom Hall where the Freeman family worshipped. *(Photo courtesy Fred Rosen)*

Salisbury Township High School attended by David and Bryan Freeman. *(Photo courtesy Fred Rosen)*

Bryan Freeman at his Michigan arraignment.
(*Photo courtesy* THE MORNING CALL)

David Freeman at his Michigan arraignment.
(*Photo courtesy* THE MORNING CALL)

Ben Birdwell at his Michigan arraignment.
(*Photo courtesy* THE MORNING CALL)

David Freeman being transported back to Allentown, PA for arraignment. (*Photo courtesy* THE MORNING CALL)

Bryan Freeman in Allentown, PA for his arraignment.
(*Photo courtesy* THE MORNING CALL)

David Freeman in Allentown, PA for his arraignment.
(*Photo courtesy* THE MORNING CALL)

Ben Birdwell being taken to court during his April 1995 trial.
(Photo courtesy Kent Allard)

Nelson Birdwell, the paternal grandfather of Bryan, David, and Ben.
(Photo courtesy Kent Allard)

David Freeman's attorneys, Brian Collins (left)
and Wally Worth (right). *(Photo courtesy Fred Rosen)*

Ben Birdwell's attorney,
Richard Makoul.
(Photo courtesy Fred Rosen)

D.A. Bob Steinberg at a press conference during Ben Birdwell's trial.
(*Photo courtesy John Reid*)

Trooper Joe Vazquez, the
primary investigator in the
Freeman murder case.
(*Photo courtesy Kent Allard*)

head, state police helicopters swooped down, photographing the participants for their files.

The sounds of Thomas's speech drifted off into the peaceful Pennsylvania countryside. Protesters outside Thomas's compound heard the shouts from inside, the *"Sieg Heils,"* and grimaced. State police cars patrolled the perimeter of Thomas's farm, tense with anticipation.

Then, visible from the roadway, a shocking sight—flames leaping from the ground, almost forty feet in the air, resolving themselves in bright orange and blue into the shape of a cross. White-hooded Klansmen carrying torches circled the blazing cross. With effort born from old ritual, they closed in on it, like their ancestors had since the Klan was formed after the Civil War. Only now, the chant was distinctly twentieth century, circa 1930s Germany.

"Sieg heil! Sieg heil! Sieg heil!"

Along to the southwest, not ten miles away, Allentown slept through the night, untouched by Thomas's anger and hate.

Sometime after the Oktoberfest, Bryan Freeman was talking to his friend Harry Liste. Harry later related how he and David were driving through Allentown one night when they hit a black kid walking down the street with an eight-ball in a sock.

In late December, Bryan showed up at home with a tattoo on his neck of a swastika made from human bones. On December 31, 1994, without his parents permission, Bryan traveled to Detroit to a New Year's Eve concert of skinhead bands.

Brenda called Frank Palumbo, the school guidance counselor. She told him, "I've lost control of my boys. I want to get Bryan and David placed somewhere. Anywhere."

Was this short-term placement she was after, or long-term? Brenda thought for a moment.

"Long-term," she finally answered.

Brenda confided in her father. She told him that she was trying to place the boys permanently. Nelson Birdwell, his heart breaking over his grandchildren's problems, told Bryan and David about those plans. He hoped they would mend their ways before things got more serious.

The site of the concert was the Clubhouse, Detroit's skinhead rock palace. One of the skins there that night was Frank Hesse, a nineteen-year-old from Midland, Michigan. Frank started talking to Bryan Freeman, who told Frank he was a skinhead on vacation from his regular job.

That night, the two teenagers celebrated their skinhead bond by drinking beer and enjoying the hate rock bands as 1995 came in at the stroke of midnight. Bryan made sure to write down Frank's name and phone number and place it in a secure place in his wallet.

Bryan returned to Allentown with a feeling in his gut that with the new year of 1995, things seemed to finally be coming to a head in the Freeman family.

* * *

Friday, January 20

At the Whitehall Mall, Martin Brownell, a student at Salisbury High School and a friend of David's, ran into Benny. Benny wanted to "rip his face off" because Martin was accompanied by an African-American friend.

Saturday, February 4

In a last-ditch attempt to make her children conform, Brenda sold their cars.

Fred Simon remembers that Bryan and David were royally pissed off that their mother sold their cars while they were sleeping. Bryan had a Camaro and David "a piece of junk," probably a Chrysler. He says that the Freemans kept a wooden bat and knives in their cars.

Sunday, February 5

Bryan and David came home from the tattoo parlor. Brenda and Dennis were shocked. Bryan had had the word "berserker" tattooed on his forehead; David had had *"Sieg heil!"* tattooed on his. When Benny came over later to visit, he, too, had had "berserker" tattooed on his forehead. Neither Dennis nor Brenda knew what to do.

* * *

Saturday, February 11

Brenda and Dennis had had it. They waited until the boys had left and then like a hurricane, the parents passed through their sons' bedrooms, turning out drawers and emptying closets of all their heavy metal and skinhead clothing. Except for what the boys had on, they left them with none of the accoutrements of their neo-Nazi lives. They took all the Nazi decorations off the walls and threw out all the posters of their hate rock stars, all their SS paraphernalia.

Tuesday, February 14

Marshall Fallon, one of the Freeman brothers' closest friends, noticed that in the last month they had changed. Fallon says they became more violent, more bizarre. They talked to Fallon about robbing a gun store, killing a cop, and "splitting" down South. The brothers also talked constantly about how much they hated their parents, Principal Platt, and some other skinheads. They talked about destroying those people.

The Freemans had told Fallon previously about getting "berserker" tattooed on their foreheads, and when they did that, it would be the final straw. That tattoo would mean that they no longer cared about anything and would go on a "path of destruction."

When Fallon saw that they had done it, it sent shivers up and down his spine. He felt that the

Freemans were out of control and would hurt anybody who got in their way, including the police.

Monday, February 20

Self-acknowledged skinhead Bob Zelinski talked with David Freeman.

"Since you're always complaining about your mother, why don't you just kill her?" Bob asked.

"I plan to," David replied. "I'm just going to kill that bitch one of these days."

Tuesday, February 21

Martin Brownell found himself in the main office of Salisbury High School with David.

"I'm going to kill my parents. And when I do, they're going to feel real pain," David told Martin.

Wednesday, February 22

Bryan took a Pennsylvania Skills Test. During a break, he spoke to Sam Ehrgott, the Freemans' paperboy and fellow classmate.

Sam noticed his tattoos. He asked him what they meant and Bryan offered an explanation.

"So what happened to your car?" Sam asked next. He had noticed that it was gone. Bryan's manner turned from friendly to cold.

"My parents sold it while I was asleep," Bryan

answered. "If I was awake while they sold it, I would have killed them."

Thursday, February 23

It was discovered that on the previous day's test, Bryan had drawn racist slogans and lewd pictures. Later that same day, Maryann Galton heard Bryan and David make threats against their parents.

"They don't deserve to live," said Bryan.

"I wish they were dead," David added, in his flat voice.

10 A.M.

Ray Seifert, his co-worker, found Dennis at his desk. Dennis was crying, staring at a photo of Bryan and David in happier times. Ray went over to comfort him and Dennis looked up, pain and anguish written all over his face.

"What am I going to do for my boys?" Dennis cried.

There was no answer. Ray didn't know what to say. All he could do was walk away, shaken up by the experience of seeing a strong man like Dennis so full of grief.

For Dennis, the problems with Bryan and David seemed to be insurmountable and he could see no solution down the dark tunnel he was staring into.

His children would not reform; they were going

straight to hell. And so was he, because he had no power over them anymore.

"He's not a bad boy," Dennis said to another co-worker, Sally Kneller, referring to David. "He's just got in with the wrong crowd."

10:45 A.M.

Harry Liste walked by the principal's office a couple of times. Each time, he noticed Bryan inside. A little after 11, Harry saw Bryan at lunch.

Principal Platt had suspended Bryan for five days. "I don't care if I get into trouble. I want to kill my parents," Bryan told him angrily.

11 A.M.

Bob Zelinski ran into Bryan in Principal Platt's office. Bryan was going to be disciplined for trashing the test. Bryan hated Platt. Eventually, Bryan's wrath turned toward his mother.

"I hope I get kicked out of school so I can go home to that ugly fucking bitch!" Bryan told Bob. "And that brother of mine? He's a piece of shit!"

11:15 A.M.

In the cafeteria, Harry Liste saw Bryan trying to scrounge lunch money. So did Platt, who came into the cafeteria and grabbed the skinhead by the arm.

Platt said something and Bryan snarled, "Shut up or I'll throw you in the oven, you kike!" Bryan pushed him away and ran out.

2 P.M.

Benny met with his probation officer, Jason Weaver. He told him that he intended to get a new tattoo, one with the image of people entering one end of a gas chamber, and smoke billowing out the opposite end. He also said that the word "berserker" tattooed on his forehead was the name of the skinhead crew he and his cousins were forming in Allentown. One other thing. He wanted to buy a gun.

3 P.M.

It was just like going home. Actually, the Freeman house on Ehrets Lane *was* home to Valerie Freeman until her nephews Bryan and David forced her out. Still, she came back as often as she could, primarily to visit her favorite nephew Erik.

She knew the problems Erik had with his older brothers. They didn't accept him, they screamed at him, they picked at him, they beat him up. But the boy was an angel and he seemed to have the patience of Job.

He was growing up nicely, too, and had worked with his parents, ministering door-to-door. Valerie worried about him in that household, though, because there was a violent unpredictability about Bryan and David.

Valerie came by to visit Erik. Up in his room, they sat quietly talking, and then Valerie asked him a question.

"How are your brothers treating you?"

With a steady gaze, Erik looked across at her. "You never know when you're going to die," he said.

Saturday, February 25

Maryann Galton saw Bryan Freeman. Now carless, the skinhead was walking so she offered him a ride, which he gladly accepted. Their conversation turned toward the subject of Bryan's car, which his parents had sold. Bryan clenched his fists so hard that he shook.

"My parents have to learn that me and my brother run this house, and until they learn that, we are going to keep doing what we are doing."

Bryan then got specific about what he really thought about his brother and father.

"Erik is a faggot," Bryan exclaimed, "and as for my father, he's a sissy."

Maryann had heard the brothers make threats against their parents in the past.

Like everyone else, she wrote it off as the disturbed ramblings of troubled teenagers.

Twelve

February 26, 1995

By the boys' recollections, it was a lazy winter's Sunday in Allentown. On Ehrets Lane, where the Freemans lived, nothing special was happening.

By early evening, David and Bryan, against their mother's wishes, had decided to go to the movies.

"I want you back by eleven," Brenda said. "You're not to be out after eleven," she warned.

They had no car to take them, but Benny stopped by and picked them up in his Camaro.

They went to Wendy's, where they ordered burgers, fries, and drinks. Bryan and Ben sat in a booth together, while David sat near them, alone and brooding. They all wore light-colored jeans and T-shirts.

All three boys left Wendy's about seven-thirty and drove to another local hangout, the Capuccino Café. After staying there for a while, they walked over to the multiplex in the Whitehall Mall. There were two movies they were interested in seeing, *Boys on the Side,* a comedy, and *Murder in the First,* a drama. They couldn't decide which film to see together, so Ben and Bryan went to the comedy and David, ever the loner, to the drama.

Dennis Freeman went to bed early that night and fell asleep quickly. Brenda stayed awake, anxious that her children should return home, unsure what to do if they came home late, a feeling of dread in the pit of her stomach.

Next door, in his bedroom, Erik lay on his bed, breathing rhythmically as he settled into a deep sleep.

Inside the theater, the boys sprayed Mace on the water fountain. They thought it was funny if they made it difficult for others to drink the water. Then it was time for the movies.

During *Boys on the Side,* some of the moviegoers heard Bryan and Ben make racist comments about Whoopi Goldberg, the film's star. Bryan wore shades during the film; he thought he looked cool. He told one of their friends who he met in the theater that the main occupation of the group of skinheads he belonged to was to party.

After *Murder in the First* was over, David went out in the lobby to wait for the others, who came out soon after.

"How was it?" Bryan asked.

David shrugged. It was a serious, dour film and he didn't have much to say about it. The clock read ten-thirty P.M.

Despite their rebellious nature, there was something about their mother's threat to lock them out that hit home. In the past two weeks, they had tried living with their aunt, Sandy Lettich, but that had not been pleasant, either, and eventually Sandy sent them home. They really had noplace to go, other than back into placement, where they knew their mother would send them. Between a rock and a hard place, they went home, reaching the Freeman house on Ehrets Lane by eleven o'clock.

They went into the downstairs family room and started making a ruckus. Bryan went upstairs and came back down with some cookies and milk. Soon they heard the heavy tread on the stairs coming down that could only be Brenda Freeman. She appeared in her nightgown looking disheveled and distraught.

"You boys have been drinking again. Benny, go home," she ordered, and "You boys go to sleep."

Ben looked at his cousins, who smiled, and Ben went out the front door. Brenda went back upstairs.

Outside, Ben went around to the downstairs bathroom. David opened it and let him in. Soon, all three were back in the family room, making noise again. Again Brenda came downstairs.

"Benny, I told you to go home. Now, go home!"

Bryan watched, his pulse racing, every sense becoming attuned to what was happening. He was beginning to feel alive, really alive, for the first time in years as the anger inside him, the resentment built up over years, produced the adrenaline that pumped like a powerful narcotic into his system.

Brenda watched as Ben left again. She gave her kids a dirty look.

"Now, get to sleep. *Now!*"

The two boys listened as her footsteps retreated up the stairs. Then they went back around to the bathroom and laughed as Ben climbed back in.

Upstairs in her bedroom, Brenda was just getting back into bed when she heard Benny's voice downstairs. Her husband was still asleep. He needed his rest because he got up early every morning around six A.M. to go to work. It was already near midnight and unless she did something, those kids downstairs were sure to wake him up.

She hurried back downstairs and lit into Benny.

"I'm telling you for the last time, go home."

It was a game now, but the stakes had changed and Brenda didn't even know it. But Bryan did. He knew that Benny was going to come back in and he knew what was going to happen.

Brenda had barely reached her bed when for the third time she heard Benny downstairs. This time she ran down the stairs like an avenging angel, and there to meet her was Bryan.

"What the heck is going on here?" she demanded of her oldest son.

"Listen, you bitch—" Bryan replied quietly.

"Don't call me a bitch. I'm your mother! I'm the adult here, I make the rules in this house, I tell you what to do."

Benny and David watched the two go at each other, awed by Brenda's anger and Bryan's unusual quiet.

"Bryan, you will do . . ."

Bryan could not hear the rest of what his mother said. He had turned on his heel and marched into his bedroom. It was a bedroom denuded of his

Nazi memorabilia. His mother had gotten rid of that, she had gotten rid of their cars, there were her stupid rules, and now she was arguing with him and she was going to send them back to prison. She was going . . .

When Bryan came out of his bedroom, he was holding a steak knife. Brenda saw him and tried to run down the narrow corridor, but Bryan was quicker. He pounced on her, grabbed her around the mouth with his left hand to stifle her cries, and thrust the knife with his right hand five deep inches into her back. Brenda gasped, and Bryan stood back to watch his mother.

Die, you bitch! Die! Die! Die!

Without a scream, Brenda fell. She should have died right then and there. It was a fatal wound, but anger overwhelmed her. She rose to her full height. She was corpulent, now in her late forties, but still a strong woman, so strong that she reached behind her, grabbed for and felt the handle of the knife, and pulled it out of her back. Then she looked at her son, her own flesh and blood, who was staring back at her, awestruck. Now she advanced on *him,* the knife held high.

Satan! It was Satan who had come from her loins.

David and Ben watched as the two struggled for possession of the knife. Bryan cut his hand on the blade during the battle, but he won—and plunged the knife one more time deep into his mother's shoulder, up to the hilt. Brenda gasped and fell to the floor.

Bryan stood over this woman he despised and watched as she gradually lost consciousness.

Brenda was on her side, breathing heavily, knowing she was dying, watching her blood spill out deep red on the floor. It was time to meet Jehovah, to be one of the 144,000, she hoped, time for Judgment Day.

Bryan turned and looked at David and Benny. "Whoever pussies out, they're gonna get stabbed."

David and Ben looked at each other, and then their gaze drifted over to the stairs that climbed toward the second floor, where Dennis Freeman and his son Erik still lay sleeping.

February 27, 4 P.M.

Downstairs, Brenda lay sprawled in her blood, her nightgown hiked above her thighs in the position in which she had fallen. She lay facedown, her face bashed in, not worried anymore about her kids, no longer concerned about answering the telephone.

Upstairs, Dennis was on the bed in the room he had shared with his wife. His blood was splattered on the walls and as high as the ceiling. His face and skull had been bashed in with a blunt object so that his features were unrecognizable and his brain had burst through a crack in his skull. His throat had been slit, and blood had oozed down his chest and onto the bedspread, where it had dried into a coagulated dark substance that looked like sticky syrup.

Erik was not in such bad shape. Considering what had happened to him, he didn't look as bad as his father. No cut throat. He had been hit three or four times by blunt objects and had died instantly. Alone in his room, he was a pathetic, frail figure huddled on his bed and covered with blood.

In his office sixty miles away in Philadelphia, Barry Morrison, regional director of the Antidefamation League, waited for someone to pick up the phone at the Freeman residence. He had not spoken to Brenda Freeman for a while and was checking in to see how she was doing and whether she'd had any luck placing her troubled kids.

After a while, Morrison hung up the phone. He'd try her later.

Someplace in the heartland of America, in the shadows of the night, Benny Freeman drove the Sunbird north toward Michigan, Bryan and David Freeman in the seats beside him.

Bryan sank back on the seat cushions. It was over, finally over, and now he could relax.

PART THREE

"Vengeance is mine; I will repay, saith the Lord."

Romans 12:19

Thirteen

The death chamber was on the mind of more than one person in Midland, Michigan. Bob Donohue, for one, was very concerned about it.

A private practice lawyer who also worked as a public defender, Donohue is stout and middle-aged, wears thick wire-framed lenses, and has large lips, a protruding jaw, and hair combed to the side. He had never worked a death penalty case, and the possibility of a client facing death terrified him. But that was not unusual. Few lawyers, if any, in Michigan have ever tried a case where the ultimate penalty for conviction was death for one simple reason: the death penalty was outlawed in Michigan over fifty years ago.

One of the first things Donohue thought about after Midland County prosecutor Norman Donker asked him to represent David was what would happen to the boys when they were sent back to Pennsylvania. Pennsylvania had the death penalty, and while no one had been executed in the state for thirty-three years, their new governor, Tom Ridge, had already signed over forty death warrants. Ridge was determined to clean the cobwebs out of the death chamber and put it back into use. That's why Donohue was very interested when he got word that David wanted to make a second statement.

Donohue hadn't been there for the first one. No lawyer had, and given David's age, there existed the strong possibility a judge would throw it out on constitutional grounds. The second statement, with a lawyer present—that would be the one that counted.

Trooper Joe Vazquez of the Pennsylvania State police and Detective Richard Metzler of the Salisbury Township police department had arrived in Michigan and taken up residence at the Holiday Inn. Vazquez was in bed on Sunday, March 5, when he got a call from Bob Donohue.

"Mr. Vazquez, my client, David Freeman, is interested in giving you a statement."

Vazquez said he'd get back to him. A short time later, the phone rang again.

"Have you seen the morning paper?"

The caller was the Midland County prosecutor, Norman Donker.

"No, not yet," Vazquez replied.

"Well, there's a long statement from Birdwell's mom in it," and Donker went on to describe how Birdwell had told his mom that he had done nothing, that the Freeman boys had done all the murders.

So that's why Donohue called me, Vazquez thought. The boys want to contradict Benny.

Quickly, Vazquez engaged the conference room at the Holiday Inn for a twelve o'clock meeting of all the participants. Precisely at noon, Vazquez, his partner, Metzler, Donker, and Donohue began their discussions.

"My client has this proposal," Donohue began. "It's in four parts."

Part one was that the defendant would give a complete and truthful statement as to the events that had occurred in the Freeman house.

Part two was that Allentown's prosecutor, Bob Steinberg, would take the death penalty off the table.

Part three was that neither Bryan nor David would give up his trial rights.

Part four was that a newsperson of their choosing would conduct an interview with them so their side of what happened would get out to the public.

After making certain that Bryan's court-appointed attorney, appointed that morning, was aware of this deal and had agreed to it and that Donohue was speaking for both of them, the cops and the prosecutor voiced a major concern about the last item. They felt that there had already been too much publicity.

"They want it," Donohue supposedly responded. "I can't stop them from requesting it. They're willing to take the rap for what they did, but once Nelson Birdwell said what he said, ratting on them, now they'll rat on him."

Vazquez couldn't agree to the deal just like that. He had neither the power nor the discretion to take the death penalty off the table. He told Donohue and Donker he'd have to call Steinberg back in Allentown to get the okay.

The meeting broke up. It had lasted all of half

an hour. That afternoon, Donker called Vazquez again to see if he'd heard something from Allentown. Vazquez hadn't. Things were still up in the air.

"I'll try to get back to you about five or six," Vazquez said.

That evening, Donohue and Donker were having dinner together when they got a call from Vazquez. The deal had been approved. Steinberg had said yes.

A meeting was set up at nine P.M. at Donker's office. A finalized agreement was placed on microcassette tape. Present for that recording were Donker, Donohue, Metzler, Vazquez and James Branson, Bryan's court-appointed attorney.

The operative paragraph of the agreement was that the defendants would give "accurate, complete, and truthful statements" regarding the events of the night in question, and that it was "an irrevocable agreement."

The agreement was then sealed in an envelope with evidence tape.

Knowingly, David and Bryan Freeman were giving the Commonwealth of Pennsylvania the motive, means, and opportunity for the crimes they had been accused of. Regardless of the fact that they had not given up their trial rights, they were, in effect, condemning themselves to life in prison. But by talking now, they would not have the death penalty hanging over their heads. And they'd get their revenge on Benny.

* * *

Attorneys who were more experienced in death penalty cases might have told the boys to keep their mouths shut. Let Steinberg make his case. With the good possibility David's first statement would be thrown out on constitutional grounds, Steinberg would have to work overtime to prove what he had done. But death is an excellent motivator.

These things are clear: Donohue was determined to keep his client out of the death chamber, and David wanted to talk.

It was March 6, 1995, 12:16 A.M. Eastern Standard Time. The place was Midland County Jail, in Midland Michigan. It was the same interrogation room David had found himself in as before, only this time the players were different.

There was his lawyer, Bob Donohue, for one, someone to protect his rights. And the cops. Not the two from Michigan, but two from Pennsylvania, Trooper Joe Vazquez, from the Pennsylvania State police, and Detective Richard Metzler, from the Salisbury Township police department.

A technician set up the videotape equipment. All was in readiness and David was anxious to begin. He wanted to get that son-of-a-bitch Ben!

Donohue and Vazquez went through the preliminaries of David's Miranda rights, how he had the right to stop the interrogation anytime he wanted, and how no threats had been made to make him talk. David agreed to it all, then signed some forms that he hardly looked at.

"David, try to use the words 'yes' and 'no,'"

rather than 'yeah' or 'nah,' okay?" Donohue reminded him.

Vazquez began.

"I'd like to start in the afternoon of February 26, 1995. Where were you around three o'clock?"

"Home. It was me and Bryan, we were talking about going to Wendy's to get something to eat, and go to the movies." They called Ben to tell them of their plans. "So maybe an hour and a half later, he came over."

"Who came over?"

"Ben did."

"You mean Nelson Benjamin Birdwell?"

"Yeah. He picked me and Bryan up. We went to Wendy's on Tilghman Street, we ate there, and after that, we went to see a movie."

"When you went to Wendy's, whose car did you go in?" Vazquez asked. His partner, Metzler, sat wearing a silent and brooding look in the corner while Donohue listened carefully.

"It was Ben's car—his dad's girlfriend's car."

"What kind of car was it?"

"I don't really know. An older model."

"About what time did you go to Wendy's?"

"Between four-thirty and five, somewhere in there."

"How long did you stay at Wendy's?"

"Until around eight o'clock. Then we went to the AMC Theater."

"Who's 'we'?"

"Me and Bryan and Ben went over there to the shopping center, to the AMC Theater, we watched movies over there and—"

"What movie did you go to see?"

"I saw *Murder in the First*."

"What time did that start?"

"Around eight o'clock or a little bit after."

"Did the others go with you?"

"They went to see this one other movie. What was it called? I forget."

"In other words, you didn't go to see the movie that your brother saw?"

"No."

"How about Ben? What movie did he see?"

"Same one as my brother."

"Did you stay for the entire movie?"

"Yeah."

"What did you do when the movie was over?"

"I went outside and I waited until they came out. They came out and when they came out, me and Bryan and Ben, we got in the car. We went over to my house, he—"

"What time do you think you got home?"

"Around ten-thirty."

"Who was there at your house?"

"Me and Bryan and Ben, both my parents, and my little brother."

"Where were they when you got home?"

"My dad and my little brother was sleeping. My mom was waiting for us to get home."

"Where was she waiting at?"

"Upstairs in the living room."

"What was she doing?"

"She was lying on a couch, reading, in the living room."

"Was she covered?"

"Sure."

"When you guys came home, how did you enter the house?"

"It was me and Bryan, we have a bathroom downstairs, we used to open the window and get in that way."

"So your mom didn't know that Ben was there when you first got there?"

"No. Not when we first got there."

"Is that a normal thing you guys used to do, sneak in through that bathroom window?"

"Yes."

"When did your mother realize that Ben was in the house?"

"Maybe fifteen or twenty minutes later she came down. We were in my room on the lower level."

"Next to the bathroom?"

"Yeah."

"Where you left the window open to let Ben in?"

"Yeah."

"When your mother came downstairs, what happened?"

"She came down a couple of times."

"Okay, the first time, what did she do? What did she tell you guys?"

"Well, she felt it was time to go to sleep, it's getting pretty late, we got to get up early tomorrow, better try to get some sleep, and then she went back upstairs."

"What did she say about Ben being there?"

"She didn't see him the first time. He was hiding in my closet."

"In other words, you heard your mom coming

down the stairs and Ben hid in the closet so as not to be discovered?"

"Yeah. Then five or ten minutes later, she came down again, she found Ben, she told him, 'You have to get out of the house now!' "

"Was she angry?"

"She wasn't really angry, no. She just didn't want him there."

"Was it because it was late or she didn't like you and Bryan hanging around him?"

"It was like a little bit of both."

"So now, it's what, a quarter to eleven?"

"Right."

"You and Bryan were there with Ben and she tells him to leave. Does he leave?"

"Yeah. He goes out the front door. And about five or ten minutes later, he comes right back in through the window."

"Did you and Bryan tell him to come back?"

David nodded.

"You just told him to come back in through the window? What happens when he comes back in?"

"We were just sitting there talking for a little bit when Mom came in. This is like the third time she caught him, or something. She goes, 'This is the last time I'm going to tell you, you're going to have to leave.' He left again."

"The front door again?"

"Yeah. I think he moved his car that time, around the block. He came back in the window and we were talking for a while, then my mom came down again."

"Just let me stop you real quick here. Did you

or your brother do any drinking or drugs that night?"

"No."

"So why did Ben go back to the house with you?"

"We were trying to call a bunch of people over to go drinking that night. That was the only reason he was over."

"Did you accomplish that?"

"No."

"You never got to go drinking? You're only fifteen. Okay, after the third time your mom found Ben, tell me what happened."

"She told him, 'This is the last time I'm going to tell you to leave.' He said, 'I'm going.' That was the time he moved his car."

"He came back in through the bathroom window, didn't he?"

"Yes."

"What happened after that?"

"We were sitting and talking for a while and got some stuff to eat. I brought down some cookies and some milk and stuff for everybody."

"Whose room were you sitting in?"

"My room."

"Everybody was in your room at this time?"

"Yeah."

"Your mom's still upstairs?"

"Yeah."

"Was she on the couch when you went back upstairs for the milk?"

"Yeah. Then she came down again. That's when everything happened."

"Go on."

"She came down pretty quick. I didn't really see what happened, but it happened then."

"What happened? You've got to be kind of specific, David."

"I didn't really see anything that happened to her."

"Where were you when it happened to her?"

"I was in that room. The family room downstairs, where my Aunt Val used to live."

"How did you know something was happening?"

"Because I heard my mom, she was saying something like, 'Bryan, what are you doing?' and stuff like 'Help' and 'Stop it.'"

"What did you do at that point?"

"I was like, 'Oh shit, fuck!'"

"Did you come out of that room?"

"Yeah."

"What did you see?"

"I saw it. It was my mom and my brother out in the hallway. He said, 'Go upstairs and get Dad and Erik.'"

"Okay. Stop. You were just about to say when I interrupted you, which I shouldn't have. You were just about to say your mom was saying, 'Stop, what are you doing,' and you said your brother was just about to say something to her?"

"No."

"What did your brother say?"

"We went up the stairway to the second floor, where the living room and dining room are. We went down the hallway to my dad's room."

"Did you have a weapon in your hand at that time?"

"Ben had the weapon."

"What was it?"

"It was like a pick-ax handle, a big wooden handle."

"Where did he get that from?"

"I don't really know. Maybe from downstairs someplace."

"Was Ben in the room when your brother Bryan—what did your brother Bryan do to your mother?"

"He stabbed her."

"Did you see him stab her?"

"No."

"How did you know he'd stabbed her, then?"

"After everything was done and we went upstairs, he told us what he did."

"Okay, so when you went upstairs after your father and your brother, Ben already had the pick handle in his hand."

"Yeah."

"What did you do?"

"As soon as you turn the corner, you go into the closet—"

"I know right where it's at, it's on the left side," said Vazquez, who had been in the house.

"He told us to go upstairs to get my dad and little brother."

"Your brother, Bryan Freeman, told you to go upstairs and get your brother and father?"

"To kill them."

"Had you ever talked about killing them before?"

"We did, but we didn't mean it. It wasn't serious."

"What did you do before?"

"We talked about killing them. We talked about killing other people. We never thought we'd ever do it."

"Did you ever talk about how you would do it?"

"No."

"Did you ever tell your mom you'd kill her?"

"No."

"Do you ever recall telling your friends at school you were going to kill your parents?"

"I don't really recall. I was like in placement for a while. A lot of them told me I said that. That's what I thought I went away for. I didn't really belong there. I never thought we'd end up killing them. You've got to believe me."

"When Bryan told you, 'Go upstairs and get your dad and your brother,' you understood what you were supposed to do?"

"Yes. To kill them. It was me and Ben, we ran upstairs—"

"Slow down. Take your time."

"Right, the closet," David agreed. "There is a big golden-colored baseball bat in there."

"Your bat?"

"Yes."

"Is it wooden or aluminum?"

"It's aluminum."

David took the bat and proceeded down the hallway.

"We went right up to my dad's room," David continued. "We argued for like a couple of seconds about who was going to go in first. Ben kept telling me, 'Go on and do it.' I said, 'You do it.' "

"Did you turn the lights on in the hallway?"

"No, they were already on."

"Was your father asleep or awake at this time?"

"He was asleep."

"Was his door closed when you got there or open?"

"Open."

"Okay, who goes into the room?"

"Ben goes in first. He hit him in the face."

"Whoa. Slow down. From which side did Ben approach your father?"

"From the left."

"And your father was in the bed facing you?"

"Yes. And I went around the right side."

"Then what happened?"

"Ben took the handle and hit him in the face, busted him up pretty good there."

"How was your father laying?"

"Straight up with his hands at his sides."

"What happened when Ben hit him?"

"He put his hands up a little bit."

"Like this?" and Vazquez raised his arms slightly.

"Yeah. And then just dropped them down. Right after that, I hit him once, and then I hit him three more times."

"Where'd you hit him?"

"All in the face. And Ben cut his throat."

"Where did he get the knife from?"

"The kitchen or something."

"Before you went down the hallway?"

"Yeah, I think so."

"Did you see him get it?"

"No."

"But you knew he had it?"

"Yeah, I knew he had it."

"Where did he have it? You told me he had the pick handle?"

"He had that in one hand and the handle in the other."

"What was the discussion about at the door?"

"Who was going to do it."

"Who was going to do what?"

David looked pained.

"Who was going to hit him first."

"How about the knife, was there any discussion about stabbing or cutting him?"

"No."

"Well, back in the room, Ben hits first?"

"Yeah, Ben."

"You hit him in the face. Who hits him in the chest?"

"Ben did. Ben hit him like four times in the face. I had, like, this real cheap knife, I tried to stab him in the chest. When I tried, it bent, so I just chucked that."

"Was it a big knife?"

"It was like about that long (indicating a few inches with his hands) with a brown wooden handle."

"What happened to it?"

"I just threw it away, I really don't remember."

"All right. This was after you struck your dad with the bat?"

"Yeah."

"What did you do with the bat after you stopped hitting him with it?"

"I put it on the side of that big tall dresser, at the corner of the bed."

"How many times did you try stabbing your dad?"

"Just once."

"Just once?"

"It didn't even go in him," David said nonchalantly, like he was describing the weather.

"Did you stab him in the head?"

"No."

"In the chest?"

"Like somewhere in there. And then Ben took the knife and cut his throat."

"What happened then?"

"All the blood, it . . . made me sick. It wasn't like all the blood, it was just the thought of what we did to our parents. We went in there and we—"

"Take your time," Vazquez soothed. He didn't want the kid getting so riled up by his emotions he left out details. He was there to build a case against this kid, and so far, things were going real good.

"Where is your brother's room in relation to your parents?"

"Right across the hall."

"Was his door open when you went up the stairs and down the hallway?"

"No."

"It was closed? Who opened it?"

"Ben. Ben opened the door."

"Was that when he went in your dad's room, he opened the door?"

"Yeah. I didn't see him, I didn't see him hit my brother."

"Did you see him turn the light on?"

"Yeah."

"Did you see him turn the light on?" Vazquez repeated.

"Yeah, yeah, I saw the light come on. I heard a noise."

"What kind of noise did you hear coming from your brother's room?"

"A crushing, it was like something snapped or something."

"Um-hum, take your time," Vazquez soothed.

"I started walking in the living room and it seemed, like, there was blood everywhere, splattered all over the wall."

"When you left your dad's room, did you look in your brother's room?"

"Yeah."

"Where was Ben at that time?"

"He was coming out of my brother's room. I looked in. I saw a lot of blood everywhere."

"Did you see your brother?"

"I saw part of his body."

"What part did you see?"

"From the head down."

"Did you see where Ben had hit your brother? Was there blood in the room?"

"There was blood on the wall."

"Was there blood on the bed?"

David nodded.

"How far into the room did you go?"

"Not far at all. I walked in, I walked out, just like—"

"Then where'd you go?"

"The dining room. I puked there."

"What did you do with the baseball bat?"

"I left it somewheres upstairs."

"Did you take it out of your father's room where you'd left it before?"

"I'm not sure. I think I did. I think I left it in the dining room."

"Do you recall taking it into the kitchen?"

"No."

"Don't remember?"

"I can't."

"Okay, but it was somewhere in the dining room?"

"Yeah, I'm pretty sure it was."

"David, at any time up to this point did Ben Birdwell have the bat in his hands?"

"No. He had the pick handle."

"Did he ever touch the metal bat you used on your father?"

"No. He had the pick handle the whole time."

"Did you hit your brother?"

"No!"

"Did you ever tell anyone else that you hit your brother?"

"When I first got arrested, I told the cops that I did. I didn't want Ben to get in trouble."

"Nice and loud," Vazquez prompted.

"When I first got arrested, I told the first detective that. I really didn't want to see him get into any more trouble."

"Why didn't you want him to get into any trouble if he had just killed your brother?"

"I knew we were going away. I just didn't want anything to happen to anyone else."

"Do you want to take a minute? Do you want to take a break?"

David nodded. The machine was turned off. A few minutes later, the videotape was turned on again.

"You okay, David? You want to go on?" Vazquez asked.

"Yeah."

"We were talking about when you were first arrested here in Michigan. Did I hear you correctly? That the reason you told the trooper from Michigan when you were first interviewed that you'd killed your brother was because you didn't want Ben Birdwell to get into any trouble?"

"Yeah, I wanted to keep him out of as much trouble as I could. Once he started to tell the press that bunch of bullshit—"

"Okay. You're referring to an article that was in yesterday's paper?"

"Yeah."

"Is there any truth to that article? Are you doing this in direct retaliation for that article?"

"No," David answered firmly.

"Are you telling the truth?" Vazquez pressed, studying his prisoner for signs that he was lying.

"Yeah."

"Nelson Birdwell III killed your brother, your eleven-year-old brother, you did not?"

"No."

"The reason you told that first trooper was to protect Nelson Birdwell III?"

"I wanted to see somebody stay out of some trouble for this. But I've had a lot of time to think about everything."

"Have you discussed this with your attorney also?"

"Yeah."

"All right. Let's get back. You said you puked in the dining room area, is that the only place you threw up?"

"Yeah."

"Did you leave the house at all?"

"I went out the sliding door. I went out to get some fresh air for a couple of minutes."

"When you came back in, did you puke again?"

"No."

"Then what happened? Did you clean the puke?"

"No. As far as I know, Bryan and Ben didn't, either."

"When you came back in, when was the next time you saw Ben?"

"As soon as I came back in."

"Where was he at?"

"He was standing in the dining room with Bryan."

"Is this the first time you saw Bryan since you left him with your mother downstairs?"

"Yeah."

"What happened after you saw these two guys standing there?"

"Bryan told Ben to go make sure that everybody

was dead, to make sure my mom, my brother, and Dad were all dead."

"Why did you decide on Ben to check them?"

"I told him I couldn't do it and Bryan said he couldn't, either. I wouldn't have been able to take it."

"You mean emotionally you would not be able to face seeing that again?"

"Yeah."

"Did Ben do that?"

"Yeah."

"Where did he go first?"

"I'm pretty sure he went downstairs to check my mom first."

"Was she dead?"

"I don't know. I didn't talk to him about that. I didn't really ask him if they were dead or not."

"So Ben goes downstairs, you and Bryan are upstairs, what is the discussion about?"

"Where we're going to go, what we're going to do."

"What did you decide?"

"We thought about going down to Atlantic City first. I believe it was Bryan that came up with the idea of going up to Ohio. He knew some guys up there, we could sort of visit them for a while."

"It was decided that all of you would flee?"

"Yeah."

"Leave your house and Pennsylvania? No matter what, you were leaving?"

"Yes."

"Okay, when Ben Birdwell comes back upstairs, where does he go?"

"I think he went in my dad or little brother's room."

"Did he come back out into the hallway?"

"Yeah."

"Did you see him go down the hallway?"

"Yeah. He said, 'They'll be dead soon, if they're not dead already.'"

"How did he say this? Was he smiling, or—"

"He was excited, he was just like nervous. Nervous."

"Then what happened?"

"Bryan and Ben went into the kitchen to get something to drink."

"What did you do during this period?"

"I smoked cigarettes."

"Upstairs?"

"Yeah."

"I'm sure all of you talked about the murders?"

"We talked about it for a little bit, but we kept trying to forget about it."

"What little bit that you did talk, what did Bryan say happened?"

"He said, my mom came down and he put his hand over her mouth and stabbed her in the back."

"How many times?"

"All I remember was that when he stabbed her in the back, he stabbed her a couple of places."

"Okay."

"And I remember him saying about her getting hit in the face."

"By what?"

"By—I don't remember, but I think he said it

was like Ben, he had—Ben, he had something that he hit her in the face with."

"How could Ben hit her in the face when Ben was with you upstairs?"

"I went upstairs first. As soon as Bryan told me, I went upstairs. I didn't want to stay around."

"Did he threaten you in any way, your brother Bryan, or Ben, if you didn't go upstairs?"

"No."

"You just understood what he meant?"

"I was real scared. I just didn't know what to do."

"What did Bryan tell that Ben did? He hit your mom in the face with what?"

"I'm not sure."

"What else did Bryan tell you afterward?"

"That's all I remember him saying. I remember Ben saying that he hit my little brother. He said when he hit him his eye popped out of his head. He said he just hit him once. His eye popped out and everything just like shattered in his face."

"He said his eye popped out? Where did that go?"

"He said it was just hanging."

"Just hanging there? Was that all Ben said? Did Ben talk about anything about your mother?"

"No."

"About hitting her or striking or stabbing your mother?"

"I don't remember him saying anything like that."

"Did you hit your mother?"

"No."

"Did you hit your brother?"

"No."

"Did you cut your brother or your mother?"

"No. The only thing I did was—I hit my dad."

"Who took the money out of the rooms?"

"On the way out of my parents' room, I grabbed my dad's wallet from his pants."

"Where were his pants?"

"On the floor in front of the bed."

"Did anyone get any money out of the closets or the drawers or anything like that?"

"I'm not sure, that's all I remember."

"Where did you get the quarters where you paid for the motel rooms from?"

"I'm pretty sure we got them from the room."

It was money their father had collected from his part-time job at a laundromat.

"Where was the change?"

"I think it was on the dressers."

"How about the rolls of quarters, where did you get those?"

"I don't remember."

"Well, that's not a problem," Vazquez said. "That's okay. You okay?"

David nodded his head.

"Try to get this over with. When you decided that you were leaving, you were going to Atlantic City, but you decided on Ohio. Who had the keys to the car at this point?"

"Ben went and got the keys on the long dresser in my parents' room. He grabbed the keys and went downstairs. He took his father's girlfriend's car home. We followed him to his house on Sixth Street in Allentown."

"Prior to leaving the house, did you take any clothing with you?"

"Well, I changed my jeans in the living room."

"Was there anything wrong with them?"

"They were ripped in the crotch."

"How did that happen?"

"When we were leaving the house, I just jumped up on the steps, they were just a little too tight."

"They just ripped?"

"Yeah."

"So yours is the longer pair. Did anybody else change?"

"Bryan did. He left his stuff in the living room."

"What was wrong with Bryan's pants?"

"He had blood on them."

"Where was the blood?"

"It was like on the bottom, below the knee."

"You saw that?"

"Yeah, I saw blood on them."

"After you left, you followed Ben to his house?"

"Yeah. He dropped his car off"

"Where did you go from there?"

"We went to get gas at the 7-Eleven on South Fourth Street."

"Did you get anything else besides gas?"

"Yeah, we got a carton of Marlboros there."

"How much money do you think you all had together that you took from the house?"

"A couple of hundred bucks, probably."

"Did you take any of your dad's or mom's credit cards?"

"We thought about it, but you have to sign for them."

"MAC cards?"

"No."

"What time of night is it now?"

"About twelve-thirty, somewhere around there."

"Did you fill up the tank?"

"Yeah, about five bucks' worth. Then we went out, got on the highway, I think it was seventy-eight, I'm not sure."

"Where did you eventually end up going?"

"We decided we'd go see these guys in Michigan."

David then related how, early in the morning, they stopped at the Truck World Motor Inn in Ohio.

"Let me stop you for this last thing," Vazquez interrupted. "Did you get injured at all, as a result of what happened with your parents?"

"No."

"Did Ben get injured at all?"

"No."

"How about Bryan?"

"He had a cut on his hand, like right there." He pointed to a place on his hand.

"What was that from?"

"I don't know."

"Did he tell you what it was from?"

David shook his head.

"Okay, so you stop at this motel in Ohio."

David went on to describe their encounter with the desk clerk Jesse Capece and how they passed that day after the murders in Ohio.

The time was 1:14 A.M. Vazquez switched video-tapes and the interrogation continued.

After leaving the Truck World Motor Inn at around eight o'clock, they headed for Michigan to rendezvous with Frank Hesse, the skinhead Bryan had met at the New Year's Eve concert at Detroit's Westside Clubhouse.

"Does anything happen between the time that you get from the Truck World until you get back on the highway?"

"No, we went straight on the highway."

"Did you discard anything?" Vazquez prodded.

"We got rid of Ben's jeans after we got on the highway."

"Where did that occur? Was that between Truck World and Route 80?"

"Yeah. It wasn't that far after we got off, but I remember we were going over a bridge. I remember at one point, I threw the jeans out the window."

"Why did Ben want those clothes discarded?"

"Because there was blood all over them."

"There was blood all over Ben's jeans? Did you see the blood on the jeans?"

"Yeah."

"Whose blood was it?"

"Probably my dad's and my little brother's."

"What time did you get to those guys' house in Michigan?"

"Around three o'clock in the morning. We knocked on the door and didn't get any answers. So we went down to the Holiday Inn and got a room."

"Who registered?"

"Ben did."

"What name did Ben use?"

"One that was totally fake."

David went on to describe their brief encounter with the Michigan uniformed cops.

"After the police left, how long did you guys stay at the hotel?"

"Till about twelve-thirty, when we went to Frank's. We stayed there and went to the mall in Midland with Frank."

"Whadja do at the mall?"

"Hung out. Ben got two Budweiser T-shirts, I think."

"Then what?"

"We ate at McDonald's and went back to Frank's house and drank and then more beer came later."

"While you were at Frank's, did anyone, you or Bryan, or Ben, say anything about what had happened—"

"No."

"—in Pennsylvania? You didn't tell anyone that you, Bryan, and Ben were responsible for the killing of your parents and your brother?"

David shook his head.

"None of those people had any clue about what you guys had done?"

"No."

"Why didn't you tell them?"

"We wanted to keep them out of it."

"Where'd you sleep that night?"

"At Frank's. The next morning, we woke up and went ice fishing with Frank. After that, we came back and got arrested."

And that was it. Joe Vazquez was finished with

his questioning. He had taken David on a tour through hell and was satisfied it would result in a "murder one" conviction.

"You got any questions, Dick?" Vazquez asked, addressing the Salisbury Township detective.

"I just got a couple of questions," Metzler answered.

Metzler has a clipped mustache and hard eyes, and he seldom smiles.

"David, when Bryan attacked your mother, what did you see?"

"I didn't see when he first did it, but when I left the room to go upstairs, as I saw him, he had his hands over her mouth," David replied.

"Were they on the floor or still standing up?"

"They were still standing, but just about like on the floor."

"Did you see the knife he had?"

"No."

"As you were looking at him, you say they were starting to go down."

"That's what it seemed like."

"Did you actually see them go down on the floor?"

"No."

"You turned around and went upstairs?"

"Yeah."

"Did Ben come right after you?"

"A couple of seconds later he was right behind me."

"As you were going upstairs, did you hear anything from downstairs?"

"No."

"Did you hear your mother screaming or anything?"

"No."

"Did you hear any scuffling noises or anything?"

"No."

"You went upstairs?"

"Right."

"Did Ben ever tell you he hit your mother with anything or have anything to do with killing your mother?" Vazquez interjected.

"I don't recall him saying anything," David answered.

"How about Bryan? Did he ever tell you what happened to your mother?" Metzler asked.

"Bryan said he hit her with something in her face."

"Did Bryan tell you anything else?"

"He said he stabbed her in the back?"

"Did he tell you how many times?"

"No."

"You told us before that Bryan stabbed your mother a couple of times in the back."

"He didn't specify how many it was."

"Who told you that Ben hit your mother?"

"Bryan."

"Was Ben there when he told you that?"

"No."

"Where was it that he told you that?"

"When Ben was going around to check on everybody."

"That's when he told you what happened downstairs?"

"Yeah."

"Getting back to the pick handle, do you know where Ben got that?"

"I don't know."

"Did he have that in his hand when he came upstairs or did he get that somewhere upstairs?"

"He had it when he came upstairs."

"You don't recall seeing that in the house anywhere?"

"As a matter of fact, I've seen it before, but—"

"Would it have been in the family room downstairs?" Metzler interrupted.

"It should have been like in the garage, but—"

"After you had gone upstairs, did you hear the garage door open?"

"I didn't hear anything."

"Okay, on the road now, did your brother drive at all?"

"Yeah."

"When did he drive?"

"I don't know, I was tired."

"Along the way, did you sleep at all during the whole trip in the car?"

"I didn't sleep."

"How about Ben?"

"He slept for a little bit."

"And Bryan?"

"No, he didn't sleep."

"While the three of you were at Frank's house, did anybody make any phone calls from there, the three of you guys?"

"I don't think so."

"You didn't make any calls yourself?"

"No."

"You don't recall seeing Ben or Bryan calling anybody?"

"No."

Metzler was finished. Donohue then had a few questions.

"In your conversations with me, you expressed remorse over this, isn't that right? In fact, you wished this had never happened, isn't that right?" Donohue asked.

"Yeah," David answered, his head sinking lower, his voice almost inaudible.

"If you could rewrite history, it wouldn't have happened, isn't that right?"

"Yes."

"Did you tell your mother you were going to kill her?" Vazquez asked.

"I didn't really recall ever telling her I was going to kill her."

"Have you ever threatened your parents to any of your friends, in or out of school?"

"No, no, never!"

"Is everything you've told us tonight true?" Metzler asked.

"Yes," David responded.

"Is there anything else that you can think of that we haven't asked you?"

"No."

Donohue looked up at Vazquez.

"I have nothing further," Vazquez concluded.

"Anything you want to talk to me about before we finish here?" Donohue asked.

"No."

"You know during this recording of this interview, you've been upset, but you've had a full opportunity to talk?"

"Yes."

David Freeman's statement of his culpability in the murders of his father, mother, and little brother concluded.

Shortly afterward, Bob Donohue had a conversation with Joe Vazquez. According to Donohue's recollection, Vazquez said, "I believe David is telling the truth."

Fourteen

Now, it was Bryan's turn to corroborate what David had said and pull the noose tighter around the rat Benny's neck. With his court appointed attorney James Branson present to represent Bryan's interests, Metzler did most of the questioning.

While he seemed coherent and alert, Bryan was clearly very annoyed. Drinking a can of diet Coke, Bryan listened as he was advised of his Miranda rights by Metzler. He waived those rights and began to give his version of the night of the murder.

"We got to Wendy's about five or six. Ben was with us."

After staying at Wendy's a few hours, they went to the AMC movies, where they split up.

"Me and Ben saw *Boys on the Side* and David saw *Murder in the First*. We got home about ten-thirty."

"Who was in the house?" Metzler asked.

"Everyone. My mom, father, and little brother."

"Go on."

"We were downstairs hanging out when my mom came down and kicked Ben out. She did that twice. The third time Ben came back in, it happened. I picked up a knife and I stabbed her."

"Where'd you get the knife from?"

"My room. A big steak knife."

"I stabbed her in the back and Ben and my brother took off upstairs."

"What happened with your mother?"

"She pulled the knife out of her back and we struggled. I closed my hand around the blade. When I got it, I stabbed her again. I tried to gag her with my hand."

"Then what happened?"

"She fell. I tried to cover her mouth with my hand. I put shorts in her mouth. I bit her hand. Then I threw the knife away."

Soon after, David and Ben came downstairs.

"Did they say anything?" Metzler asked.

"Ben said, 'Is she dead?' Then Ben hit her over the head a few times. She kept trying to get up. He struck her with the pick handle."

After that, Bryan went upstairs and went into the rooms. As he talked, he kept his head down. When he looked up, his face was streaming with tears.

"I went into my dad's room and took his wallet. Then we changed. Blood was all over us. We left the clothes in the living room and brought along some socks and underwear. Ben went around to make sure everyone was dead, then I went outside and moved my dad's van to get the car we were going to take."

"What were you wearing when you left?"

"A plain white T-shirt and jeans."

"Okay, then what did you do?"

"After that, we went to the 7-Eleven to gas up, where we got gas and cigarettes, then straight up Interstate 78 to Ohio and then Michigan."

"Where'd you meet the Hesses?"

"I met the Hesses at a New Year's Eve concert in Detroit."

"Was Michigan the first place you thought of going?"

"No. I was thinking of Atlantic City, but I changed my mind. I took Route 22 to the turnpike to Exit 35 and across the state."

He related how they'd checked into the Ohio motel for the day, how they threw Benny's bloodied clothes away, and their flight to Michigan, where they checked into the Holiday Inn.

"At the Holiday Inn," Bryan continued, "the cops came because we'd paid in small bills. The hotel clerk had gotten suspicious. So the cops checked it out."

"What did you say when the cops asked you where you got the small bills and coins?"

"I told them the truth. I said I got it from my dad's wallet."

By 12:18 P.M., they had gotten to the Hesses' house. "Frank was there. We talked a lot and drank beer. We watched a movie that night. We slept on a bed downstairs. We got up the next day around noon. Dave and Frank went ice fishing. I went to Farmer Jack's Market."

After that, the cops got them.

"Go back to the night it happened. How was it decided who would go upstairs?"

"We had an argument about that." Eventually, David and Ben went upstairs. "Ben went over and hit my brother. Ben said he hit my father and brother. He said he cracked my brother's skull and hit him in the face. He said it didn't take that many times to hit Erik. He said his skull just shattered."

"Where did he say he hit your dad?"

"He said he hit my dad in the face."

"And David?"

"He said he hit my dad with a baseball bat. He didn't say where he hit him."

"Did David change his clothes because they were covered with blood?"

"David split his jeans earlier in the day kneeling down. That's why he changed his jeans."

"Did you tell David and Ben to kill your father and little brother?"

"No way! I never told them anything like that."

"Why'd you kill your mother?"

Bryan looked down and his voice broke.

"I just lost control."

Bryan cried. Metzler gave him a moment to compose himself

"Did Ben stab your mother?"

"He stabbed her more times, yes."

According to Bryan, his mother was still alive and Ben went back to finish the job.

"Did Ben say anything to you about what had happened?"

"Ben said if we were caught, I should take the rap because I had a documented history of mental illness in a state hospital."

The interview was over. In the early morning hours, Bryan was returned to their dank cell he

shared with his brother, there to await formal arraignment.

They were tired, spent, worried. Nearby, Ben refused to speak to anyone but his mother. Ben had
not given a statement. He was too smart for that.
He had been arrested before and knew the drill.
You do not speak to cops. Let them prove their
case.

Ben Birdwell relaxed in his cell while his cousins
sweated in theirs.

Fifteen

Later that same day, a week after they were murdered, Dennis, Brenda, and Erik Freeman were laid to rest. It was March 6, 1995.

The funeral service was held at Allentown's new Kingdom Hall on Emmaus Avenue, the one that had replaced the old one in Salisbury Township. The hall was relatively plain with theater-type seats facing a stage with a simple podium.

During the funeral service no one talked of David or Bryan, or Benny, for that matter. Instead, those who were present listened to biblical teachings of hope.

"It's the same message we preach when we go door-to-door," said one Witness who was there. He wouldn't give his name because to do so glorifies the individual, which is anathema to JW teachings.

"We want to comfort the family, and what will comfort the family and what will comfort them most is that these people believed in the resurrection of the dead."

Radio, TV, and newspaper reporters converged on the funeral service like a pack of wild wolves, ravenous for a story. Their hunger remained unsated when they were barred from the Kingdom Hall.

They were even stopped from going into the parking lot. So they stayed on the perimeter of the property, right off the avenue, stopping traffic as they photographed whoever they could, grabbing anyone walking by for a comment. They had stories to file.

Inside, during the hour-long service, friends of the family, Dennis's co-workers, all those who attended, listened to one of the Elders, Andrew Grencer, who only briefly mentioned the dead by name. Other elders explained that Jehovah's Witnesses don't eulogize the dead, focusing instead on Jehovah's religious teachings.

Outside, after the service, the press milled around, looking for further comments.

"For me and a lot of us, it brings closure," said Francis Kaye, a secretary at Salisbury High School. She was there along with about twenty-five from the school district.

"Spiritually, we're all a family," explained Susan Crater, a Jehovah's Witness from Reading. "That's why I came. It's our brotherhood."

An anonymous church Elder said, "We sense it's going to be months and even years before we can deal with this."

A few days later, David and Bryan Freeman and Ben Birdwell came before a Michigan judge for a formal reading of the charges against them. It was a scene played over and over again on national television.

There they were, the menacing-looking skinheads in their prison jumpsuits, the tattoos readily apparent on their shaven heads. Led into the courtroom by guards, shackled hand and foot, they took seats in the jury box while the lawyers stood before the judge going over their cases.

The defendants waived their rights to fight extradition.

Before they left Michigan, David and his brother Bryan sat down together with Michigan State police. Using an Ohio road map, they indicated the spot where they thought Benny had dumped his alleged bloodied clothes. The coordinates were conveyed to the Ohio State police, who mounted a massive search. After hours and hours of searching for the valuable evidence to no avail, they finally had to call the search off

Either the Freeman brothers were telling the truth and had just gotten the coordinates wrong, or maybe someone had come across the clothing and for whatever reason gotten rid of it. Of course, there was the other possibility: the Freeman brothers were liars and Ben Birdwell was an innocent pawn in this game of life and death.

There was no physical evidence to connect Benny to the murders, simply the brothers' word that he had been responsible for killing Erik and helping to kill Dennis. And Ben thought that with no physical evidence to connect him directly to the murders, all he could be charged with was hindering prosecution by driving the escape vehicle.

Someplace in the depths of the Midland County Jail, a police technician was at that moment examining the clothes Ben Birdwell had been wearing when he was captured. There was the jacket he had on that said "White Power" across the back. There were the jeans. There was the good luck pin he had in his pocket that said "KKK." And there was his dark blue T-shirt.

The technician looked at the T-shirt. It appeared clean to the naked eye but looking closer, the technician saw something else. He examined it under a microscope.

It took a few seconds to adjust the magnification and the light, the fabric of the shirt getting clearer and clearer. Then . . . yeah, that was it . . . yeah, yeah . . .

Under the microscope what the technician had seen faintly with his eye became clear. There were spots all across the front of Benny's T-shirt.

Blood spots.

After their arraignment, Connie Chung and a camera crew from CBS showed up at Frank Hesse's house. He declined to be interviewed.

ABC's news magazine *20/20* also decided to present the Freeman/Birdwell case to its viewers. They dispatched ace reporter Tom Jarriel to Midland, where he was dramatically photographed walking down the same road the Freemans and Birdwell had walked before their capture. He went on to interview some of their friends and to focus exclusively on their neo-Nazi beliefs as the causative agent in the family tragedy.

Newsweek came in the following week with a report on the case that once again focused on neo-Nazism and its threat to America. Nothing was mentioned about David and Bryan's formative years or Benny's record.

Fearful of transporting them back to Pennsylvania on a public aircraft, the Michigan State police chartered a plane to fly the heavily shackled skinheads directly into the Allentown International Airport. No stopoffs in Philadelphia or Baltimore to change planes.

The media thronged to the airport to see the skinheads emerge from the plane. Despite the fact that it was still winter and the temperature hovered in the low thirties, the three boys were clad in their short-sleeved prison-issue cotton jumpsuits. The press got as many close-ups as possible of their foreheads with the indelible Nazi symbols standing out like fiery brands of hate. They were led quietly down the steps to waiting police cars.

The motorcade sped from the airport onto Route 22 briefly and then down Sixth Street, arriving at the Lehigh County Jail, which was right behind the courthouse.

They were issued new jumpsuits and given cells. Bryan and David requested and were allowed to share the same cell. Since the crimes, the brothers had gotten even closer than they had before.

For his part, Ben was content to be put in a cell alone. The last thing he wanted was to be with his cousins. He knew he wouldn't survive five minutes in their presence.

In the newspapers that evening, Erik's death was portrayed as being the most brutal. Why did Erik have to die? What had he done? The only thing Erik appeared to be guilty of was obeying his parents. Would this be enough to make David and Bryan kill him?

The media had no knowledge at that point of the content of the brothers' statements. They assumed that since Birdwell had been charged only with hindering the brothers' capture, he was merely along for the ride.

The police looked at the crimes as one, yet to anyone familiar with parricide, the murder of parents by their children, it was two different crimes.

There were the deaths of Dennis and Brenda, in which the Freeman brothers had implicated themselves. They had also implicated Ben in particular in the deaths of Erik and Dennis.

The only blood relation of Ben Birdwell's who wound up dead on the second floor of the Freeman house was Erik; Dennis was his uncle by marriage. If Ben had participated in the murders, he was not guilty of parricide. He had no blood relation to Dennis.

As for an emotional relationship, it was tenuous at best. And while Erik was Ben's first cousin, the difference in their ages (six years) plus the fact that they saw little of each other growing up, practically assured that Benny would have little feeling toward the boy. The emotional and societal barriers to parricide and fratricide that were present in the Freeman brothers' psyches were not present in Ben's.

* * *

Once they reached Pennsylvania, a new problem existed: in that state, the boys did not have counsel. For Ben Birdwell, that problem disappeared almost immediately. His parents hired Richard Makoul, one of the state's best defense attorneys to represent him. The dapper and bearded Makoul, had previously defended Ben's father, so he was familiar with the family history. Makoul, though, had been warned about taking the case on.

He had had an off-the-record conversation with Allentown district attorney Bob Steinberg who had heard he was going to take the Birdwell case. "Don't get in, it's death penalty," Steinberg warned. Steinberg indicated to Makoul that there were three weapons used in the murders, implying three people had wielded them. One of those, Steinberg felt, was Ben Birdwell.

Rather than watching out for Makoul's skin, Steinberg may have been watching out for his own. The last thing he wanted was an expert attorney like Makoul on Benny's case. It would be much easier to defeat a less experienced attorney in court.

Makoul doesn't take kindly to warnings. He took Benny on as his client.

As for the Freeman brothers, they did not have the luxury of private counsel. With no assets between them, and with no one from their family coming forward to help them—their grandfather, Nelson Birdwell III, called for them to be executed for their bloody crimes—their cases were assigned to the Allentown Public Defender's office. Public defenders Earl Supplee and Jim Netchin represented Bryan and David, respectively. But almost immediately a legal conflict developed.

The Allentown public defenders were privately critical of Bob Donohue's willingness to broker a deal for the Freeman brothers' cooperation in return for the death penalty being waived by prosecutor Steinberg. They felt they could have gotten a better deal, but they were now hampered by the binding agreement.

Then there was the matter of complicity. David seemed to be less culpable, at least legally, than his brother Bryan. After all, it was Bryan who'd started the ball rolling. It could be legally argued that when David struck his father, he was already dead from the blows he had received from Benny, making David only guilty of maiming a corpse. Also, it was conceivable that given David's acknowledged history of alcohol and drug abuse, he was stoned the night of the murders and didn't know what he was doing.

A conviction of first-degree murder requires that the state show that the defendant was in his right mind and knew precisely what he was doing and had formed an intent to commit murder prior to the crime.

It therefore became clear that the brothers' interests might be different. There also existed the possibility, that David might testify against his brother to avoid extensive jail time. For all these reasons, presiding Judge Lawrence Brenner kept the public defender's office from representing David.

"It's because of a possible conflict, and that's all

I'm going to say," said Chief Public Defender Robert Long, in explaining the change. Long and his office were known for their taciturn replies to reporters' questions, and this case would prove no different.

Reports began circulating that a deal might be brewing between prosecutors and defense attorneys. Richard Makoul was publicly quoted as saying that David was trying to strike a deal with Steinberg by implicating Birdwell.

"If he charges Ben (with the homicides), there's going to be a real fight in the courtroom," Makoul warned. As to Ben's part in the whole thing, Makoul said, "Basically, he said he saw Mrs. Freeman being murdered. Bryan just snapped. David Freeman vomited after watching his brother stab his mother. Bryan Freeman then threatened to harm his brother and cousin, who followed him out of fear." Makoul would not reveal Ben's recollection of the other murders.

Makoul is excellent at playing the media card. He knows how to utilize the media to get his point across, which is especially useful in cases where one knows the defendant is guilty. After interviewing Benny, who adamantly maintained his innocence of any crime, Makoul became convinced that his client was actually innocent. In confidence he told one reporter who was writing a book about the case that it would be a tragedy if he was charged with murder.

For his part, Steinberg revealed that he had spoken to the defense attorneys, but he would not reveal whether their conversations had covered any substantive issues. He did say that neither he nor his investigators had sought a meeting with the Freemans since their return from Michigan.

Steinberg was tightening the noose. He had trouble with the statements of David and Bryan, and especially Ben. He felt they weren't consistent; there were too many holes; and the accused had not been truthful.

In preparation for the upcoming formal arraignment, he dispatched Joe Vazquez and other investigators throughout Lehigh County to gather any more evidence that could be used against the Freemans and Birdwell.

Steinberg had made a deal and he would adhere to it . . . maybe. If he felt that the accused were lying, the death penalty would be brought back to the table, despite the Michigan agreement.

David's case was subsequently assigned by presiding Judge Lawrence Brenner to Wally Worth and his associate Brian Collins. They made an interesting team.

Worth is a crusty Matlock type, a force in Republican politics in Lehigh County and probably the county's most respected defense attorney. Worth's associate was Brian Collins, a young attorney with a pugnacious manner and a keen legal mind. Collins had a lot of experience working death penalty cases. Despite the Michigan deal, he knew there was always the possibility it could fall apart and his client would once again be facing death.

A profound opponent of the death penalty, he knew death was a real possibility in this case, that a fifteen-year-old could be sentenced to die and killed by lethal injection. He was determined to do everything in his power not to let that happen.

After accepting the case, the first thing Worth did was give out a public statement in which he said, "Our client has not talked to us about any deal." Mindful of the fact that none of the defendants had given up their trial rights, Worth continued, "We don't have anything to say about a deal."

Privately, after they had had a few more chances to talk to David, Worth and Collins decided that the best they could hope for was to cut a deal reducing the charges against their client from first- to third-degree murder. If David pleaded guilty to third-degree murder, he'd go to jail for ten to fifteen years, but at least when he got out he'd be young enough to start a new life.

If David, or for that matter, Bryan, was convicted of first-degree murder, even without the death penalty, each would be sentenced to life in prison, and in Pennsylvania, life means life. There is no parole. The only way to get out is if the governor gives you clemency, and in a state as conservative as Pennsylvania, that was not likely to happen anytime soon.

The arraignment was set for April 26. Prior to that, Nelson Birdwell, the grandfather, announced to the press and all who would listen that he had changed his mind, that he didn't want any of his grandsons executed, and that it was in everyone's best interests that the boys just serve time.

Birdwell visited his grandchildren in jail.

"Keep your brother and cousin out of trouble," Birdwell implored Bryan. "Set the record straight."

Birdwell said Bryan responded, "Don't worry, I'll take care of the whole thing when the time comes."

Birdwell senior then told the press that he did not believe Benny had participated in any of the killings. As for David, "I just asked him how everything looked to him and he said, 'It looks like I'll be in here the rest of my life. I asked him if he could handle that and he said, 'I don't know.' He was sad."

Asked by a reporter what that sadness signified, Birdwell replied, "I would say that it means that he is very remorseful, almost hopeless."

Having made his decision to stand by his grandsons, Nelson Birdwell, Sr., then went national with his campaign to "help" his grandsons. He went on a national talk show where he told the studio and viewing audience how his grandchildren were actually good boys who had gone bad and how they could be helped. One of the guests on the same panel was the widow of Alan Berg, the Denver radio talk show host who had been executed by white supremacists because of his liberal beliefs and his religion.

Mrs. Berg told Birdwell that he had no idea how evil his grandsons were, how virulent hate was. He just didn't have any concept. Birdwell listened, but with a glazed look in his eyes. He didn't know what the hell she was talking about.

* * *

Bob Steinberg does not look like a tough-as-nails district attorney. He is a lot sharper than can be imagined, however.

Steinberg began his professional career working as a public defender in the same Allentown office that was now defending Bryan. He worked for Bill Platt, the head public defender. They became friends and allies.

When Platt became district attorney, he brought Steinberg along as his assistant. When Platt left to become a county judge, one of the last things he did before he left office was to appoint Bob Steinberg to serve out his term.

Originally a Democrat, Steinberg switched his political allegiance to the Republican Party because the Republicans control Lehigh County politics.

Despite his PD background, Steinberg took a hard line toward lawbreakers, preferring to put 'em in jail and get 'em off the street, and to hell with analyzing them. He knew the system was imperfect, he knew that stringent sentences did nothing to stop crime at its root cause. Jails are there for one reason and one reason alone: to punish. And his job as district attorney was to make sure the bad guys, and gals, got all that was coming to them.

After a preliminary investigation, Steinberg had discovered the dysfunctional nature of the Freeman family. There was enough there to make the defendants slightly sympathetic, and so Steinberg had been willing to go along with the deal that Donohue had brokered: if they'd tell the truth in their confessions, he would take the death penalty off the table. He had that power.

All they had to do was give the truth in their statements and they would not face death. They could be tried without that hanging over their heads.

Steinberg had confessions, motive, means, opportunity. So why didn't he feel completely satisfied?

Closeted alone in his office, Bob Steinberg was surrounded by law books and diplomas, awards and file after file of pending legal cases.

Outside Steinberg's window was a grand view of Lehigh County, a place that had in the past few years started to see more than its fair share of crime as the gang problem that had plagued the rest of the country had moved within the county's borders. Out there, too, were the hate mongers.

So the DA passed the night reading the defendants' statements, trying to reconcile what he felt were inconsistencies. In the end, the statements just didn't feel right. The boys *hadn't* answered truthfully, after all.

The deal was off.

He announced publicly that he would accept a plea from any of the defendants to murder in the first degree with a recommendation of life in prison. Otherwise, if they went to trial, he would death qualify the jury. In Pennsylvania, a prosecutor does not have to ask for the death penalty until after the defendant is convicted of first-degree murder.

During voir dire, the early stage of a trial when the attorneys question prospective jurors, they simply ask them if they could apply the death penalty upon conviction. The prosecutor does the best he can to get twelve jurors who say they could, and who he believes, given half the chance, would condemn the prisoners at the bar to death.

Steinberg intended to hold the death penalty over David and Bryan as long as he could, right up until sentencing if he got a conviction, which he was sure he would get, given their statements. As for Birdwell, he began to see him as an instigator.

Steinberg made public statements that whenever trouble occurred in the Freeman household, Ben Birdwell was there. Despite the fact that no one his office questioned said that Benny had made any threats against the family, Steinberg became convinced that Benny had killed Erik, battered Dennis, and then, as the brothers had said, gone around with the pick handle and finished the job.

Benny, with his bland, babyish face, with the polite manner, with the "berserker" tattoo on his forehead—*Benny* was the one Steinberg wanted to get. But how could he get him when there was only the boys' word against his?

"The district attorney can't charge Ben without evidence," asserted Ben's attorney Richard Makoul.

Steinberg pored over the details of the case and then he found it: the shirt, the blue T-shirt Benny had been wearing when he was captured. According to the Michigan police technician's report, it bore blood spots.

And it was now in the possession of the Pennsylvania State police. Steinberg made immediate plans to send the T-shirt out for DNA testing. If it came back positive for any of the decedents' blood, he would charge Nelson Benjamin Birdwell III with murder in the first degree.

Sixteen

April 26, 1995

Metal detectors had been set up outside courtroom number two on the second floor of the Lehigh County Courthouse.

The courtroom is old-fashioned by today's standards, with row upon row of wood benches separated by a central aisle, a slatted divider, and then the main part of the floor, with prosecution and defense tables side by side flanking the judge's bench and to the left the jury box. The place was packed, filled with thirty or so reporters, the rest witnesses, lawyers, and spectators who wanted to be in at the beginning of what promised to be an exciting trial.

At the defense table on the left sat two of the defendants, David and Bryan. Alongside David were his defense attorneys, Wally Worth and Brian Collins. Next to Bryan were Earl Supplee and Mike Brunnabend, from the public defender's office.

Each boy wore a sky blue nylon jacket. Ben Birdwell wore the same outfit, but he sat in the jury box. He was there more as a matter of courtesy, because he was going to be arraigned separately at a later date. His attorney, Richard Makoul, dapper in a double-breasted worsted suit, sat on one of the benches for counsel that lined the railing encircling the courtroom.

Makoul immediately made a motion before Judge Lawrence Brenner to sever Benny's case. The last thing he wanted was for his client to be tried alongside the two Freeman Brothers, who the media had made out to be the next coming of Jack the Ripper. Steinberg agreed with Makoul's motion and the judge moved on to the business at hand.

"Mr. Steinberg, ready to begin?" the judge asked.

"The state calls Isidore Mihalikis."

Mihalikis is the coroner for Lehigh County.

The purpose of an arraignment is to present the basic facts of a case necessary to hold a defendant over for trial and to see that he's charged with the crime indicated. It is a formality, because everyone knows that unless the state has an exceptionally weak case, the judge will bind the defendants over for trial. What it does do, though, is force the prosecution to show the outlines of their case. And while it is a hearing, the same rules of evidence and examination apply as at a trial.

Steinberg is nothing if not thorough. He had spoken to all his witnesses before they'd testified, and like any good lawyer, he knew what they would say before they said it and tailored his questions accordingly.

Steinberg asked Mihalikis to review his findings for the court.

"Dennis Freeman was struck first," Mihalikis began, consulting a looseleaf binder full of notes and reports that he had set up on the railing of the witness box. "He had injuries on the face, and the right upper arm and hands, which I would say were defensive wounds." That is, as he was being struck, Dennis had reflexively raised his arms to ward off the deadly blows.

"There was blunt force to the head, about six blows, I should say. To the chest, where there was an extensive amount of bruising, seven blows."

"Could you be more specific?"

"Yes. His ribs were fractured, and so was his breastbone. His heart and lungs were bruised. There was a transverse cutting wound of the neck. It was superficial, though, going from side to side. His nose was injured, the orbits, the nose. The left jaw was fractured."

Mihalikis turned the page.

"There is a gaping four-inch fracture of the entire frontal area of the skull. It lacerated the covering of the brain."

"Which resulted in?"

"The brain mushroomed outside the skull."

"How many blows did Mr. Freeman take to the face?"

"He was struck in the face approximately three to five times. The bones projected through the skin."

The courtroom was silent.

At the defense table, David and Bryan hung their heads. They were either tired or ashamed of what they were being accused of doing.

"Could you describe the kind of instrument used to inflict this type of damage?" Steinberg asked.

"A rounded, broad-based weapon. The blood splattered because a flat instrument was used to the head while the weapon that damaged Mr. Freeman's right arm had a projection," Mihalikis replied.

That made two types of weapons. Mihalikis theorized that the flat side of a pick-ax handle and a baseball bat recovered at the scene probably were used to inflict the head injuries. The supposition was that David had wielded one, Benny the other. As to the weapon with a projection that Mihalikis referred to, a piece of exercise equipment, a bar to a dumbbell, was recovered at the scene. That had done the arm damage.

"Mr. Freeman died from massive head injuries and facial trauma induced by blunt force," he concluded.

Steinberg then asked the coroner to describe the injuries to Brenda Freeman.

"Sharp-force injuries. Cut and stab wounds. Blunt-force stab wound to the tip of her right shoulder that went through and through to her right arm, five and a quarter (inches)," he testified.

"There was a stab wound to her back," Mihalikis continued. "To the right scapula."

"What kind of damage did that blow do?"

"It perforated the chest wall, the right lung, into the vena cava, the vein to the heart, and caused the blood to leak into the right side of her chest."

"Can you determine what kind of weapon was used?"

"It was done by a sturdy, single-edge blade that was two millimeters wide."

"Would you please describe the head wounds of Mrs. Freeman?"

"Eight blunt-force blows to the scalp. Seven to the central part, the top and frontal areas, and one to the back. The handle of a pick-ax was most likely the object that caused the blows."

"What was the cause of death, Doctor?"

"The cause of death were the stab wounds to the back and the cerebral injuries."

Brenda had apparently survived for a time after she had been stabbed by Bryan. But then, someone had inflicted the final death blows with the pick-ax handle. Which of the boys had bent over her while she was dying and pounded her head till the life drained from her body?

Bryan and David continued to look down as Mihalikis continued his testimony. But Benny looked up, his innocent face unlined, his cheeks rosy red, like a cherub's. A smile seemed to play at the corner of his mouth.

"Now, Doctor," Steinberg continued, "would you please describe Erik Freeman's injuries?"

This was the one the spectators had been waiting for. Teens killing adults was one thing, but to kill a small, innocent child was another matter altogether, a matter of the utmost depravity. Every spectator in that courtroom leaned forward to hear Mihaliklis's testimony.

"Erik Freeman had injuries to his forehead, the

left part of his face, the left arm, and the back of both hands. They were blunt-force injuries."

Mihalikis gazed down at his notes.

"There were two transverse injuries low across his forehead and above the eyebrows that caused skull fractures, which then caused the brain to mushroom.

"There was a massive fracture to the frontal bones and the nose and facial area. There were four bruises to the temple and the left side of the face and two lacerations. There was a defensive injury, a bruise on the left forearm and the back of both hands. The metacarpals (hand bones) were fractured."

His voice ringing out in the hushed courtroom, Steinberg asked Mihalikis, "How did Erik Freeman die?"

"Erik Freeman died from cerebral front-force injuries delivered by an aluminum bat."

During his cross examination, Wally Worth asked Mihalikis how much blood Brenda Freeman lost after she was injured.

"About one and a half to two liters," Mihalikis answered. "The average person would have about five litters in their body, but Mrs. Freeman was heavy-set, so she had about eight."

"So if she lost one and a half liters, how long would it take her to die?" Worth wondered.

"In that case, it would be a matter of minutes for the victim to die."

Which meant that someone was not satisfied to wait; they had to bludgeon her to death to finish off the job. Would Bryan have stabbed his mother, waited, seen she wasn't dead, and then picked up another weapon to finish the job?

Officer Michael Pochran was next to the stand. The cop testified that on February 27, 1995, he was working the three-to-eleven shift, in uniform, when he received a transmission at 5:15 P.M. to proceed to the Freeman house. He got there in two minutes. In the next part of his testimony he summarized his arrival and discovery of the bodies.

Steinberg then played a tape of the crime scene shot by police photographers to reinforce Pochran's testimony and show what a bloody scene of carnage it was. It was eerie, watching that tape, looking at the bodies and the blood.

After Pochran finished his testimony, Steinberg called Valerie Freeman to the stand. Wearing large, black square-framed glasses that did nothing to soften her features, and a conservative suit that set off her blond hair, Valerie took the stand. Looking more fragile and meek than usual, she spoke in a soft voice.

Valerie testified that she was fifty-two years old, that she worked at the Lehigh Valley County Parks and Recreation Department as a clerical technician, and that she was Dennis Freeman's sister.

"How long did you live in the Freeman home?" Steinberg asked.

"Seventeen years," she replied.

"When did you leave?"

"November of 1994."

"Why?"

"Because of a confrontation with David. Dennis

said to leave. David had gone wild, and Dennis was afraid for the safety of the family."

Valerie went on to describe the relationship between the cousins, and how David and Benny seemed the closest. She told how the family owned three cars, a new van, the Chevy truck Dennis drove to work, and the Sunbird that Brenda drove, and how the boys' driving privileges had been revoked.

"When was the last time you saw Erik?" Steinberg asked.

She had seen him the Friday before the murder. When she had asked him how his brothers were treating him, little Erik had responded, "You never know when you're going to die."

There was an audible gasp in the courtroom. The reporters scribbled hurriedly in their notebooks.

Valerie spent the next fifteen minutes testifying about how she'd found the bodies, what her reaction was, and the altercations she'd had with her nephews, who, sitting at the defense table, would not make eye contact with her.

Next up to testify was the Freemans' paperboy, Sam Ehrgott. Dressed in a suit and tie, looking neat and well groomed, Sam presented quite a contrast to the skinheads at the defense table.

Sam testified about his relationship with Bryan Freeman. "We'd been friends for a while, but for three or four years we didn't speak much to each other," he said. Then he related the conversation he'd had with him in school prior to the murders in which Bryan had talked about wanting his par-

ents dead. Sam described how he had delivered
the paper to the Freeman home the day of the
murders, how he was surprised not to see Dennis
Freeman coming down the steps of his house at
5:45 A.M. like he did every day, and how Bryan was
absent from school that day. Finally, he told how
Valerie had come over after discovering Erik's
body, how his mother called the police, and how
she sent him to his sister-in-law's after she'd made
the call to protect him.

After Sam Ehrgott came Steinberg's best witness,
Jesse Capece.

Capece is the type of witness every lawyer loves.
She remembered every detail of the skinheads' stay
at the Truck World Motor Inn in Hubbard, Ohio,
where she had been working the seven-to-three
shift when she'd checked them in. Capece remembered in exacting detail how they'd lied about their
license number and what their movements had
been while they'd stayed there. She wasn't surprised when she was later questioned about them
by the Pennsylvania State police; they'd just seemed
so weird.

Greg Pavledes, Capece's counterpart at the Holiday Inn in Midland, Michigan, testified to the same
things: what time the boys came into his place, how
he called the cops because they suspiciously paid
with change and small bills, and how their overall
appearance just made him wonder.

Steinberg was tracing the boys' activities minute
by minute and that meant it was time to call Ser-
geant Thomas Mynsberge of the Michigan State po-

lice. He testified to how they caught and questioned the suspects, and how David Freeman had confessed to the killings of his father and brother, how Bryan had killed his mother, and how Benny wasn't responsible for any of it.

Trooper Joe Vazquez came to the stand. Under cross examination by Brian Collins, he was forced to admit that he had told Donohue in Michigan that he felt David's statement was truthful.

Then the videotapes of David's first confession and Benny's statement were played. Bryan's statement was the last to be played.

At the end of the hearing, the judge ruled that the district attorney had proved his *prima facie* case. Bryan and David Freeman were bound over for trial.

After the hearing, Steinberg distributed copies of David's and Benny's statements to the Michigan State police. But when local television stations asked if they could get a copy of the crime scene videotape for broadcast on the evening news, Steinberg demurred. He felt it would compromise the defendants' opportunity to get a fair trial in Allentown.

In private and public pronouncements in the days that followed, Steinberg once again made it clear that he did not believe the statements of any of the defendants. They would all face the death penalty if they went to trail. But if they pleaded now, he would accept first-degree murder and life in prison.

Not one of the attorneys or their clients went for the deal.

David and Bryan had one hope of avoiding trial as adults.

Since they'd been underage when they'd committed the crimes, they could be tried as juveniles, in which case the worst sentence they could get would be confinement in a state prison until they were 21.

Worth and Collins, representing David, and Supplee and Brunnabend, representing Bryan, decided to try it. The judge set a date for the juvenile certification hearings in the fall. In the meanwhile, all the defendants would continue to be held without bail in the Lehigh County Jail.

Brenda's surviving sisters, Linda Solivan and Sandy Lettich, went back to the Freeman house.

A big dumpster was brought in, set up in the driveway, and they went through the house and threw out the stuff that every family accumulates over the years and keeps until the time they move. Since the Freemans had already left the temporal plane, it was a good idea to do this now, considering the auction that was about to come.

The house on Ehrets Lane was no longer a crime scene. Bodies had been removed, photographs taken, evidence gathered. Linda and Sandy and their husbands went through the house and cleaned everything up. By the time they were finished, the blood was gone.

They had had the house painted, which was important, because no one wanted to buy a house with walls splattered with blood. But blood seeps into the pores of the plaster; no matter how much it is painted over, the blood is always there. Blood became part of the very fabric of the house.

Seventeen

Steinberg took nothing for granted. He was not satisfied with his case. He wanted more. Joe Vazquez was sent out to interview more witnesses with information on the murders. At the Lehigh County Juvenile Detention Home, he interviewed Jason Philip Conlan.

"About a month or so before the murder," Conlan told Vazquez, "I met Bryan, David, and Benny at the home of a friend of ours."

"Who was the friend?" Vazquez asked.

"Sean Crossland."

The name wasn't familiar to Vazquez.

"Anyway, Bryan told me that that night he was going to kill his parents. The reason was that they were treating him badly."

"Did he say anything else?"

"Both Bryan and David said they hated their little brother, but neither of them said anything about killing him."

"Why'd they hate Erik?"

"Because he was spoiled. That's what they said. Anyway, during this time I was with them—"

"This was the first time you were with them?"

"Yeah. And what happened was, Bryan got

drunk and tried to start a fight with me. This girl named Melanie stopped it."

Vazquez knew that Bryan had for a while been seeing a girl named Melanie who seemed to be his girlfriend. It was common knowledge.

"When was the last time you saw the Freemans and Birdwell?"

"I saw them at Crossland's home on a Saturday or Sunday night before the murders. Bryan said he was going to kill his parents by blowing their heads off and that he was going to take their money and head for Alabama."

Vazquez hadn't heard that before.

"How about Birdwell? Did he make any threats?"

"I never heard Birdwell say anything about killing anyone."

Vazquez knew from experience that many people come forward with information during a murder investigation. Some are legitimate; they have good information and they want to help. Some claim to have intimate knowledge but are in trouble with the law and hope to get a break if they open up.

Conlan could be either.

As the executor of Dennis and Brenda Freeman's estate, Sandy Lettich had decided to liquidate their worldly possessions during an auction on Sunday, May 21, 1995.

It was an auction like any other, with veteran bargain hunters arriving early and sitting down on lawn chairs set up in front of the auctioneer's podium that had been set up in the driveway where

David and Bryan had played basketball with Dennis.

Sandy Lettich had made certain that no one could get any actual souvenirs of the crimes. The beds the family had been killed in had been put into the dumpster. The bloodied bedclothes were in the police labs and would not be released until after they had been thoroughly examined for further evidence.

Auctioneers Mark "Dutch" Kistler and Kim Kistler kept things moving during the actual auction process and cracked a couple of well-timed jokes to remove tension.

"I'm here for a very practical reason, to get a car. And if I can get it for three grand less than at a dealer, great," said Mike Ryan, an Allentown resident hunting for a bargain.

"I got a great van and no, I had no problem buying it," said Gene Braden, the man who bought the family's 1995 Ford Windstar minivan for the bargain price of $18,000. The speedometer only showed twenty-five miles.

A short time after noon, after a lot of the smaller items, like Brenda's jewelry, Dennis's tools, and Erik's bicycle, had been sold, Mark Kistler began his pitch for the prize of the afternoon: the house itself.

The interior of the house still smelled from fresh paint, and new carpeting had been installed throughout. The kitchen cabinets had been painted a pristine white, and new appliances and a new kitchen countertop had been installed. On the back porch, a hot tub overlooked trees and shrubs that since the murders had overgrown to the point that weeds were overtaking the backyard.

An attorney for the estate, John Greisamer, read the conditions for the sale of the five-bedroom house. It was the only time during the afternoon that the name "Freeman" was mentioned.

Kistler opened the bidding at $130,000. It was a good price for the house. It was in excellent shape and this was a nice neighborhood, certainly not the type of place where one expected a triple murder to take place.

The crowd had grown silent, hushed, as Kistler went through his spiel. "$130,000, $130,000, do I hear $130,000?"

People looked around. No one raised his hand. No one signaled a bid. Finally, a brave couple who did not fear death or murder and knew a bargain when they saw one, shouted, "$72,000."

People turned to look at them as the auctioneer sounded out the bid and raised the price higher. But no one was biting. They put the house bidding aside.

Kistler moved on to Dennis's 1985 Chevy S-10 pickup, the one Sam Ehrgott had seen parked in the driveway the day of the murder, the same car Bryan had moved to get the Sunbird out of the driveway. The S-10 sold for $5,400.

When Kistler resumed the bidding for the house forty-five minutes later, only the one brave couple bid. With no one competing against them, there was no reason to raise their bid from $72,000.

"We reserve the right to reject your bid, and that's what I'm gonna do," Kistler announced to the crowd. "I'm willing to negotiate with you. You know where to find me."

Lawyer Greisamer later explained that the estate had a sale price in mind, that the proceeds from the sale of the house and its contents were needed to pay off two mortgages and outstanding taxes.

"We're not going to let it go for nothing," he explained. "If we don't sell it today, we'll sell it some other way. It's unfortunate what happened here. But it's still a valuable piece of real estate."

Inside the Allentown jail, David and Bryan Freeman had still not been convicted of anything. Whether they were or not, one thing was certain: they could never go home again. If they did, all they would see was an empty shell.

"Toy soldiers," David responded. David was concerned about the auction. He asked Worth to make sure that his prized possessions were well taken care of while he was in jail.

"What are those?" Worth asked.

Tuesday, May 23, 1995

Politics make strange bedfellows. The same might be said for the Constitution.

When Steinberg showed the crime scene videotape at the arraignment, he had opened up a Pandora's box. He had declined the media's request that he furnish them with a copy for the evening news. He thought that would be it. It wasn't.

Channel 6, a local Philadelphia station that was covering the Freeman/Birdwell case avidly, filed a brief with Judge Brenner demanding access to all the videotapes and audiotapes, including those of the boys' statements and the crime scene, citing First Amendment rights. The station claimed that the tapes are judicial records that can be released. Steinberg, Collins, Worth, Supplee, and Brunnabend countered that the tapes are not public record and would compromise the defendants' right to a fair trial.

All the lawyers went before Judge Brenner and pleaded their case for three hours. Seated in the gallery was Brenda's sister, Sandy Lettich. Allowed to address the court, she said, "We feel it would be terrible to have something like this shown to the general public." She felt that airing the tapes would be an invasion of the Freemans' privacy and an insensitive exploitation of them.

Brenner promised to rule on the motion but gave no indication of exactly when that would be. Meanwhile, Nelson Birdwell Sr., the grandfather, was engaged in media action of his own.

"I'm dickering with a man from Warner Brothers' studio for the rights to my story," he told a reporter. He was exploring the possibility of writing a book about the case. Asked how he was coping since the murders, he explained, "I'm sixty-two years old. My mind can control my body and emotions."

About Bryan and David, who he now visited in prison regularly, he said, "The older one is keeping the younger one intact. I am, you might say, their person outside. Everybody needs one"

He said that they spent their days writing letters and watching television. The brothers still shared a cell, while Benny was housed in a separate unit. Apparently, they figured they had nothing to worry about regarding the death penalty. They still figured that the deal they'd made in Michigan was on.

"They don't look to get out for the rest of their lives," the elder Birdwell said.

As to the current matter before Brenner's court, Birdwell gave an interview to one of the local papers in which he said that the prosecutors should indeed release the tapes in question to the press.

"I don't think anything should be kept from the public," Birdwell said.

At first he hadn't wanted the tapes released, particularly a shot that showed the body of his daughter Brenda lying on the floor in her own blood, her nightgown hiked above her waist. Now, he said, he wanted the tapes, with a bit of judicious editing, released, because their release would help ensure his grandchildren of a fair trial.

Birdwell explained that the reason for his change of mind was that after prosecutors showed the video in court, he figured he would trust a jury to be fair in the case more than the officials within the court system, whom he referred to as "dictatorial."

"Why didn't Steinberg practice his own counsel from the start instead of now contradicting his own action?" Birdwell said in a prepared statement.

Behind the scenes, Steinberg had been informed that the elder Birdwell had anti-Semitic tendencies that had been communicated in letters to officials in the judicial system. That raised an interesting question:

Could Birdwell have communicated those same sentiments to his neo-Nazi grandchildren, who had then ultimately embraced anti-Semitism?

Maybe the answers would come out at the certification hearing in the fall.

June 15, 1995

It was a warm, dry day, a perfect day for the Salisbury High School seniors graduating into the sunshine of their lives.

Principal Michael Platt described the Class of 1995 as a mosaic. "It is the portrait beneath the surface that I would like to address. Each of our graduates carries with them a powerful palette of colors with which to dream. Our graduates are the artists and the artisans of their dreams. Make each brushstroke meaningful to you, consistent with who you are and what you believe," he said, in addressing the graduates at the hour-long graduation ceremony at the high school stadium.

Platt mentioned nothing about Bryan Freeman, who, when he'd last seen him in person, was arguing with him. He mentioned nothing about the murders, or the fact that Bryan had been an honors student who would have graduated. But one graduate, Stephanie Kramer, seemed to be addressing the Freeman brothers when she told the crowd, "We need to keep our eyes open to find the happiness we all desire. We can find it in our friends, in our family, and in ourselves."

Beautiful words, with more than a hint of truth—but what she had not said was that in order to reach those goals, it is best to grow up in a household where everyone loves and respects everyone else and shows it. And if you happen to grow up in a house where those things are not present, life might not work out the way you'd like.

June 30, 1995

Acting on a tip, Joe Vazquez headed sixty miles south to Philadelphia and the federal courthouse at Sixth and Market Streets. There, he met with Assistant U.S. Attorney Joseph G. Poluka, who had arranged for the state trooper to interview Ivan Smith.

During the interview, Smith was represented by Assistant Public Defender David Kozlow. Smith, who hailed from Brooklyn, New York, had some information about the case that he wanted to share.

"I was in the county prison on March sixteenth and seventeenth."

"This year?" Vazquez asked.

"Yeah. This year. And I spoke with Nelson Birdwell. We were both in the same unit at the Lehigh County Prison."

A jailhouse informant. Maybe the guy had heard

something from Benny that they could use.
Vazquez was interested.

"Go on."

"Other guys in the unit, they would ask Birdwell
why he did what he did, and Birdwell would just
smile and then talk about it."

"You talked to Birdwell about that night?"

"Yeah. And I made notes of my conversation
with him and I still have them."

"So what did Birdwell tell you?"

"I asked Birdwell why he had been involved in
the murders. Birdwell told me that the two brothers did it, not him. Birdwell told me that the brothers had been planning it for years."

"Did Birdwell say anything about what he saw?"

"Birdwell told me that he had seen the mother
being killed. He said he did not see the other two
being killed because that took place in a different
part of the house."

"Did Birdwell say how the murders were committed?"

"He said that the two brothers used bats, knives
and clubs to kill the family. Birdwell didn't specify
who killed the mother, he kept saying 'they.' "

"What did he say about the mother's killing?"

"Birdwell said that when the mother was on the
floor, there was a lot of blood and that she was
screaming a lot."

That contradicted what David and Bryan had
said, Vazquez thought. They'd said she'd never
screamed.

"Birdwell said that prior to everything happening, he and the Freemans had been at Wendy's,

eating, and then they went to the movies. He said that the brothers talked about killing the parents while at Wendy's and at the movies.

"Birdwell said that while in the car on the way home, they had listened to racist music. He said the music talked about killing. I said to Birdwell, 'Man, I know you all didn't mean to do that shit.' "

"What did Benny say?"

"Birdwell, he replied, 'Naw, they deserved it.' "

"Did he say why they deserved it?"

"Well, Birdwell told me that the younger brother wanted to kill his parents because they put him in a mental institution. And afterward, when it was all over, they started to drive. Birdwell said he was the one driving the car. He said they stopped at a hotel and saw a report of the murders on the news."

"Then what did he say?"

"Birdwell told me that they left the motel and went to a farm where the cops got them. He said that while they were in Michigan, they talked about going back to Pennsylvania to make the murders look like a robbery that had happened when they were not there."

"Did he say anything else about the night of the murders?" Vazquez asked.

"Birdwell said that after it all happened, the oldest brother wanted to stop at his house for some tapes, but he told him that if they did, he might just stay there. So they didn't stop at his house."

Not quite true. They did drop the car off that Ben had been driving, but it was true that it was a quick stop and no one went inside.

"Did he say anything else at all about the crime?"

"Yeah," Smith answered. "Birdwell said that Steinberg knows he's involved. Birdwell said that he was going to say that since he saw the mother get killed, he got scared and went on the trip with the Freemans because he was scared they might kill him. Birdwell told me that he was going to stick to that story."

"What else?"

"Well, just one thing more. I asked Birdwell why they killed the little brother and he told me, 'We had to kill him because he was a mama's boy and he would have squealed anyway.' " Birdwell went on to say that they were talking about killing their parents the day they did it and they were planning to do it the night it happened.

Smith then provided copies of notes he had written regarding his conversations with Benny.

There was enough truth in Smith's statement that it could be used at trial to show Benny's culpability in the crimes. Things were going Steinberg's way.

The summer wore on, a hot one in Lehigh Valley, but no one sweated more than Ben Birdwell. He was worried about the results of the DNA testing of his T-shirt.

Steinberg kept assuring the press, "the results will be forthcoming next week," and then next week came and went and nothing happened. Steinberg explained that the reason for the continual delay was that DNA testing is very exacting and it takes time.

The DA was hoping that at least one of the decedents' blood would show up on Benny's shirt. If he was wrong and it didn't, Benny could not be charged with murder.

July 6, 1995

Steinberg called Makoul. He told Ben's lawyer that if Benny pleaded guilty to murder one, he'd take the death penalty off the table and tell the judge he was cooperating with the prosecution. Makoul ran the deal by Benny, who nixed it. Benny adamantly maintained that he hadn't killed anyone.

July 24, 1995

The document was filed quietly with little fanfare in Judge Brenner's court. But in terms of legal strategy, it spoke volumes.

NOTICE OF INSANITY OR MENTAL INFIRMITY DEFENSE

The Defendant, David Jonathan Freeman, by his attorneys, Worth Law Offices, PC, Wallace C. Worth, Jr., Esquire, and Brian J. Collins, Esquire, do hereby give notice pursuant to Pennsylvania Rule of Criminal Procedure 305 (C)

(1)(b) that he intends to enter a claim of mental infirmity at the time of trial and that he has served notice of the intention on the Office of the District Attorney on July 24, 1995. Defendant gives notice as follows:

A. Defendant intends to enter a claim of mental infirmity at time of trial. Defendant has been diagnosed as mentally ill and treated for his mental illness. Defendant has long-standing personality problems, mental illness, and substance abuse. A pathological relationship existed between Defendant and his parents. On the night of the incident Defendant was intoxicated to the point of being unable to form the requisite specific intent to commit first-degree murder and was overwhelmed to the point of losing his faculties and sensibilities. Defendant started drinking at approximately the age of 6. Further details to be provided in expert reports.

Under ordinary circumstances Collins and Worth's petition would have been greeted with a chortle of humor; with no other way to explain the crimes, they were going to use an insanity defense.

Contrary to the public perception that an insanity defense usually provides a guilty defendant with a way out, it is anything but. In a court of law, insanity is probably the most difficult thing to prove and juries rarely accept it as a defense, especially in a capital case.

But the case of Jeffrey Haworth had sent a long

shadow across the DA's office. Steinberg was worried about lightning striking twice.

Jeffrey Haworth was a twenty-one-year-old Lehigh County man who had killed his parents by firing repeatedly at them with a shotgun. When he was arrested, police confiscated his notes on the crimes, in which he said that what the Freeman Brothers did to their parents was "cool."

His attorney decided to use an insanity defense. Steinberg never believed the jury would buy it and was confident of a conviction.

The case brought the DA a lot of publicity. And when the verdict came in that the jury had, indeed, bought Haworth's assertion and acquitted him, you couldn't find a more surprised individual or a more disappointed one in Lehigh County than Bob Steinberg. Not only did Steinberg feel a guilty man had gone free, his political capital waned because he had not gotten a conviction in what appeared to be an open-and-shut case. That made the pressure to get convictions against the Freemans and Birdwell that much more immediate.

Judge Diefenderfer, who was scheduled to hear Benny's case, was stepping down from the bench at the end of 1996. Steinberg wanted his job. A conviction in the next high-profile case, the Freemans and Birdwells, couldn't hurt.

Now, one of the defendants, David Freeman, had stated that he would use an insanity defense, the same insanity defense that had gotten Jeffrey Haworth off.

* * *

July 25, 1995

If Steinberg was going to renege on the deal, the defense attorneys were going to take him to task publicly.

Worth and Collins, along with public defenders Supplee and Brunnabend, filed papers in court in which they claimed that Steinberg broke his promise not to seek the death penalty, and that the brothers were coerced into giving statements. "Bryan's court-appointed lawyer in Michigan was not familiar with Pennsylvania law, and Bryan relied on his advice in giving a confession," said Bryan's public defenders, Earl Supplee and Mike Brunnabend. Not to be outdone, David's lawyers had a little surprise of their own.

Worth and Collins filed a brief in which David Freeman claimed that imposing the death penalty on someone his age constituted cruel and unusual punishment under both the federal and state constitutions.

"David Freeman consumed alcohol and marijuana and got very little sleep on the trip from Allentown to Michigan," Collins said in the brief he had prepared. "He was tired, hung over, and partially under the influence of intoxicating beverages and substances, with the result that the defendant's confession was not the product of a rational intellect and a free will but was rather the result of the defendant's will being overborne."

"They can't get a fair trial here in Allentown,"

all the lawyers agreed, and they said so in their legal papers. "There's no way we can get an impartial jury in Lehigh County or the surrounding area because of prejudicial pretrial publicity that has flooded and saturated the area."

For his part, Steinberg continued the pressure: since the Freemans and Birdwell did not tell the whole truth in their statements, the death penalty would still apply. If they went to trial, he fully intended to death qualify the jury.

July 27, 1995

Steinberg got back the DNA test results on Benny's T-shirt. The results were positive.

Ben's blue T-shirt had been sent for testing to the FBI labs in Washington. The spots on his shirt were a positive match for Dennis Freeman's blood.

"The impact stains could not have occurred unless the defendant, Nelson Birdwell III, was in the bedroom of Dennis Freeman while Dennis Freeman was being murdered and in close proximity to the body," Trooper Joe Vazquez wrote in the affidavit that called for Birdwell's arrest on murder charges.

As he had promised, Steinberg, pleased that his hunch had proved correct, hauled Benny into court and charged him with three counts of first degree murder. Since he was apparently present when Dennis was killed, it was a logical assumption he was there for the other two as well. David's second statement, along with Bryan's, provided more than enough justification in Steinberg's view to charge him with killing all three victims. Benny had a triple murder charge lodged against him.

Shackled hand and foot, his hair grown out so you no longer could see the "berserker" tattoo on his forehead, Benny stood before the bench of District Justice Joan Hausman. Judge Hausman read the charges against him.

"How do you plead?"

"The defendant pleads not guilty to all charges," said Richard Makoul.

"I have to let you know how serious this is. You could face the death penalty," Judge Hausman warned. Benny didn't look too perturbed. The judge ordered him back to Lehigh County Prison without bail.

Downstairs in the lobby of the courthouse, Steinberg held his usual post-court press conference. "Now, he's in the bedroom," Steinberg said of Benny. "I'm probably going to file court papers preserving the Commonwealth's right to seek the death penalty in this case, as I did with the Freeman brothers."

Steinberg pointed out that the stains were barely visible to the naked eye, but under infrared photography, they came up clear. "They could easily have been overlooked." He commended the state police and the FBI lab for their work on the case. "If not for the work of the scientists in advancing the cause of DNA testing in criminal cases, this case probably would not be in this posture today," Steinberg continued. Then he said publicly what he had only discussed privately.

"Whenever there was trouble in that house, Mr. Birdwell was in the thick of it," said Steinberg.

Only Brenda's sisters and Dennis's sister could have given him this information, since the Birdwell family wasn't talking, except for the grandfather. The district attorney was convinced that Benny was the real culprit in the case, because he had no real motive to commit murder, yet he had, apparently, done it.

Steinberg concluded by saying that he had decided to prosecute the Freemans and Birdwell separately, because the defendants' statements might be used against each other.

For his part, Makoul waited until Steinberg had finished his statement and gave one of his own. It was terse and biting.

"Well, I'm not surprised by the new charges. But that blood on my client's shirt does not prove he killed anyone. The bloodstains could have occurred in many different ways. How about if Ben tried to stop the killings? He could have gotten blood on his shirt then. How come no one is exploring that possibility? The district attorney is proceeding on a circumstantial case, and it's tenuous at best," Makoul declared confidently, and then strode off down the courthouse steps and back to his office a block away.

A few doors down from Makoul's office, David's lawyer, Brian Collins, was in his, fielding questions from the press, all of whom wanted to interview his client. Collins received interview requests from *Rolling Stone* magazine and other media outlets. Like any good attorney, he turned them all down.

"I can't answer ninety-nine percent of their questions," Collins said. "I can talk about court procedures, but I can't talk about anything my client has told me. That's privileged."

Privately, Collins and his boss, Wally Worth, were hoping against hope to make a deal with Steinberg, to reduce the charges against David. Second-degree murder was not applicable in this case, because second-degree murder occurs only when someone is killed during the commission of a robbery, which this clearly wasn't. That left third-degree murder, which is murder committed without premeditation.

Collins and Worth had some doubts whether they could achieve that goal. Steinberg's offer was still on the table: life without parole instead of death. But they did not like the idea of pleading David guilty to first degree. To a sixteen-year-old, life behind bars *is* death.

As the case wound toward the juvenile certification hearing in September, once again Steinberg sent Vazquez out to bolster their case. The object was to find out as much information as possible about the Freeman Brothers and Benny Birdwell that could be used to try them as adults.

August 23, 1995

Vazquez arrived at Salisbury Township High School, where he had an appointment with Nick Palumbo. The forty-eight-year-old Palumbo was the Student Assistance Director for the Salisbury School District. Vazquez was there to see what

Palumbo knew about a rumor that surfaced which indicated that the Freemans had told him that they were going to kill their parents.

"They never said they were going to kill their parents," he told Vazquez. "But they expressed a severe hatred toward their parents."

He told Vazquez that due to disciplinary problems in school and at home, he had assisted Brenda Freeman in placing the boys in various treatment facilities. But he never heard from any of these facilities regarding the actual treatment the boys were getting. "Those records would have been maintained by the individual treatment facility," Palumbo continued.

Steinberg later tried to obtain the treatment records of the Freeman brothers, but because of confidentiality laws, he could not.

After Vazquez had finished with Palumbo, he drove back to Steinberg's office, where an interview had been set up with Todd Reiss. Reiss, then an inmate in Lehigh County Prison for several months, had an interesting story to tell.

"Well, about July nineteenth," Reiss began, "I was in the 'hole' at Lehigh County Prison at the same time as Nelson Birdwell."

"Did you talk?" Vazquez asked.

"Yeah."

"I didn't know who he was at first." But after they talked for a while, Reiss figured out who he was. "Birdwell told me about the Freeman killings and that he was only charged with taking the Freeman brothers out of the state."

"That's all?"

"No. There's more. Birdwell said that he had helped kill the mother."

Vazquez was an experienced interrogator. He hid his excitement, though he knew this was hot stuff.

"Birdwell told me that he had gotten her attention (Brenda's) and she was then attacked from behind (by Bryan). He said that all three of them had been involved in planning the murders a week or two before at his (Birdwell's) house."

If that were true, then Steinberg's hunch about Birdwell's complicity in the crimes was even greater than the district attorney thought.

"What else did he say?" Vazquez asked.

Reiss continued, "Birdwell said that the mother was the hardest to kill because she was awake and the others had been asleep. He also said that he had discussed the idea of killing his (Birdwell's) parents also."

"Did Birdwell tell you anything about how the murders were committed?" Vazquez said.

"Birdwell told me that Bryan went upstairs and killed the father with a bat. He said that he and the younger brother stayed downstairs and killed the mother. The brother and father were quiet deaths because they were asleep at the time.

"Birdwell said the father and brother were killed first and the mother was the hardest because she was screaming and yelling. Birdwell said he was scared to be in the house and was intimidated by his older cousin. He said he found the car keys in the house for the car they used to leave the state."

"So why are you giving us this statement?"

Vazquez asked. Did Reiss expect a sentence reduction?

"No, that's not it. I just don't like the fact that these people had killed their own parents." He especially did not like the fact that the younger brother had been killed.

That ended the interview, which left Vazquez, and ultimately Steinberg, with a problem: despite the obvious discrepancies, there was enough truth in Reiss's statement that it could not be wholly discounted.

Maybe Benny had been in the process of preparing his lies and was trying the story out on Reiss. A lie always sounds more plausible with an element of truth in it.

All eyes now focused on the coming juvenile certification hearing. It was highly doubtful that Judge Brenner, an elected official, would throw the Freeman case into juvenile court. Political considerations aside, and they were many, the defense would have to present an overwhelming case for a change of court. Even in the Haworth case, where not only the defense psychiatrists but the prosecution psychiatrists said Haworth was amenable to treatment, the judge had refused to certify Haworth as a juvenile.

Under Pennsylvania State law, and a process called discovery, the defendants are entitled to read any statements the police have gathered which prove their guilt or innocence.

Steinberg made up those packages and sent them out to the lawyers.

Eighteen

September 5, 1995

It was now six months after the boys had been captured. David, shackled hand and foot, was led into Judge Brenner's courtroom by sheriff's deputies.

"He's lost weight," one reporter said to another.

"Yeah, looks like about forty pounds," answered the second reporter.

"I heard he told his lawyers that he missed his mother's cooking."

"Oh yeah? What's he gonna do now? Ask the court for mercy because he's an orphan?"

Sandy Lettich and her sister, Linda Solivan, stood back as David shuffled down the aisle toward the slatted railing. His eyes did not once drift to his aunts. They noticed that his red hair had gotten longer, covering his forehead tattoo, but he still had the red beard that made him look like a Viking.

After court was convened, David got to his feet and with Collins and Worth on either side, shuffled up to the bench. Brenner looked down from on high at the defendant.

"Mr. Freeman, when were you born?"

"February 9, 1979," David answered with his flat affect. "I'm sixteen years old."

"How far have you gotten in school?"

"I finished the ninth grade at Harry Truman High School and I was in the tenth grade at Salisbury High School."

"So you've gone as far as tenth grade?" the judge asked.

"Yes."

"Have you continued your education during your incarceration?"

"No."

The reporters wondered where the judge was going with his questions. This was supposed to be a juvenile certification hearing.

"Mr. Freeman, you are aware that to be judged a juvenile by the court, your attorneys would have to prove that you are amenable to treatment through the juvenile justice system?"

"Yes."

"You are aware that the court makes a determination of your mental capacity?"

"Yes."

"That the court takes into consideration the nature and circumstances of the alleged homicides, which could require lengthy incarceration?"

"Yes."

"All right. Now, Mr. Worth and Mr. Collins are your court-appointed counsels?"

"Yes."

"You've had sufficient time to consult with them?"

"Yes."

"They've informed you about the procedures for this hearing?"

"Yes."

"You are satisfied with their services?"

"Yes."

"Your honor," Wally Worth interrupted. "Mr. Collins and I met with the defendant many times."

"Good."

"Are you prepared to go forward today with the certification hearing?"

"Your honor," Wally answered, "we feel that is in the best interests of our client to withdraw our petition for juvenile certification."

"Is that accurate, Mr. Freeman?"

David didn't answer.

"Mr. Freeman?" the judge repeated.

"Yes," David answered

"You understand you would then face these charges as an adult?"

"Yes. I do."

"If this matter is tried with you as an adult, there is a presumption of innocence. You may be tried before a judge alone or at your option, before a jury of your peers who must render a unanimous verdict."

"I understand."

"During such a trial, your lawyers have the right to cross examine and the right to confront witnesses, to look 'em right in the eye. But if you are found guilty of murder in the first degree, then there is a separate penalty phase. The jury will then consider your sentence: death or life. Do you understand that?"

David was nervous, but he held it in and answered in an unwavering voice, "Yes."

"If the jury finds one or more aggravating circumstances, then the sentence could be death. Do you understand that?"

"Yes."

"Anyone make any threats or deals to make you give up certification?"

"No."

"Have you consumed any drugs or alcohol in the last twenty-four hours?"

"No."

"Your honor," Steinberg interjected, "the defendant has average intelligence. His IQ is over 100. He has the capacity to understand these proceedings. He has also been examined by a psychologist and a psychiatrist, and found competent to stand trial."

"Mr. Worth," Judge Brenner asked, "why are you not moving forward with certification?"

"We have our strategic reasons for doing this," Worth replied.

Judge Brenner looked down and began writing on the papers in front of him.

"The court finds the motion for withdrawal intelligent and voluntary. The motion is withdrawn."

It had been a surprise. David and his lawyers had elected to have him tried as an adult. While not stating the reason publicly, privately, Worth and Collins figured there was little chance of the judge kicking the case into juvenile court. Worse, at the certification hearing, they would have had to lay out their trial case, including expert opinions about David's troubled family background and how it had led him to participate in the murders. In effect, they'd be giving Steinberg a free peek at their trial defense.

No way were they going to lay out their case for the prosecution. If anyone wanted to find out what had made David do it, they'd have to wait for trial.

Downstairs at the press conference, Worth and Collins simply reiterated that they had decided for "strategic reasons" to remove their petition. They wouldn't elaborate. But they were willing to talk about David's actions on the night prior to the murders.

"There's no question he'd been drinking," Wally asserted, as the press huddled around him and video cameras were pressed into his face. "The father drank. That's why alcohol was in the house since he was six."

For his part, Steinberg told the press the only alcohol in the house was the bottle of Chivas that Dennis had bought to celebrate Valerie's marriage. It had remained unopened.

Responding to questions about David's demeanor, Wally said, "He kept asking me, 'How long will it be in court? How long will it be?' "

"Why'd he say that?" a reporter asked.

Wally smiled. "Because he said, 'I want to go back and watch the cartoons.' He thinks as a *kid.* He follows other people. He certainly follows his brother and cousin."

And then Wally put a little spin on his client's background in placement.

"You know, he got three citizenship awards. He won them at the Paradise School."

As for his incriminating statement to the Michigan State police, Wally said, "The Michigan police officers didn't give a damn about the alcohol and marijuana he'd used prior to being captured. It certainly diminished his abilities."

Attempting to mount further public support for his client, Wally continued, speaking about "certain religious disciplines" David had to adhere to. "His faith barred him from celebrating holidays, or even his birthday. He was not allowed to have kids of other faiths in his home. His parents wouldn't allow it. David looked up to the military, but he was barred by his religious teachings from serving in the armed forces."

All of this encouraged his rebellious attitude toward his parents, and then, when his parents had trouble controlling him, "They put him in an institution."

Steinberg countered that David Freeman was far from a good citizen. He was an evil kid who had killed his parents, and he was going to pay for it.

Shortly thereafter, Bryan's lawyers also removed their petition for juvenile certification for the same reasons. They were all headed for trial. The lawyers were banking on Judge Brenner ruling that since the Freeman brothers gave statements that were "truthful," Steinberg could not obviate their agreement to take the death penalty off the table. They also figured there was a chance that the judge would throw out the boys' statements because they were underage and did not have adequate counsel when they confessed.

At least, that's what they hoped. If they were wrong, there was no guarantee that Steinberg would still be there with his offer. The brothers, who liked being together, might have to face the death chamber together.

Upstairs in his office, Steinberg took out the *Death Book*, the book of parricide and neo-Nazi clippings that Bryan had compiled, and the note Brenda had written to document her discovery of it. What was even more curious than the *Death Book* itself was why Brenda Freeman had felt the need to write a note authenticating her grisly find.

Brenda must have felt her death at the hands of her children was imminent. If that were so, she wanted to leave something behind that showed their intent.

The *Death Book* showed that either or both boys were contemplating murder before the actual event. And if a jury saw it that way, they would have no choice but to convict them of premeditated first-degree murder.

November 13, 1995

All the lawyers were back in court for the most crucial phase of the case. Supplee and Brunnabend for Bryan, and Worth and Collins for David, would argue that Steinberg had reneged on his agreement regarding the death penalty. If they won, the prosecution might have to make a deal, because there is never any guarantee of conviction, even if there is a confession. If the brothers lost, they, in turn, might be anxious to accede to Steinberg's deal to avoid the death penalty.

The Michigan cops who had taken David and Bryan's statements, Mynesberge and Harms, testified to what the brothers had said to them. Norman Donker, the Midland County prosecutor, testified to the circumstances under which the statements were given and the plea agreement that was put on tape and sealed with evidence tape. Trooper Joe Vazquez gave testimony as to his involvement in the case, and how he had gone to Michigan to question the boys.

The hearing, which was supposed to last one day, stretched into two. The whole thing was becoming a lengthy, drawn-out process. The judge, for one, felt there was a better way.

In chambers, Judge Brenner told Bob Steinberg to make a deal. "I might as well jump out an eight story window," Steinberg replied.

"With Wally Worth representing David Freeman, you might as well jump out a fifteen story window," Brenner countered.

Steinberg, though, was right: if he made a deal now, it was political suicide. What's more, the people in the county, whose passions had been inflamed by the case, did not seem willing to settle for a reduced sentence.

The district attorney was between a rock and a hard place.

November 14, 1995

In the back row of the courtroom sat a mysterious man with a face like a prune. He carefully took notes in a little notebook throughout the day's proceedings. He identified himself as a Jehovah's Witness who knew the Freeman family. When asked if the notes he was taking would be delivered to the JW congregation in Salisbury for inclusion in their permanent files, his terse reply was, "No comment." Asked if he knew why Dennis Freeman had resigned four years before as an Elder, he replied again, "No comment," though a little smile played on his lips.

Throughout the first day of the hearing, a young man sat in the front row of the courtroom. He had a close-cropped haircut and big hands. No one noticed him until Brian Collins rose and said, "The defense calls Frank Hesse."

Frank Hesse was the skinhead who the brothers had hid out with in Michigan. He was being called as a defense witness.

Hesse had a good memory. He recounted how Bryan had called him from the road and said he'd be in the neighborhood, and how he, Frank, had invited him and his brother and cousin up to visit. He recounted their activities during the day, everything up to the time they were captured. His most relevant testimony for the defense was that in the day and a half they'd stayed with him, David was drunk on beer and stoned on marijuana much of the time, giving credence to the defense's contention that when David gave his statement to the Michigan police, he was under the influence and therefore that statement, the most incriminating one he gave, should be thrown out.

After Frank left the stand, he was followed outside by a phalanx of reporters who wanted to interview him further about his skinhead beliefs and what the boys had said to him. Frank was polite, though most of the questions he was asked were only tangential, such as "When you hunt, what do you prefer—bow and arrow, or rifle?"

"What does that have to do with this case?" Frank asked.

It was raining outside, and Frank, wanting to get to the airport to get a flight home, got a ride from a reporter. On the way, he spoke about the case and his beliefs.

Of Benny he said, "He was a loudmouth." Considering what Benny was accused of doing, "It scares me in light of later facts that I put a loaded assault rifle in the hands of that braggart."

Frank hastily reiterated his testimony: when Bryan called him from Pennsylvania, he didn't at first remember him from the New Year's Eve concert they had attended together. When he remembered, Bryan said, "Listen we're here in Ohio, off Route 80, and we were thinking, you know, of going up to Detroit and seeing what's happening there."

"How did you reply?" the reporter asked.

"I said, 'Well, stop by for a beer.' "

To Frank, they were his brothers in the skinhead movement. He could not deny them his hospitality. But had he known what they had done, it would have been a different story.

"What they did is horrible, awful," Frank said. "And one thing you never, ever do is kill kin if you're a skinhead. All the skinheads I know would love five minutes with those guys. Those guys set our movement back. What they did has nothing to do with the skinhead movement."

Frank, who was born and raised in Iron Mountain, Michigan, explained that he is a white separatist. He basically believes in the voluntary separation of the races.

"There are two different types of skins—rural and urban. Rural skinheads, like me, read a lot and watch and wait. I'll be ready if the government comes after me." But rural skins do not believe in violence, he says, as opposed to urban skins, who, because of their close proximity to urban conditions, are more prone to violence and confrontation.

"I believe in working within the system to change it," Frank continued, as the rain came down and the windshield wipers beat back and forth.

He waved goodbye and ran into the airport terminal, back to Michigan and armed readiness.

Back at the courthouse, Bob Donohue testified. He was the Michigan attorney who'd brokered the plea arrangement with Steinberg and he testified as to how it came about and what the plea said. After his testimony, the judge recessed for the day.

Outside the courtroom, Donohue was angry. He had never seen anything like it. Here he'd brokered a deal to save these boy's lives and they were taking the whole thing apart! What the hell was going on?

Right from the outset, both David and Bryan said they wanted to plead. They wanted the deal. They never wanted to go to trial. And yet when they got back to Pennsylvania, all of a sudden their lawyers were finding ways of maneuvering them out of the deal.

How on earth could you do this deal, public defenders Supplee and Brunnabend wondered? Donohue got furious. What was this, a game to these guys?

"If you don't think these two kids could lose their lives, you're sadly mistaken. You don't believe for a minute someone will impose the death penalty given the political climate. Let me tell you something.

"You all want the same thing, don't you? To save their lives! Those boys vigorously delivered on their agreement, and that agreement has to be honored!"

By the next morning, the rain had cleared out and Donohue was on a plane back to Michigan. The hearing concluded at noon, with Judge Brenner saying he would soon rule on the matters before him.

Back in jail, David and Bryan were worried. If the judge ruled against them, they would face death.

Nineteen

December 7, 1995

Bryan Freeman got up early. He shaved and showered and put on his blue prison jumpsuit. He parted his hair on the side and combed his beard and mustache. His youthful, unlined forehead was speckled with pimples.

A van picked him up and transported him the few blocks to the depths of the Lehigh County Courthouse. In shackles and chains, he was taken up in a private elevator to Judge Brenner's third-floor courtroom. He entered the packed courtroom and took his seat next to his attorneys, Earl Supplee and Mike Brunnabend. After the judge came in and court was convened, Bryan marched up to the bench with his lawyers.

"Mr. Freeman, have you twice been hospitalized for mental illness?"

"Yes."

"Can you read, write and understand English?"

"Yes."

"I understand you wish to enter a plea?"

"Yes, Your Honor," Bryan responded in the hushed, crowded courtroom.

"Did you kill your mother?" Brenner asked.

"Yes, I did," Bryan answered.

"Do you have any doubts about admitting to murdering your mother and accepting a sentence of life in prison?"

"I have no reservations."

"Then I sentence you, Bryan Freeman, for the murder of your mother, Brenda Freeman, to life in prison without parole."

The deal, which had come together in the previous few days, did not require Bryan to testify against David or Benny.

Brunnabend told the press after the hearing that he and Supplee had considered negotiating a plea bargain for weeks, but had decided to pursue it after a meeting on Sunday.

"We gave him a chance at life," Brunnabend said.

Steinberg, meanwhile, defended his decision to take the plea bargain.

"There's no guarantees that a jury would impose the death penalty nor that it would be carried out. There are certain punishments worse than death. Sentencing a seventeen-year-old to life behind bars is one of them."

Upon hearing of the deal, Wally Worth immediately responded that he had discussed possible deals with Steinberg but insisted he would not agree to one in which David plead to first-degree murder. "David's a follower," Wally maintained. "His history of emotional problems lessened his culpability in the crimes."

Richard Makoul, Benny's attorney, was surprised

by the plea arrangement but said it wouldn't affect Birdwell's case.

"You only plea bargain when you're guilty," Makoul told the press.

After Bryan's plea, Brian Collins was called down to the jail. His client, David Freeman, wanted to see him.

"I want the same deal as my brother," he told Collins. He didn't want to go through with a trial; he just wanted things over with.

Collins and Worth tried to convince David to hang in there. They felt they could do better for him than murder one and life in prison. David, though, wanted to be together with his brother.

The attorneys explained that no one could guarantee that, not even Steinberg. That was up to the guy who headed the prison system. David didn't care. He wanted it over with—now!

December 15, 1995

Brian Collins stood on one side of David, Wally Worth on the other. Judge Brenner went through the same basic set of questions he'd asked Bryan the week before.

Did he understand what he was doing? Yes.

Did he read, write and speak English? Yes.

"Did you kill your father?" Brenner asked.

"Yes, I did," David said.

"Why?"

David thought for a moment. "I don't know," he replied.

Sitting in the visitors' section, Brenda Freeman's sisters, Linda Solivan and Sandy Lettich, looked at their nephew.

They knew.

February 22, 1996

It was early morning. The phone rang. The reporter let it ring a couple of times and then, half awake, picked it up. An automated voice told him he had a collect call from David Freeman. He accepted the charges and then a low voice with a flat affect came on the line.

"Hello, this is David Freeman. You wrote me a letter."

"How ya doin', Dave?"

"Pretty good. I got your letter about interviewing me."

"Uh huh."

"It'll cost you."

"Oh, really? How much?"

"More than ten thousand." He chuckled.

"Well, David, I'm not in the habit of paying for information."

He chuckled again. David Freeman continued to talk.

"I should be leaving next month some time."

"Where you going?"

"The prison at Matahoy."

"Are you with your brother?"

"Not in here, but he got classified to Matahoy, too."

"At least you'll be in the same place."

"Yeah."

"You know, I don't think you should have pleaded. You had a good shot at murder three."

"The way I look at it, one's better than three."

He offered no further explanation. He would have the rest of his life to figure it out.

April 3, 1996

It was during a phone conversation with Brian Collins that the reporter discovered Bob Steinberg's oversight.

Through a source, he had gotten a hold of a complete set of interviews that the police had done with all the relevant players. He had assumed that since he had the complete set, so did Collins. After all, Steinberg had to turn everything over to the defense during discovery that could prove the defendant's guilt or innocence.

As he discussed the jailhouse statements of Todd Reiss, who claimed that Benny had told him that David had not killed his father, the line got ominously silent.

"Brian, you still there?"

A long pause.

"That's the first time I ever heard about that statement."

He called his colleague, Wally Worth. Worth hadn't heard about it, either.

They both went through the discovery packets Steinberg had supplied them with. The statement was not included; their conclusion was that Steinberg had never supplied it.

Wally Worth was furious. "That statement contradicts the prosecution's case. No matter how cockeyed a jailhouse statement may be, it certainly doesn't warrant the court allowing a plea bargain of first-degree murder. Third is more like it. We never ever would have let him plead guilty to first-degree murder if we knew that statement existed."

They might go to Judge Brenner with a copy of the police report and tell him Steinberg had deliberately not included it in the discovery packet because it exculpated David. Brenner had the power to set aside the verdict and order a new trial.

To make matters worse, David and Bryan were cooling their heels in the Lehigh County Prison right down the street. Steinberg had brought them in to testify against Benny. But neither brother wished to comply. Why should they? What was Steinberg offering in return?

"You drag us into court, we'll plead the fifth," the brothers told Steinberg.

Richard Makoul knew that Ben Birdwell had a big chance of being convicted of the first-degree murder of Dennis Freeman. Despite telling the media that Steinberg had a weak circumstantial case, privately he knew better.

There was the blood spatter on his T-shirt. Prosecution experts would claim that it showed beyond a shadow of a doubt that Ben had been close enough to Dennis to have beaten him with the ax handle. As to his character, he'd be shown at trial by the prosecution's psychiatrists that he was the next coming of Hannibal Lecter.

Given all the pretrial publicity, most of the public already was eager to see Benny killed by lethal injection. Finding a totally impartial jury in Lehigh County was impossible. The only break he got was that the presiding judge, James Diefenderfer, disallowed Steinberg from introducing any evidence of Benny's participation in the skinhead movement. "That would be inflammatory," the judge said.

Despite this ruling, Makoul was still in a dire circumstance.

Makoul knew what was really on the line—the boy's life. Whether he'd done it or not, Makoul was determined to keep him out of the death chamber. Steinberg, he knew, would do *everything*, to get him there.

Makoul's defense would be this. First, Benny was a dullard, or more precisely, his IQ of 78 proved he was mildly retarded. He was barely capable of comprehending the events transpiring that night.

Second, after witnessing the murders, Benny had suffered from an acute anxiety disorder. Fearful his cousins might kill him, he was so stressed out that he'd accompanied them on the run to Michigan.

"You can't allow this mind science to permeate this courtroom," Steinberg told Judge Diefenderfer at a pre-trial hearing. Makoul's experts believed Birdwell's version of events. Allowing their testimony took away the jury's "right and function of deciding the defendant's credibility."

"No, Your Honor," Makoul shouted in the courtroom. "If Mr. Steinberg has his way, simply the appearance of being at a crime scene will be punishable by a conviction. The court has to allow the defendant's constitutional right to a fair trial. And that right can only be upheld if you allow the testimony of our experts."

"If the type of testimony defense counsel seeks to present is admitted, we might as well do away with the jury system and let psychiatrists and/or psychologists decide credibility," Steinberg countered. "While much has been written on the role of emotions in patterns of human behavior and in the causation of crimes, at best, a courtroom makes an awkward psychiatrist's couch.

"Does a psychiatrist know what a defendant was feeling? Did he have an intent to kill when his acts would cause the death of another?"

On Friday, March 15, Judge Diefenderfer ruled that Makoul would be allowed to introduce the reports from shrinks that stated Benny had suffered from acute stress disorder after witnessing the crimes.

Makoul had his defense.

Twenty

Jury selection in the trial of Nelson Benjamin Birdwell III on the charges of conspiracy to commit first-degree murder and the first-degree murders of Dennis, Brenda, and Erik Freeman began on the morning of March 25, 1996, in the third-floor courtroom of Chief Judge James N. Diefenderfer at 9 A.M.

For the next nine days, Makoul and Steinberg questioned potential jurors one by one as they were brought in from the jury room. Steinberg did as he'd promised: he death qualified the jury. Each and every juror was asked whether, if he found Benny guilty, he could impose the death penalty, if asked. All the jurors answered "yes."

For his part, Makoul tried to choose jurors who would not, in his words, be snowed by the mountain of evidence he anticipated Steinberg would throw at them. He looked for compassionate, intelligent people who wouldn't be swayed by prosecution or media rhetoric.

After they questioned 118 potential jurors, 12 were chosen, and 4 alternates. Steinberg said that only twenty of the 118 people questioned said they couldn't be objective because they had firm opinions that Birdwell was guilty. As Allentown was a small town, some had actually known Dennis and Brenda. They had been rejected.

As to pretrial publicity affecting the jury's verdict, "People in their ordinary lives don't pay as much attention to these things as we do, and we tend to overreact to what the public is paying attention to," Steinberg told the media, at one of his noontime press conferences.

Makoul was still concerned that given, the vast amount of pretrial publicity, Benny wouldn't get a fair trial in the county. But there was nothing he could do about it. The judge had refused a venue change. The jury had been picked, nine women and three men, ranging in age from their thirties through their forties, representing a cross section of society, including a customer service representative, a housewife, a financial analyst, and a computer analyst.

Together, in the coming weeks, they would decide Ben Birdwell's guilt or innocence, and whether he would live or die. His grandfather, though, had one or two things to say on the matter.

On April 4, Nelson Birdwell sent the following letter to his daughters.

April 4, 1996

Dear Sandra & Linda:

Our family has experienced some terrible things in the past year. Once, it was thought of as a model family. Perhaps, it wasn't a model family even then. I understand now, there have been some terrible things happening for a long time. I believe the worst is yet to come.

Legally, up to this time, there's only one way to view Ben's case. No one can declare him anything but innocent and everyone should hope he is innocent. The law says he is innocent until proven guilty. Everyone should view the evidence carefully before they find him guilty. Allow the uninhibited evidence to speak for or against him.

You two well know what the rules were when God exercised sovereignty over the nation of Israel. Two eye-witnesses were required before a person could be put to death. And, in the case of stoning a person to death, the two eye-witnesses had to cast the first stone.

God ceased to exercise sovereignty over that nation for two reasons: 1) First. He did it to allow that difficult nation be disciplined; 2) Second, He selected the judge [over] the sovereign nations in their conduct. Allow them to prove whether they would regretfully take a life or to politically misuse the office for selfish gain and to learn if they did indeed feel regret that they had to take such drastic measures.

God's requirements, in exercising justice in behalf of humankind, didn't lessen any. He simply placed the duties in different hands. You can rest assure that His requirements didn't change since He made it a point to say, "I change not." He no longer intervenes in the affairs of humans except to make sure "The Word" is fulfilled.

To determine one's guilt, before one is found guilty by the evidence, is to bring God's judgment upon oneself. "The judgment with which you judge is the same judgment from which you will be judged." I would shiver for everyone involved if one is found on circumstantial evidence and indeed his life is taken—alive or dead.

Love,
Pa

April 9, 1996
Opening Statements

Robert Steinberg, representing the people of Lehigh County and the Commonwealth of Pennsylvania, rose to address the jury and a packed courtroom.

"Nelson Benjamin Birdwell III was an active participant. He was no spectator. This is about a gang of three that committed mass murder," he began.

Steinberg went on to summarize evidence he characterized as massive, but which really consisted of Dennis's blood on Benny's T-shirt. Steinberg also pointed out the inconsistencies in Benny's statements to police as evidence of his guilt.

It was a weak case, built totally on circumstantial evidence, but convictions have been had with less, and at least in front of the jury, Steinberg remained confident that they would see things his way and convict Benny of first-degree murder.

"What was his motive to kill? He never had any problem or conflict with them whatsoever," Dick Makoul began. "I want to know what the prosecution thinks the motive was."

Of course, the prosecution hadn't presented one. By law, they didn't have to in order to gain a conviction.

Makoul, who had formulated his opening argument while standing on a jetty at his seaside home in New Jersey over the weekend, pointed out that his client was borderline mentally retarded, only a *witness* to the murders, nothing more. As to the blood on his T-shirt, the blood in Dennis's room was spattered up to ten feet from the body. "Anybody who walked into that room for an instant, even just to see what was going on, could have gotten that much blood on them. Why was there so much blood everywhere else, but a small amount on him?"

The inference was that he had walked in while David was killing Dennis and had been innocently spattered.

"He had acute stress trauma brought on by the horror of what he had seen; coupled with a low IQ of 78, that impaired his decision-making," Makoul maintained, which explained Benny's decision to run with the brothers.

After the opening statements were concluded, Steinberg put on the stand Officer Pochron, who had found the bodies with his partner, Officer Renninger, who also testified.

After the day's proceedings, Steinberg held his post court press conference downstairs. When asked if the brothers would testify, Steinberg said, "Probably not. There has been some interference by a family member, and in all likelihood, neither brother will take the stand."

He didn't bother to explain until the next day that the brothers had been in Allentown for two weeks.

As to the family member who'd "interfered," it was clearly their grandfather, Nelson Birdwell, who held his own impromptu press conference in the courthouse lobby.

Birdwell told the assembled throng that he didn't feel Benny was guilty. As to Steinberg's "interference" charge, Dan Kelly, a reporter for the *Reading Eagle,* discovered that Birdwell was depositing money into all three grandsons' prison accounts and that he had established an 800 number they could call whenever they wanted to talk with him.

What was left unsaid was the possible result if the brothers testified against their cousin. Their grandfather, their only contact with the outside world, could cut off all contact with them, and freeze his contribution to their prison bank account, which allowed them to buy small luxuries in prison.

April 10, 1996

Jesse Capece testified about David, Bryan, and Ben's stopover after the crimes at the Truck World

Motor Inn, in Ohio, where she worked. Under Steinberg's patient direct examination, she explained that it was Bryan who'd actually checked in, under Ben's name. She also testified that they had lied about their license plate number.

Next to the stand came a clerk in the motel variety store who recalled seeing Birdwell buy a pair of jeans, bolstering the prosecution's claim that he threw the ones he'd worn at the time of the crime, soiled with blood, out the car window in Ohio.

Greg Pavledes, the desk clerk at the Holiday Inn in Michigan, testified that Birdwell checked into his establishment under the name "Mike Burr," and that David and Birdwell paid $66.68 for the room in one- and five-dollar bills.

Suspicious about the way they'd paid, the clerk had called the police, who'd come to the motel, checked out the boys, and made no arrests.

April 11, 1996

The jurors listened to the twenty minute audiotaped statement Birdwell had given the Michigan cops in which he'd declared his innocence in the murderers of Dennis, Brenda, and Erik, and implicated his cousins David and Bryan.

Eight days after the taped statement, Ben had called a girl he knew in the Allentown area. "He told me he was hiding in a closet," she testified.

During his cross, Makoul kept trying to show that Ben had no reason to kill the Freemans, while David and Bryan did. Steinberg, in turn, tried to show the jury that Birdwell's statement was designed to throw suspicion off himself

April 12, 1996

Dr. Barbara Rowley, of the state police crime lab, told the jury of her analyses of the victims' blood.

With charts on easels facing the jury, Dr. Rowley described the genetic markers found in blood. Then she went on to describe the blood on Ben's T-shirt.

"I counted eighty tiny specks of blood, some that were so small they could only be seen under ultraviolet light."

"And whose blood was it on Ben Birdwell's T-shirt?" Steinberg asked.

"Dennis Freeman's."

Rowley said small drops of blood can't travel far, bolstering the prosecution's claim that Birdwell was on one side of Dennis's bed and David the other and both were beating him to death.

April 15, 1996

Christine Tomsey, the DNA laboratory manager for the state police in Greensburg, Pennsylvania, and Dr. Harold Deadman, a retired FBI man, bolstered the prosecution's case by testifying that the pickax handle had a mixture of Brenda and Erik's blood, and possibly Dennis's. This fit in neatly with

the prosecution's theory that Ben had wielded it
to finish off all three victims.

Dennis's blood was also found on an aluminum
baseball bat and a pair of soiled jeans and T-shirt,
allegedly left by David in the house after the murders. Also, a green Philadelphia Eagles jersey was
stained with Bryan's blood. The prosecution con-
tended that he'd cut himself when he'd stabbed
his mother.

Testimony about Bryan and David's presence at
the scene of the crime was irrelevant to Ben's guilt
or innocence, but by tying Ben in with them at
the scene of the crime, Steinberg knew their guilt
could rub off on Ben and lead to the conviction
he was seeking.

That night, Nelson Birdwell sat down and wrote
his grandson Bryan the following letter.

April 15, 1996

Bryan:
    Opportunity is knocking at your door! Will
you answer it?
    This is your opportunity to get your case re-
opened with emphasis on the medical aspect
rather than the criminal. I will get you a lawyer, not a public defender and with the medical records and the publicity that is needed,
hopefully, we can turn the tide.
    We can have a representative of the press or
more than one. We will air the interviews by
satellite to about ten local television stations

and newspapers at the same time. The interview will consist of the press, you, Mr. Bo and me. We will be well prepared.

Both David and you are losers at this point in time. The D.A. commented after your sentence. He said a life sentence for a 17 or 18 year old is worse than death.

Your lawyers stood by and watched Steinburg offer you a plea bargain that was full of loopholes while they sat on your medical records and didn't come to your rescue. I would like to see you fire your lawyers right on television.

If we attempted to get your case re-opened, they would try to prevent it. But if we create a big scene, they will automatically re-open it. That is why I feel that now is the opportune time. We have a chance right now to blow the current trial away and re-open yours at the same time, along with discrediting Steinberg, the judge and the court system all.

With the proper publicity, we will get justice for you both. Every person is guaranteed by the Constitution, to a speedy jury trial. They railroaded you both and you didn't get a fair shake. Don't fear a jury trial! With your medical records and the fact that you were juveniles, you only stand a chance of bettering yourselves. They dare not sentence a juvenile to death.

Bryan, this is the greatest opportunity you will ever have again. Don't pass it up. You can prevent another innocent person to your blame. At the same time, get public attention with opportunity to get free sooner.

Call me on this soon.

Love,
Pa

P.S.

Bryan, I am asking you to testify for the defense in Ben's trial if you can truthfully say:

"Ben saw it all only because I ordered him to be there, on the threat of his life."

"Ben had no part of what happened at Ehrets Lane on February 26, 1995."

"The tape of March 5, 1995 was made to hurt Ben because he ratted on Dave and me."

For justice sake, this must take place!

April 16, 1996

Voodoo forensics: that was the only way to describe Dr. Barbara Rowley's subsequent testimony.

Steinberg called Rowley to the stand to testify as to how far the blood of Dennis Freeman could have spattered onto Ben's shirt. If it was a good distance, it would seem to prove Makoul's initial claim that Ben was in the room, standing back, and did nothing. If it was a short distance, Steinberg's contention would be proved.

"I set a piece of wood vertically on the floor and put plastic over it with a thin layer of horse blood. I set poster board and T-shirts on cardboard boxes at various distances from the wood, and then beat the top of the wood with a baseball bat to observe the patterns the blood made on the shirts and poster boards," Rowley testified, as explanation of her blood-spatter experiment.

The jury listened intently to her testimony, but most impartial observers in the courtroom thought it sounded unscientific. On cross, Makoul got her to admit that in beating wood, not flesh, she was testing wood's different tensile strength, and the force she used probably was less than that used by the Freeman brothers, who were stronger than she was, not to mention the fact that she was not using the same exact weapon as the ones that had killed Dennis Freeman.

April 17, 1996

Bob Steinberg put the jailhouse informant, Ivan Smith, on the stand.

Smith testified that Birdwell told him about the murders and how he felt about them while both were incarcerated at the Lehigh County Jail.

Smith said Birdwell smiled when he talked about the murders and didn't show sympathy for the victims. "He told me that the older brother [Bryan] was the mastermind of the whole thing."

Birdwell told Smith that he knew something like the murders was going to go down because Bryan had once forced his mother against a wall and held a knife to her neck.

Smith said Birdwell told him that on their way home from the movies, they were listening to skin-head rock with the message to Kill everybody.

"They talked about the murder, and they planned it out, what they were gonna do," Smith said.

Birdwell told Smith that he saw Brenda get killed. He showed no remorse.

"He said the two brothers did it, not him, and they were not sorry afterward. He said, 'They deserved it.'"

Makoul scoffed at Smith's testimony. "Why would Birdwell confide in you, a stranger? You're not his friend!"

Smith had no real answer.

Makoul got Smith to testify that in a statement Smith gave to a detective, he did not say that Birdwell admitted killing anyone.

Next was Dr. Isidore Mihalikis, the forensic pathologist, who duplicated most of his testimony from the hearing a year before. Mihalikis testified to the cause of death of the three victims. Mihalikis testified that the attackers had used different weapons, one for each of the three boys, including Ben.

Makoul tried to show that David had used two weapons, freeing Ben of guilt. But Mihalikis didn't agree with that theory and stuck to his guns.

Three weapons. Three assailants. David, Bryan, and Ben.

April 18, 1996

Steinberg took the day to tie up loose ends in his case by calling the lead investigators in the case, Trooper Joe Vazquez and Detective Ken Metzler, who implicated Ben as being part of the murder and its conspiracy. Then the prosecution rested.

"I'm very satisfied with the way all the witnesses testified," Steinberg told the press at the conclusion of his case. He was standing in front of microphones, with the flags of the state and the nation as his backdrop in the rear of the Lehigh County Courthouse, that had been set up for the press conferences.

"He hasn't proven it," Richard Makoul countered a moment later, taking his place in front of the flags. "It's total confusion," Makoul added, in characterizing Steinberg's case.

April 19, 1996

Makoul opened the defense's case by calling witness after witness to testify that while the Freeman brothers repeatedly threatened their parents prior to the murders, none could ever recall Ben making such threats.

Although Makoul tried to show that Birdwell had no motive to kill the Freemans, some of the defense witnesses didn't appear to help his case when questioned under Steinberg's strong cross examination.

"Ben might have been the leader. He may have had influence over David and Bryan," said Maryann Galton, who had worked with Bryan and Ben at Wendy's.

Bob Zelinski testified that Bryan had pushed him

during a confrontation and that when Bryan had started hitting him, Ben had joined in.

Hal Jordan told Steinberg that Bryan said he was mad at his parents and wanted them dead.

Many of the youngsters testified that all three teens dressed alike and had the same skinhead haircuts. Steinberg's implication was obvious.

They dressed alike.

The looked alike.

They killed alike.

Sitting at the defense table, Makoul squirmed. He had called these kids to be his witnesses, and Steinberg was turning their testimony against his client. As much as he tried to separate Ben from the brothers, Steinberg kept reeling him back in.

To others, it might have appeared that only Birdwell was on trial, but to Makoul, he knew that the Freeman brothers were seated with him at the empty chairs at the defense table.

April 20, 1996

It was a day off for the jury but not for Nelson Birdwell. Pen in hand, he wrote his grandson Ben:

Ben!

I can halfway imagine how you must feel, sitting there innocent of the charges, and legally innocent until proven guilty, in chains, with all eyes focused on you and the confused press writing their mixed emotions.

I am writing this for two reasons: 1) to strengthen you to face the foe: 2) to entertain those would-be mail fraud, law-breakers that tamper with your mail. The cowards, cheats, clowns that are participating in the big carnival at courtroom #3.

These hypocrites will bring you down the corridor, hobbling in chains, rushing you along to save face before the jury arrives. They can't allow the jury to see you in chains. They are pretending to the jury that this isn't happening.

However, this is perhaps the only jury *ever* to live at home, watch the evening news, see you hobbling down the corridor, and next morning go down to the coffee shop and read the newspaper while drinking their coffee. I understand from the new rules that will be imposed on the jury after your trial is over, will change this. They will get strict again.

Ben, the God of Heaven not only sees their hypocritical pretense, but he can read their evil thoughts and the intent of their rotten hearts. Let me share my faith with you that these hypocrites will not escape. They are simply selecting their own judgment.

God often allows one to select one's own destiny by what that one sought for another.

Ben, Mr. Bo and I so far have been able to defend ourselves against that prosecution-blonde attending to your mourning aunts and the pretending public servants, *but* more accurately said, court stooges who wear badges and guns, only because we are law abiding. They would like to throw us out, but dare not because the public is present.

Oh!, how I wish we had freedom of press. I wish the cameras were in the courtroom to hold these people in line, but with a dictatorship as we have, they can escape human punishment and blame.

Ben, I feel better expressing myself. I hope you do as well. Also, we entertained our guest. Head High!

> Love,
> Pa

April 22, 1996

Makoul called to the stand psychologist Dr. Peter Badgio and psychiatrist Dr. Peter Bloom. Between them they testified to the heart of the defense's case.

The traumatic events of the Freemans' deaths triggered in Birdwell acute stress disorder, and that had forced him to flee with the brothers, because he feared they would hurt him. That explained why he didn't do what an innocent man would have under the same circumstances: call the police.

According to the test results, and adding to Benny's confusion, was an IQ of 78, which they characterized as "borderline mentally retarded." Both doctors said the disorder could be triggered by a traumatic event such as war, a plane crash—or murder.

Under cross, Bloom acquiesced that stress disorder tests ideally should be given within a few weeks of the traumatic event for best results, not almost a year later, as in Ben's case. In addition, Steinberg raked the experts' qualifications over the coals; neither, it came out, had testified before in a criminal case. Bloom had never even evaluated anyone charged with a crime.

"Do you think it is important to consider that after the murders, Mr. Birdwell and the brothers checked into a motel and Mr. Birdwell signed a false name on a registration card?" Steinberg asked Bloom. "Do you think he forgot his name?"

Bloom said he couldn't explain Ben's behavior, but that it was a sign of the disorder.

"Maybe he was just trying to deceive the police. Isn't that a reasonable interpretation?" Steinberg countered.

April 23, 1996

"Carol Russell," Makoul began.

A bleached blonde, Russell was Nelson Birdwell Jr.'s girlfriend. Ben had been driving her car the night of the murders. The police discovered that shortly thereafter, the seat covers had been changed. Police theorized that the reason was that they were bloodied. Steinberg had brought this up during his opening statement. In addition, there had been the matter of the jeans Ben had bought at the Ohio truck stop which the prosecution alleged were to take the place of the jeans Ben had dumped out of the car. With Russell's testimony, Makoul was seeking to counter both contentions.

Russell testified that she recognized the jeans Ben was wearing when he was caught. She did the wash for the family, and she could tell those jeans were not new but had been washed.

She also testified that weeks prior to the murders, she herself had removed the car's driver's seat cover because it was dirty. A friend then took the stand and said she was at an Allentown car wash when the cover was removed and thrown away by Russell prior to the murders.

Outside the jury's presence, various machinations were occurring. Nelson Birdwell's letter to Bryan, that asked him to testify "truthfully" that Ben had not been involved in the murders, was intercepted by prison authorities in a standard review of inmates' mail; it never got to Bryan. It wound up on Steinberg's desk.

The district attorney was furious. The old man was trying to ruin his case, not to mention tampering with a witness. He contemplated charges, then decided against them. The trial had already alienated family members, with Birdwell senior and junior on one side, and Sandy Lettich, Linda Solivan, and Valerie Freeman on the other. (Birdwell never spoke to his daughters; they never spoke to him).

Sandy and Linda believed in Ben's guilt and wanted him to go away for life. He was an agent of the devil; the Birdwells thought of him more as an angel.

Clearly the family had been ripped apart by the blood crimes. That night, Nelson Birdwell sent another letter. This time, it was to Linda.

April 23, 1996

Linda:

I am sending you a copy of the letter mailed to Bryan on 4/15/96, which he never received. They shipped him out on Thursday, 4/18/96. Bryan called me today, Tuesday, 4/23/96 and said: "I never received your letter of 4/15/96."

You called me around 5:00 P.M. on Wednesday, 4/17/96, in which time you said your brother, Nelson Jr. (Mr. Bo) and I, your father, are both from the Devil. At the same time, you accused me of asking Bryan to be a witness for the defense.

Bryan also called me on Wednesday evening about two hours after you did and informed me that he had not, at that time, received my letter. I am very interested to learn just how you came to know what I had written to Bryan since the letter was still in the mail route.

The Federal Law of mail fraud may permit a prison system to examine mail to ascertain if it contained metal objects or drugs, but I feel certain that the Federal Legislature didn't give the prison authorities the liberty to confiscate the person's mail and share this with an outsider.

I'm sure, if you were called on to tell how you came into this knowledge, you would be more than happy to do so. This is how I taught you in life—to be honest and truthful and never become a party to the hurt of an innocent person.

This act reflects a good number of the stated things that the God we know hates. Prov. 6:16 N.W.T. (16) "There are six things that Jehovah hates; yes, seven are the things detestable to his soul; (17) 1) lofty eyes, 2) a false tongue, and 3) hands that are shedding innocent blood, (18) 4) a heart fabricating hurtful schemes, 5) feet that are in a hurry to run to badness, (19) 6) a false witness that launches forth lies, and 7) anyone sending forth contentions among brothers."

I feel certain that you must realize by now that you are supporting the wrong side of something that is dirty business and getting you more and more involved.

I feel sorry for you.

Love,
Your father, Nelson

April 24, 1996

For the twelfth day in a row, Benny was led out of the basement bullpen in the Lehigh County Courthouse. Shackled and chained, he trudged along, an innocent expression on his angelic face, his hair long now, down to his collar. Wearing an inexpensive gray suit, he looked like an average teenager with time on his hands.

At that moment, Benny's father was speculating on why the murders had occurred. "David and Bryan, their parents gave them too much freedom," he told a reporter. Benny's father felt that was a primary reason they had murdered them. "I tried to give my son a structure," he stated proudly, rationally, explaining that was why his son was not guilty of the crimes he was charged with

Birdwell never bothered to explain how that structure had included his own convictions for crimes, both misdemeanors and felonies, or how that structure was enhanced by his abandoning his son in a New Jersey hotel years before.

"Do you sleep? Are you worried?"

Birdwell Jr. said he slept well, and he certainly looked well rested. As for worrying, he believed the jury would find his son "not guilty."

A short while later, court reconvened. Birdwell Jr. and Birdwell Sr. sat in the front row, in the section reserved for family. Next to them was a victims aid person who separated them from Sandy Lettich and Linda Solivan. The Birdwells had not talked to the women since the trial had started.

In the second row of spectator seats, Carol Russell kept leaning on Birdwell Jr., who sat directly in front of her. They exchanged whispered confidences and gum, and then Birdwell sat back to listen, crossing his knees in a manner of utter relaxation. He didn't look in the least worried that his son was on trial for his life.

Watching all this in the back row was Ben's

mother, Donna. She was bitterly estranged from Nelson Jr. Her eyes shot daggers into Russell's back.

"Dr. Neil Hoffman," Makoul called in the courtroom, after Benny was seated. A thin man in a gray suit and with a thin mustache, Hoffman was a forensic pathologist Makoul had hired to bolster his case. He took the stand.

Hoffman was a blood spatter expert. He had reviewed the reports filed by the prosecution's blood spatter expert; examined the murder weapons and gone over the crime scene shots.

"How did Dennis Freeman die?" Makoul asked.

"The cause of death to Dennis Freeman were multiple blunt impacts to the head and chest," Hoffman replied. "The most severe injuries were those inflicted by the baseball bat," (which the prosecution theorized David had been wielding).

Makoul tried to get Hoffman to state categorically that the blood on Ben's shirt was expirated (exhaled through the nose and mouth), which could account for it going a long way, possibly up to eleven feet, and landing on Ben's shirt. If Makoul could prove that, then the jury would believe Ben had not been close enough to inflict any blows.

But Hoffman wouldn't agree. He qualified his answer: "The blood *could* have been expirated in bursts of blood droplets from the nose and mouth across the room," he answered. "Or, it could have been spattered from the blows," which he estimated at about ten.

He also testified that Dr. Barbara Rowley's blood

spatter experiments had a reliability factor of "virtually nil" because scientifically, "the variables of her experiment couldn't be duplicated."

Eventually, after all the technical testimony, Makoul got Hoffman to admit that he believed "the blood on the shirt was projected a considerable distance, eight to eleven feet."

On cross-examination, Steinberg was able to show that Hoffman had come to his conclusions without conducting his own experiments. He shook his testimony so much that at one point, Hoffman couldn't even recall the name of the defendant!

"This is Nelson Birdwell," Steinberg intoned, pointing at the defendant. "He's on trial for three counts of murder." Sarcasm dripped like honey. "Never met him?"

"No," Hoffman answered sheepishly.

After the court broke for lunch, Steinberg ushered Sandy, Linda, and their families, whom the prosecutor described as "the good side of the family," up to his office for a repast. For the Birdwells, it was back to cafeteria food. They didn't seem to care. Nothing fazed the father and son.

At the noontime press conference, Dick Makoul said he might put Ben on the stand. Steinberg came to the mike afterward with a big smile on his face. He would relish the prospect of tearing into the defendant. But off camera, he asked a reporter, "Is Dick really gonna put Ben on?"

Court reconvened and the judge wanted to know if Makoul was putting Benny on.

"The defense rests," Dick said, almost inaudibly. It was time for the rebuttal case.

Sharon Reiss Kratzer, a registered nurse at the Lehigh County Prison, testified that Ben was intelligent enough to fill out a complete health history. "I'm fine. I eat well and sleep well," he stated in writing, implying that he was not the dullard Makoul was suggesting. He also denied he had any medical or mental problems.

School psychologist Barbara Miller testified, "The defendant is not mentally retarded. He had some learning disability."

Dr. Robert Gordon came to the stand. A clinical psychologist and associate professor at Widener University in Pennsylvania, Gordon said that according to a psychological test the defense shrinks had given Ben, "Birdwell shows no anxiety whatsoever. Clearly, his anxiety level is in the normal range."

But the test showed something else: "The test supports a diagnosis of psychopathic personality."

Benny was a psychopath, a person who felt nothing, least of all guilt and needed no logical reason to commit murder. "There are no signs he felt residual anxieties at the time of the crimes."

Makoul's defense had just been shot to hell and then some. He had to do something and he did, trying to goad Gordon into losing his temper, making a mistake, anything to damage his catastrophic testimony. But the more he needled and probed, the more bemused Gordon got. He just wasn't going to break. Finally, Makoul asked, "Doctor, why do all of you doctors with degrees disagree about the defendant's emotional state?"

"I think you have different levels of expertise," Gordon answered amiably. "And I'm sure all these doctors who testified, while I don't know them, are well qualified. I just happen to be well qualified in the area I'm testifying in."

April 25, 1996

Closing arguments. Makoul went first. He kept stressing "reasonable doubt," saying there was no evidence proving that Ben had killed Brenda, Dennis, or Erik, or helped or conspired with his cousins to do it.

Makoul tried to explain away Ben's disingenuous statements to police and why he'd chosen to run with the brothers if he really was innocent.

"Ben was in shock by what he witnessed," Makoul said. "He may not have told the whole story to police because he was afraid that just being in the home during the killings could get him in trouble."

The jury kept staring at Ben. There was nothing there, nothing behind his eyes.

Makoul emphasized the testimony of his experts. Ben had a low IQ, was marginally retarded and suffered from stress disorder that prevented him from doing anything either to stop the murder or call the cops. He was afraid if he did do something, Bryan or David would kill him.

As to the testimony of the prosecution's forensic

experts, "Was there even a speck of Brenda's blood on this boy?" Makoul wondered aloud. He walked over to Ben at the defense table and gently placed his hand on his shoulder.

With his cherubic cheeks, Ben looked as innocent as a baby.

When it was Steinberg's turn, he argued that Birdwell was a willing accomplice to the murders and had indeed actively participated in them. "I can't tell you what motivates killers," Steinberg said, knowing full well that a psychopath does not need motivation to kill. "These people were joined. I would suggest to you that they are joined in murder."

They did everything together, Steinberg suggested. Including killing.

Steinberg argued that after Bryan stabbed Brenda, Birdwell beat her with the ax handle, ran upstairs, and killed Erik with it. And in between all that, Ben also helped to kill Dennis.

Steinberg argued that Ben was not the dullard the defense had tried to portray him as. If anything, he was a cunning young man, cunning enough to help plan a murder, commit it, make a successful escape, and then lie to police, once captured.

"It doesn't matter what weapons you believe Mr. Birdwell used, nor does it matter how many people you believe he killed. Whether it was one or three, he is still an accomplice, a murderer, and you should find him guilty."

In the back row, the little man from the Jehovah's Witnesses Kingdom Hall in Allentown, who had attended the Freeman brothers' hearings and all of Ben's trial, scribbled madly in his notebook.

With final arguments concluded, the judge charged the jury and sent them out to deliberate. An hour and a half later, they asked to have some testimony reread to them, including Ben's statement to police that he'd had nothing to do with the murders.

By 10:30 P.M. they had still not reached a verdict. They turned in for the night.

The next morning, Richard Makoul arrived at his office early, waiting for the verdict. The hours passed.

Ten o'clock.

Eleven o'clock.

In the bullpen, Ben Birdwell waited, still dressed in his suit, calm, waiting to find out his fate.

Twelve o'clock.

One o'clock.

The phone on Makoul's desk rang. Heart pounding, he picked it up.

"There's a verdict," said the judge's clerk.

Makoul got up, smoothed down his sleeves, straightened his tie, and walked out into the afternoon sunshine for the one-block walk to the courthouse.

In his office, Steinberg, too, got the call. He walked downstairs from his fourth-floor office to Judge Diefenderfer's third-floor courtroom. Waiting in the front row, he assured Linda and Sandy that Benny was about to be convicted.

"Let's go, kid, there's a verdict," said one of the guards. He turned Ben around and handcuffed him while his partner applied the shackles. For the last time Ben shuffled off to the courtroom. Outside, in the corridor next to the elevator, TV cameras shone lights in his eyes.

He smiled for the cameras.

Epilogue

April 26, 1996

From combined national news sources:

ALLENTOWN, PA—An eastern Pennsylvania man, Nelson Birdwell III, eighteen, was found guilty today of first-degree murder for his role in the death of his uncle, Dennis Freeman. The jury immediately recommended life in prison. "No parole," they wrote in block letters on the verdict slip.

The Allentown jury found him "not guilty" in the murders of Dennis Freeman's wife, Brenda, and eleven-year-old son Erik citing insufficient evidence tying him directly to their deaths.

Ruling that there were no aggravating sentences to bring the death penalty into play, Judge James Diefenderfer sentenced Birdwell to life in prison.

Richard Makoul, Birdwell's defense lawyer, had admitted his client was present at the time of the murders but denied he had participated in the killings.

Birdwell's cousins, David and Bryan Freeman, had previously pleaded guilty, Bryan to his mother's murder and David to his father's. No one was convicted of their son Erik's murder.

Afterword

Richard Makoul was depressed after the verdict. He believed in Ben's innocence and felt he should have been found "not guilty" because of reasonable doubt. He wondered if he could have done more.

Makoul had no reason to feel disappointed, though. His noble effort had resulted in Ben Birdwell's life being spared. Besides, he was going to appeal.

Ben Birdwell is now a convict in the Pennsylvania State prison system. He and his cousins David and Bryan, who are in different prisons, talk to their grandfather frequently. The old man remains their staunchest supporter.

David's lawyers, Wally Worth and Brian Collins, are still contemplating taking some legal action regarding Steinberg's alleged failure to turn over exculpatory discovery material. However they probably won't. They fear if David's verdict were set aside, the teen would have to face not one but three counts of murder at his next trial, with the death penalty still looming on the horizon.

Bob Steinberg continues to bask in the glory. His future looks brighter than ever.

The rift in the Birdwell/Freeman family will probably never be repaired. To date, neither side talks to the other, though Linda Solivan has tried to contact Bryan and David. They have ignored her.

The Freeman home on Ehrets Lane in Salisbury Township has not been sold. With the blood soaked into its floorboards and plaster, it remains the one true eyewitness to what really happened.

As for the victims, the Jehovah's Witnesses in the Allentown congregation continue to look at them as martyrs. Dennis, Brenda, and Erik would probably settle for resting in peace.

Soon after the verdict, Nelson Birdwell issued the following statement to the press:

Memorandum

SUBJECT: My Evaluation of Matters

TO: Those Supporting The prosecution

(My Daughters Linda and Sandy)

Girls, this was your test-of-a-lifetime. One never knows how it is coming about. You allowed a tool-in-the-hands of God's adversary to use your less than mature emotions to maneuver you to the wrong side of the issue. Hopefully, Mr. Bo., and I, with our more mature emotions, saved Ben from his fangs. If not, *we* escaped the snare.

If you had maintained all your thinking faculties and had heeded the warning from your teachings, you could have prevented this from happening. You could have simply stopped and reflected on what the clowns were trying to do in their carnival. They were trying to conceal the truth, not reveal it. They were out to kill, not save a life.

A WORD ABOUT SOURCES

When I first decided to write this book, I had no idea that I would have to penetrate three worlds to do it—that of the Jehovah's Witnesses, that of the Pennsylvania neo-Nazis and most important, that of the Freeman family.

Jehovah's Witnesses make it a point to remain silent. While Linda Solivan did finally grant me an interview, which provided tremendous insight into the family's feelings, the challenge was to find Witnesses who would talk further. I got lucky when Paul Blizard, an ex-Witness, put me in touch with other ex-Witnesses in the Allentown area who gave me background on the Freemans, whom they had known.

Barry Morrison, of the Anti-Defamation League in Philadelphia, gave me an extensive amount of information on neo-Nazi activity in the state and country. But it was Mark Thomas himself, through his Internet site, who provided the most information.

As to the Freeman family, information there came from the attorneys involved: Brian Collins, Richard Makoul, Wally Worth, and Bob Steinberg.

They all were kind enough to spend many hours filling in much-needed information about the family and, of course, a real understanding of the legal proceedings. No one from the Allentown public defenders' office, however, would provide information, so I was unable to research Bryan as fully as Benny and David.

As to what the boys said in their statements, wherever possible, I quoted them verbatim.

The names of many of the participants have been changed to protect their privacy.

Finally, if I have shown any insight into family dynamics, it is because of my wife, Leah. A family therapist, with whom I argue frequently about structural, narrative, and all those other family therapy schools of thought, in the end, it turns out, she was more right than wrong.

—Fred Rosen

Biography

Fred Rosen is the author of several books, including *Lobster Boy* and *Chameleon*, which is now in development with ABC-TV. He has been a columnist for the *New York Times* and has written for publications ranging from the in-flights to *The Saturday Evening Post* and *Cosmopolitan*.

He has been a professor of journalism for Hofstra University and an "almost" professional baseball player, playing in Firebird Stadium in Phoenix, Arizona, the spring training home of the San Francisco Giants.

SINS AND SCANDALS!
GO BEHIND THE SCENES WITH PINNACLE

JULIA: THE UNTOLD STORY OF AMERICA'S
PRETTY WOMAN   (898, $4.99)
by Aileen Joyce
She lit up the screen in STEEL MAGNOLIAS and PRETTY WOMAN.
She's been paired with scores of stunning leading men. And now, here's
an explosive unauthorized biography of Julia Roberts that tells all. Read
about Julia's recent surprise marriage to Lyle Lovitt—Her controversial
two-year disappearance—Her big comeback that has Tinseltown talking—
and much, much more!

SEAN CONNERY: FROM 007 TO
HOLLYWOOD ICON   (742, $4.50)
by Andrew Rule
After nearly thirty years—and countless films—Sean Connery is still one
of the most irresistible and bankable stars in Hollywood. Now, for the first
time, go behind the scenes to meet the man behind the suave 007 myth.
From his beginnings in a Scotland slum to international stardom, take an
intimate look at this most fascinating and exciting superstar.

HOWARD STERN: BIG MOUTH   (796, $4.99)
by Jeff Menell
Brilliant, stupid, sexist, racist, obscene, hilarious—and just plain gross!
Howard Stern is the man you love to hate. Now you can find out the real
story behind morning radio's number one bad boy!

THE "I HATE BRENDA" BOOK   (797, $4.50)
By Michael Carr & Darby
From the editors of the official "I HATE BRENDA" newsletter comes
everything you ever wanted to know about Shannen Doherty. Here's the
dirt on a young woman who seems to be careening through the heady
galaxy of Hollywood, a burning asteroid spinning "out of control!"

THE RICHEST GIRL IN THE WORLD   (792, $4.99)
by Stephanie Mansfield
At the age of thirteen, Doris Duke inherited a $100 million tobacco fortune.
By the time she was thirty, Doris Duke had lavished millions on her lovers
and husbands. An eccentric who thumbed her nose at society, Duke's circle
of friends included Jackie Onassis, Macolm Forbes, Truman Capote, Andy
Warhol and Imelda Marcos. But all the money in the world couldn't buy
the love that she searched for!

*Available wherever paperbacks are sold, or order direct from the
Publisher. Send cover price plus 50¢ per copy for mailing and
handling to Penguin USA, P.O. Box 999, c/o Dept. 17109,
Bergenfield, NJ 07621. Residents of New York and Tennessee
must include sales tax. DO NOT SEND CASH.*

INFORMATIVE—
COMPELLING—
SCINTILLATING—
NON-FICTION FROM PINNACLE TELLS THE TRUTH!

BORN TOO SOON (751, $4.50)
by Elizabeth Mehren
This is the poignant story of Elizabeth's daughter Emily's premature birth. As the parents of one of the 275,000 babies born prematurely each year in this country, she and her husband were plunged into the world of the Neonatal Intensive Care unit. With stunning candor, Elizabeth Mehren relates her gripping story of unshakable faith and hope— and of courage that comes in tiny little packages.

THE PROSTATE PROBLEM (745, $4.50)
by Chet Cunningham
An essential, easy-to-use guide to the treatment and prevention of the illness that's in the headlines. This book explains in clear, practical terms all the facts. Complete with a glossary of medical terms, and a comprehensive list of health organizations and support groups, this illustrated handbook will help men combat prostate disorder and lead longer, healthier lives.

THE ACADEMY AWARDS HANDBOOK (0258, $4.99)
An interesting and easy-to-use guide for movie fans everywhere, the book features a year-to-year listing of all the Oscar nominations in every category, all the winners, an expert analysis of who wins and why, a complete index to get information quickly, and even a 99% foolproof method to pick this year's winners!

WHAT WAS HOT (894, $4.50)
by Julian Biddle
Journey through 40 years of the trends and fads, famous and infamous figures, and momentous milestones in American history. From hoola hoops to rap music, greasers to yuppies, Elvis to Madonna—it's all here, trivia for all ages. An entertaining and evocative overview of the milestones in America from the 1950's to the 1990's!

Available wherever paperbacks are sold, or order direct from the Publisher. Send cover price plus 50¢ per copy for mailing and handling to Penguin USA, P.O. Box 999, c/o Dept. 17109, Bergenfield, NJ 07621. Residents of New York and Tennessee must include sales tax. DO NOT SEND CASH.

HORROR FROM HAUTALA

SHADES OF NIGHT   (0-8217-5097-6, $4.99)
Stalked by a madman, Lara DeSalvo is unaware that she is most in danger in the one place she thinks she is safe—home.

TWILIGHT TIME   (0-8217-4713-4, $4.99)
Jeff Wagner comes home for his sister's funeral and uncovers long-buried memories of childhood sexual abuse and murder.

DARK SILENCE   (0-8217-3923-9, $5.99)
Dianne Fraser fights for her family—and her sanity—against the evil forces that haunt an abandoned mill.

COLD WHISPER   (0-8217-3464-4, $5.95)
Tully can make Sarah's wishes come true, but Sarah lives in terror because Tully doesn't understand that some wishes aren't meant to come true.

LITTLE BROTHERS   (0-8217-4020-2, $4.50)
Kip saw the "little brothers" kill his mother five years ago. Now they have returned, and this time there will be no escape.

MOONBOG   (0-8217-3356-7, $4.95)
Someone—or some*thing*—is killing the children in the little town of Holland, Maine.

Available wherever paperbacks are sold, or order direct from the Publisher. Send cover price plus 50¢ per copy for mailing and handling to Penguin USA, P.O. Box 999, c/o Dept. 17109, Bergenfield, NJ 07621. Residents of New York and Tennessee must include sales tax. DO NOT SEND CASH.